The Confession

Peter J. Dellolio

DEDICATION

For The One

All men naturally have an impulse to get knowledge.
A sign of this is the way we prize our senses; for even
apart from their utility, they are prized on their own account,
especially sensing with the eyes. For not only from practical
motives, but also when we have nothing practical in view,
we could be said to prefer sight to any of the other senses.

Aristotle, *Metaphysics*
Book Alpha

Dear Mr. Loki:

Enclosed for your approval is the Final White draft of Detective Dialogue at one of the generic crime scenes. I've written the details so that this scene is not necessarily time-specific. That seemed to be the inference from your last memo. I know that you are still waiting to purchase rights to the killer's diaries and that is the material we need, obviously, to construct some kind of chronological story.

There is, however, some cut-away material as you'll notice: the reference to Sgt. Jauntley at another location where a different homicide has occurred. You'll recall that Jauntley is the detective with the sick interest in victims of extremely violent serial killers. He loves to gaze at the gruesome details and here one of the detectives refers to a telephone call in which a friend of his, a fellow investigator, just informs him that Jauntley has to be removed from the house because the killing is so horrific that even Jauntley cannot endure it without reaching the point of nausea and vomiting.

I still have some of that trial transcript dialogue which refers to Jauntley's ulcer, but you had indicated that you weren't sure about plausibility, etc. Until that journal becomes available, I know we're trying to keep everything pretty much generic about location, time, identity, etc. However, there is merely the reference to this scene being "upstate." This was to suggest that Jauntley may be in a slightly different time zone, but we can change that later if necessary.

Also, I lengthened the opening with Capt. Jake Becker ranting on and on about all the misery he's witnessed, etc., and how this murder goes beyond anything he's ever seen, etc. When we last discussed this, you indicated that you wanted a long, convoluted tracking shot to follow him from room to room as he gives this tirade. You were emphatic about wanting it to appear that, although the rooms are filled with detectives and evidence technicians, he's speaking more or less in soliloquy fashion. We can also have some of the non-speaking actors pop in and out of the frame from behind the camera while Becker is carrying on and the camera is weaving through the rooms following him. I know you wanted the apartment to be sprinkled with bird imagery and I think we should have a few large paintings of pelicans in the room where the body is discovered.

One of the things that intrigued me in the telephone message you left last night—I missed some of it, unfortunately...my answering machine is dying apparently and the tape kept clicking and skipping— was the biographical information you've already uncovered about the killer or supposed killer, I should say. I think we can do a lot with the so-called religious theme. The fact that this guy was a priest can work for us or against us, given the recent climate concerning the Catholic Church, but I think we can find some interesting angles to play it from nevertheless. If we play it from the angle that he somehow lost his faith and turned to pornography and murder, we can suggest that the world of imagery and illusion is a potent temptation in modern society; if we play it from the angle that the priest was innocent and wanted to sacrifice himself because he lost his faith, we can suggest that Christianity is still a powerful force within the collective conscience of the 21st century. As you can see, there's a lot to work with here without necessarily becoming heavy-handed which, of course, we want to avoid at all costs.

Please let me know what you think about these suggestions as soon as you can.

Best regards,

J. Wakdjunkaga

INTERIOR. DAY. A LARGE, NICELY FURNISHED APARTMENT.

A crime scene in the home of a murdered young woman. She is the latest victim of a serial killer being hunted by the authorities. The rooms are filled with uniformed policemen, plainclothes detectives, and evidence technicians. Everything is in disarray: furniture knocked over, objects scattered throughout the floors, shredded clothing, bloodstains everywhere. The woman's body is not yet visible. The camera backtracks on *Captain Jake Becker*, who is in charge of the investigation. He is a large man in his fifties, with that world-weary, sarcastic demeanor of homicide detectives who have seen too much misery. He saunters through the rooms wearing an imposing, dark grey fedora and raincoat, smoking a fat cigar, supporting himself with an old wooden cane to assist the leg that was permanently injured by a bullet that was meant for his partner. While Captain Becker is speaking, more or less to himself, the camera zigzags through the rooms with other detectives moving in and out of the frame. After he's finished, the camera moves on to a series of two-shots and group shots where other conversations are already taking place. This entire scene, therefore, is a continuous take.

CAPTAIN JAKE BECKER: Thirty years! Thirty years of dirt and crummy pay! Bloody palm prints on green elevator doors! Spent syringes stuffed up the nostrils of a mounted gorilla head! Smell of clay and fresh newspaper! Old men in the back of a closet hanging from wide checkered neckties, pathetic farewell messages carved by razor on their white-haired sandpaper chests! Little kids mutilated beyond recognition, flung down the incinerator hog-tied! Jism still warm inside hookers' holes! Used to find 'em with their throats cut open squatting in the blow-job position at the end of some filthy brick alley, blood frozen like a twist of cherry licorice vibrating in the winter wind! A poor mutt crucified in some cult basement rust hole, a two-foot spike jutting out of its helpless forehead! Thirty years of newborn babies, aborted fetuses lodged real stiff between a bunch of chunky milk bottles and an old typewriter! New dead life left inside some garbage can half a mile from where the mother squeezed her oily twat lips, punching out the life of a human being she had no intention of speaking to, no desire to cradle or caress or nurture or love. Love? Christ, I gave up on that loony tune crap long ago! Read some article once on how motherhood has gone through an existential revolution! What the fuck is this about? Who can tell me why the baker makes bread for forty years and then one day he decides to put a shotgun in his mouth after stabbing his wife so many times her body looks like a gigantic fish gill? I remember when I first joined the force...I wanted to save the world...wheat and grapes, wheat and grapes. I don't believe this lukewarm shit about the moral breakdown of the family in the twentieth century. Or maybe we came from aliens experimenting with genes and all the psycho violence in the world is just Mr. Outer Space getting his kicks at the control board! Loaded idiot bullshit! You tell me why some truck driver or a traveling salesman or a postal worker just snaps and then from city to city or state to state he starts leaving a trail of mangled bodies? Because maybe he got fist fucked when he was nine? Or maybe on the first day of kindergarten he saw some disfigured stranger's prick? So the poor bastard was emotionally "damaged," right? And now every goddamn body he leaves butchered in some sewer or filthy flop house is just his way of telling the world he's getting even, that he's finally worked out a nice satisfying revenge formula so he can smell fresh blood and get from day one to day two? So here we are with another thrill boy who loves the knife. Thirty years in homicide, thirty years of bodies burnt, shot, stabbed, hacked, hung, what have you...and I'll be damned if I've ever...

SGT. VARGAS: Hey, some light, some light will ya! Will you throw a little of that damn light over here! No, not by the window seat, idiot! We're in the basement!

The basement, I said! There's lots of blood in the hallway. Should I get some samples there too? Hey Browser, Browser!

CAPTAIN JAKE BECKER: ...seen it done like this! He must be sleeping only a few hours a week, not even a split personality case could shut this much horror out of his mind!

INSPECTOR GRISBY: That's where you're off, Jake...lot of these sex deviants go into a normal routine just as pretty as you please, lot of them always turn out to be unusually

likable, and they remember, too, but what they do don't really interfere with their everyday life.

DETECTIVE BROWSER: Yeah Sergeant, what's up?

SGT. VARGAS: Have you collected enough physical evidence, Browser? You wearin' the halo, huh?! Innocent?! Got the aureole over ya, huh?! Do you think his fingerprints are gonna jump outta her fucking panties?! Or maybe this one's gonna be like the corsets with *The Uptown Stuffer*?

SGT. BROOM: *The Uptown Stuffer*? What the hell was that?

UNIFORMED OFFICER NO. 1: I'm not so sure we can identify this person at this time because of the manner, ah, because of the...please be calm and wait outside for now.

DETECTIVE BROWSER: Aw, c'mon Sarge, that whole thing got blown way outta proportion.

INSPECTOR GRISBY: No, I don't think so, I don't think you'll find any skin under the fingernails, but take some samples just in case.

SGT. VARGAS: Yeah, Browser? It got blown outta proportion, huh? Maybe that's why you got the nickname *Browsing Browser*, you degenerate fuck that you are!

LT. DOYLE: Here's the light now, what about those auxiliary cables for power in the house?

SGT. BROOM: *Browsing Browser? The Uptown Stuffer?*
What the hell are you guys talking about?

SGT. VARGAS: There was this guy, see, ran a little candy and
cigarette joint up in the 90s, East Side, retiree district, lots of old bags on
Social Security or theircroaked husband's pension…

SGT. THORWALD: Yeah, that's it, Connors, shine it to the left
so I can take a mold from this breast, or at least what's left of it…Christ,
will ya look at those cuts, my god!Wait a minute, is that a dove under
her neck?

SGT. VARGAS: …checks with just enough left over to buy
underwear entertainment.

UNIFORMED OFFICER NO. 2: Eighteen feet from the
bedroom to the phone…jeez, wouldn't think she could crawl that far
after losing so much blood. Funny how people want help even when
they're already almost dead.

LT. DOYLE: Hey Mike, I've got the coroner on the line, says it's
urgent!

SGT. VARGAS: Yeah, wait one second, Vin…so anyway, this
guy's closing up his placeat lunchtime, see, just so he can go hang around
the corset place down the street, you know, one of those dusty old
shops where they sell old women's twat junk, right?

UNIFORMED OFFICER NO. 3: One night me and Sal get a
call to one of those old buildings with the walk in shit closet that has the
pull chain thing, you know?

SGT. THORWALD:_Oh shit, sew that up, will ya! Every time I
turn her sideways all this crap comes squishing out of her, goddammit!

LT. DOYLE: Hey Sergeant, the coroner wants puncture
identification as soon as possibleso he can compare these wounds to
the other bodies. He's pissed, Mike, he says…

SGT. VARGAS: Tell him to puncture his ass with the receiver for ten minutes! Anyway, to make a long story short, this guy, see, he starts to follow these crusty old witches out the store on his lunch hour, but he waits 'till they buy corsets with appliqué roses on 'em, OK? Those are the only victims he picks, right? So he follows them back to their apartments, pretendshe's from the store, the garment store, that they made some mistake on the receipt and the placeowes them money, right? Soon as he gets in, ties the poor old bag of shit to the refrigerator, the fuckin' open refrigerator door! Shoots two, maybe three loads in the corset right there infront of them, then he puts on one of those rubber Popeye masks, starts playing *Somewhere Over the Rainbow* on a miniature harmonica, and finally this sorry psycho bastard stuffs the goddamned come-soaked corset down their poor grandma throats! Now Browser here…

UNIFORMED OFFICER NO. 4: What was that, back in the 50s, early 60s, when they still had a lot of those old fashioned johns?

UNIFORMED OFFICER NO. 3: Yeah, right, was about '58, '59, like that. So we find this poor old fairy impaled on a goddamn pipe that he rigged up on the toilet seat. He made a garland of pomegranates for his head. He hoists himself up with the toilet pull chain so he can lower himself slowly onto the pipe to get his thrill, only the goddamn chain snaps and all his weight goes straight down on the pipe. Wow! Instant death. Nobody came for a week and it was the middle of the summer. Roaches made a nest inside his mouth.

SGT. VARGAS: Browser comes in with forensic and collects evidence, see, but by theseventh or eighth victim we're pulling out dishtowels and brillo pads instead of corsets!

LT. DOYLE: What about that one time when it was the same MO with the eighty-five yearold retarded Russian midget broad and they pulled a *Sad Sack* comic book outta her miserable throat, huh Mike! Ha ha ha!

SGT. VARGAS: Yeah, oh yeah, I almost forgot, Frankie! The comic book, yeah…

SGT. THORWALD: No damn it, I said try the other outlet, use that one and the whole house'll go up, you'll overload the fuse box, asshole!

INSPECTOR GRISBY: Send those prints to Washington. Maybe we'll get lucky with a quick I.D. if the bastard's already in the FBI computers.

SGT. VARGAS:_…so one day we look in this lunatic's locker and, guess what? The prick's got stiff little dried jism corsets standing all in a row like a bunch of stale fruit or somethin'! You shoulda had some lilies in there, too!

DETECTIVE BROWSER: Those were from some bitch I was seein', she was into kinky stuff!

SGT. VARGAS: Aw give it a rest already with that story! You couldn't get laid in awoman's prison with a fist full of pardons! You're just lucky I could cover, jerkoff! Could'vehad Internal Affairs crawl up your ass with charges of suppressing evidence! Goddamn clothing freak! Are you done with the fuckin' panties now?!?! Christ! All right, give me thereceiver, give me the damn…

INSPECTOR GRISBY: You should talk to Mike about that line, Dave. I think he went through the whole application process with the FBI stuff.

SGT. BROOM: Who wants pastrami? Some of this meat looks like toilet paper froma leper's shit house.

SGT. HAINES: You know, to tell the truth, I never really trusted Jauntley. I mean,he did his time and I don't mean no disrespect, but he's always acted funny in homicide,you know, like he enjoyed it all. He'd spend hours with the photographer when something really disgusting popped up.

LT. DOYLE:_Didn't they have a hung jury on *The Uptown Stuffer*, like the defenseproved he wasn't working alone, or some other shit like someone else did it, and hewas just some lonely twisted jerk gettin' off sayin' he did it?

SGT. VARGAS: I don't buy that crap. I was on the case. He was I.D.'d more thanonce coming and going in three buildings where women were killed. And he waswearing a corset when they picked him up. Had long stem roses taped to his legs.

SGT. BATES: You never know about these nuts. Sometimes they're involved witha guy who does the real thing, and they're just like a psychic passenger or somethin'.

SGT. VARGAS: Oh, do tell us more, Herr Doctor!

SGT. BATES: Fuck you, Tony! You went to I. H. S. University, "Institute for Heads Full Of Shit"!

SGT. VARGAS: This whole thing reminds me of a case we had a few years ago, remember, Jake? That crazy Chinaman with the wolf-man mask he made ouf otincontinence bags? Total psycho bastard! Thought his restaurant was built over Larry Talbot's sacred burial ground or somethin'! We even booked him once on a health code violation, he was using pigeon meat in the dumplings, but that wasbefore the murders started.

INSPECTOR GRISBY: See the way the wrists are tied, two double bows...make a note of that. If this is the same guy, he's changing his act: before it was always asloppy knot, nothing tidy.

SGT. THORWALD: OK, I think the mold is dry, I just hope we get enough of an impression for the lab boys to work from. Christ it's hot down here, wish we coulduse the goddamn fan!

LT. DOYLE: Yeah, I remember that guy! The heroin gangs used to call him Wong Dong. Always took out a big artificial dick when he went to screw thewhores, had a growth defect or something, a thimble for a prick.

SGT. VARGAS: Right, that's the guy! He'd take out his little Mickey Mouse whistle and when the broads started to giggle he'd grin like an idiot and say'Oh, solly, so solly, wong dong, wong dong!' then he'd pull out ol' Rubber Ralph and finish the job by remote control!

SGT. BATES:_What's all this crap got to do with Browser starting a deceased chick's panty artifact collection like some Smithsonian Institution freak?

SGT. BATES: No, no, you don't get the idea, Norm. Wong Dong liked suffocation, just like the *Uptown Stuffer*, that was his MO. One of the waiters we talked to said he liked it so much he used to go out of his way to get live chickens for his joint just so he could strangle them himself. Crazy bastard used to sit behind the kitchen on Nimbus street in his boxer shorts, middle of the summer stinking sweat and heat, put the bird's head through the piss flap of his shorts, then twist the flap like a tourniquet 'till the fuckin' neck snapped. Waiter said he liked the way the bird pecked all crazy at his tiny weasel while it croaked.

SGT. HAINES: No, originally I wanted to get into the behavioral sciences unit in theFBI, I even applied to the academy, wrote to my Congressman for a recommendation.

INSPECTOR GRISBY: So what happened? How'd you wind up in homicide scrapin' some poor broad's massacred tits off a cement staircase?

SGT. HANES: Too many weirdo's in the FBI. It freaked me out.

SGT. VARGAS: Hank told me a story about some old bastard who was a cannibal. Liked to roam through low-income tenement neighborhoods, allall minority kids, this was back in the 30s and he figured there wouldn't be too much fuss if some little black or Hispanic kid disappeared. Clever bastard.

Was a building maintenance man, did little handiwork stuff, painted. His act was to go nude under the painter's overalls, this way he could be raw in aminute when he grabbed some poor kid, did his thing, then later on if he let'em go the kid would never recognize him in street clothes, and he only ate chubby boys with real plump asses.

UNIFORMED OFFICERS NO. 2:_How many angles do you think he stabbed her from? Jeez, there's hardly any skin between most of these wounds!

She looks like somebody put her torso through a paper shredder! And this was all done with a pocketknife?! No way!

INSPECTOR GRISBY: Yeah, my grandfather was a private dic in the 30s, he told me about that old maniac, managed to get an invitation as a witness to hiselectrocution. Said the psycho geezer looked forward to the chair, liked to torturehimself too and figured the juice would be some kind of ultimate thrill or somethin'.

SGT. HAINES: I remember Mike Jauntley came in when the forensic boys lifted the body off the pipe. You know Mike with the goddamn chili dogs, what withhis fuckin' rat breath and the stink of the corpse, Christ! You almost passed out!

SGT. VARGAS: Yeah, and he's still up to the same sick shit. Just spoke to one of my pals at a homicide upstate on Trefoil Boulevard, some Jane Doe nailed to a wallor somethin'. Jauntley had to have his look, only this time they had to carry his ass outta the house so he could throw up his stinkin' guts!

LT. DOYLE: Hey Vargas, just talked to the coroner again, says the hooker he cut open before had a rubber dork inside her with the inscription: *Thank You MiguelFor A Romantic Evening.* Says he always new you were a real tiger with the girls!

SGT. VARGAS: Next time that morbid corpse fucker calls tell him we found his wife's bra in the retard ward for deformed animals!

SGT. THORWALD: I'll take pastrami. What the hell, maybe my ulcer'll give me some sick pay, I could use a vacation.

SGT. BATES: So what was the deal with the crazy Chinaman?

SGT. VARGAS: He finally strangled his ninety-two year old grandmother with a shredded Daffy Duck mask. Couldn't resist the temptation to get off so the family comes home and finds the moron with his shorts wrapped around a chicken's head, makin' the scared silly bird peck his prick head bloody. Committed suicide during the trial.

LT. DOYLE: How?

SGT. VARGAS: Somehow he managed to dislodge a sink pipe from the courthouse john, rammed it up his ass 'till he punctured his intestines. Died instantly.

SGT. BROOM: Yeah, I was there. Weird way to die. All his shit came up through his throat.

UNIFORMED OFFICER NO. 3: Haha! Maybe the old faggot I found used to eat in his joint!

LT. LECHTER: Nicky, get me a few of those empty grapefruit bottles, these organs are gonna bake under the klieg lights. Find out if there's any new leads in the "Chi Rho" case.

This one looks like it could be related to it. Tell Sam to take his damn pictures already, before we all pass out from the smell.

The Son: Chapter I

Fear rules the heart. You learn that in prison. Here it is worth something to be feared. Privileges extend to those who command respect and intimidate the weak. It matters little if innuendo and rumor color your reputation. The lack of hard knowledge only adds to the abominable character of an inmate. Myths are the most potent source of terror. Human nature is drawn towards folklore and legend the way molasses attracts the fly. We need to be threatened by the monster, the devil, the goblin, the nameless thing. An ancient dread of the unknown, an addict's craving for the thrill. I remember going to films with my father when I was a boy. The horror pictures especially entranced me. My father told me stories of the silent cinema days, then the first "talkies," how all the frightening creatures achieved new life. Now I am part of a sacred group, on death row in a maximum-security prison, a convicted serial killer, waiting to die. By lethal injection or electrocution, I am not sure what they have decided, but it is scheduled for tomorrow morning. I refused my right to an appeal; I refused to help those who wanted to save me from death. But I embraced my role as a figure of evil, a man without soul, conscience, or compassion. I have played the part with consummate artistry, as though I too were from the world of the screen, a conjured object of perfect illusion.

I remember the cool darkness of the enormous theatres filled with circuitous passageways and shadowy alcoves. There was always the sense of something waiting for you, some dormant force waiting to take over your senses. Riding the escalator, holding my father's hand, I tried to see past the other patrons so I could glimpse the color posters lining the walls. At that age my limited height prevented me from seeing the outstretched fingers of the screaming cowering ladies overtaken by the stalking fiendish creature. Then came the murmur of voices as everyone groped through the energized gloom in search of a seat. The blank screen silver and quiet, soon to unveil its hypnotic power; the transformation from ridiculous void surface to opened magic case twisting space, time, and reality to its whims.

It was from the cinema screen that I gained wisdom. The images lied. Little did I realize that these would become the most truthfully constructed lies I would ever know. It is said that Christ enters the hearts of the condemned, so they may know the light of redemption before the end of mortal life. I am the Light. I am the Truth. I am the Way. I studied the words and teachings of Christ. I still have a copy of the New Testament. My father gave it to me. It is on my shelf, next to some movie postcards I collected as a boy and a priest's collar that I made out of thick white cardboard from the prison workshop. It was my father who explained the mechanics of film to me. For example, from the beginning, at a very young age, I already understood the technical basis for cinematic illusion. My father seemed to know everything. It seemed that my father somehow knew the outcome of things; that he had foreknowledge of events divined from relationships between things that he alone could see. I practiced this divination. I practice it still. I wanted to be one with him in this regard, to associate things so that I too could see and know. He used to tell me he thought it odd that everyone called them "moving pictures." There was no movement, he used to say. For every second of film, explained my father, there were twenty-four still photographs. When these individual pictures were moved at a certain speed in front of a projected light, people and things appeared to be in motion. *I am the Truth.* How many times did I quote those words for someone's enlightenment within the confines of a space not much smaller than this cell? My father was obsessed with truth. Sometimes it seemed that our film viewing was more of a theological education for me, rather than a recreational activity. There is no movement, he would say to me. This is not real, he would insist. And when there was any expanse or depth of space on the screen, such as a desert or a tunnel, again my father would give me a strict dissertation on the role of illusion in the manufacture of "the real."

Look, he would say to me, it is a flat surface, it is a lie. There is nothing beyond the two-dimensional plane of the screen, he explained. My father was a devoutly religious man. He encouraged me to study Christianity. He was particularly keen on the writings of St. Augustine. I studied the gospels, the parables. I read Augustine's *Confessions* over and over again. I wondered often about what makes man ultimately divine but temporally evil, the great paradox that confused Augustine's mind for so many years. I saw myself, even when a child, as a modern day model of Augustinian debate. The physical world became for me a macrocosm elucidated by the microcosm of cinema. Images. Reflections. Parallels. Associations. Illusions that represented reality. One could think of the physical world in those terms, too. One could view all matter, the modalities of the senses, and the demands of the body as a radiation of deception, of original sin. This must have been my father's rationale. If my father wanted me to have knowledge of the eternal, these distinctions must have formed the basis of his thinking. He would never draw absolute conclusions. He would point to things and make declarations about them, but I was left to pull everything together, to associate one idea with another until a radiance of understanding was achieved. How often has it been said that the Word of God, as expressed through Christ the Son, is not presented to man in the form of a command? I am certain that if Augustine had lived and thought in my century, the metaphysics of cinema would have resonated in his mind, as it does in mine, with all sorts of religious significance. One of the most compelling aspects of his argument is that man, because he is human, is born evil. Even the infant, who knows only the need to drink and eat, is already a slave to the dictates of the finite body, a servitude that expands with age into more complex forms of evil. The appetites of the body, literally and figuratively, consume man at the cost of spiritual communion: food, drink, sex, property, profession, ambition, pride. I was always deeply attracted to the idea that there is no innocence. Even those who think and act honorably are technically evil simply because they must use their senses as a mediator between the mind and the world. They must survive, so they must eat and drink. They must reproduce, so they must engage in sexual activity. They must have shelter, so they must work and spend and acquire. To be human, they must not only smell, see, hear, taste, and touch; they must attribute meaning to this ceaseless phenomenological inventory. Where does that meaning come from? For many years I wondered if this was the same kind of meaning that came from the screen. Remembering my father's discourse, that feverish belief in the magic of cinema was a great temptation to resist, I would often look upon photographs of holy places with special attention. Jerusalem, Cavalry, Golgotha, Bethlehem...places where Christ walked and spoke and taught. The edges of the frame were the key. Without the frame, there could be no sense of time. When one looks at a photograph, one knows that something is happening at that moment only because the frame edges create the present by implying a past and a future for the current happening. The little boys building their snowman with the frozen lake behind them exist in the present moment only because they previously came out of the big house that is not in the picture and will swim in the lake when the summer makes the empty trees bloom. In the beginning, said my father, there were little films that lasted only a few minutes. These were tiny stories made out of ordinary, everyday events. The masses were so fascinated by this new invention, this incantatory box that brought people, places, and things to life. There was endless interest in the viewing of the commonplace: all across the civilized world, image-hungry humans flocked to see streetcars moving back and forth, couples sitting on benches in gardens, workers entering factories, sick elephants being electrocuted. My father saw what was probably the most famous of these mini-narrative films of a real-life event, *The Arrival of a Train at La Ciotat Station*. He described it to me many times. A motion picture camera, placed at the end of a railway station, recorded the entrance of a locomotive in the middle of the day. This film was pivotal, my father explained to me. The illusory logic of the cinematic reproduction of the world began here, said my father. The edges of the frame were the key. Why, I used to ask as a boy, sitting at my father's feet as we looked down upon the flickering lights of all the cities we could see from the hilltop, where my father often brought me for hiking trips, why was the frame edge so critical? And as my father directed my attention to all the glitter and material comfort and pleasures of the senses, in being and doing and having, within the world that contorted before us below, he explained that I could have all of this, if I chose to be sinful, or I could embrace the truth and be one with God. He said that the deception of the frame edges was like the imposture of the senses, the corruption of pure mind when it succumbs to what is apparently real but inherently false. Did you know, explained my father, that many who saw the film gasped and even jumped away from the screen because the train past beyond the frame? They feared a locomotive crashing into the very rooms and halls in which they had ceremoniously gathered to watch the illusion unfold! Now a world of time had been born, said my father, for to those who watched, the train could exist in an imaginary past, it continued to exist in an imaginary future, only because the frame edges, together with the trickery of motion and depth, made the spectator think of the present event within a broader context. How many passengers were on the train? Where were they all going? There were those who had disembarked at the station, exiting out of the right side of the frame. What were their lives like? What would they do today, and where in the city would they go? What about all of the stops the train had already made, before it entered the frame? And one wondered too about all of the new stops that, having mysteriously disappeared out of the frame, the train had yet to make. The fascination with what is included becomes irreversibly linked to the mystery of what is excluded. In a sense, the frame becomes a figure, a metaphor, a vehicle for Augustine's concept of the "today" of God. For everything that has already happened to those passengers, everything that is presently happening as the viewers watch them, and everything that will eventually happen to them after the train leaves the frame and they become an abstraction that lives only within the memory and imagination of the viewer...all of this is contained by the "now," the "today" of the frame. Just as Augustine's perception of human time hinged upon the notion that a supreme being such as God can exist only in a perpetual present, through which all of the successive generations of man and all of the details of the lives of those generations passed, so too would all viewers of cinema, from this point forward, perceive the content of the world and the logic of time as elements passing through the immutable dimension of the frame. I would never forget that lesson. I would never again submit to the belief that perception and matter must necessarily have a logical relationship. I knew the truth.

It is a square cell. Not very large, but unusually high walls. I know that is not unique. When you are a prisoner, you become interested in the obvious; you tend to focus on the everyday. Twitching shadows of morning birds. The branches must not be far. I can discern only the insubstantial outline of the little creatures, yet I know I am unaffected by the evening medication. Sparrows? Cannot be certain. Appealing, though, the silhouette dark against pale stone. Frozen until they notice something, then fluttering, hopping, sudden pointing of beaks. Shadows, however insignificant, are important to a condemned man. Many possibilities exist in even the tiniest index of movement, human or otherwise.

The certainty that each morning is in fact a new day, and not a fantasy produced by one of my trances, or by the drugs, depends on the umbra. I rely on many pieces of secret evidence to draw this conclusion and comment is inappropriate, but the criteria I examine most judiciously are the shadow phantoms, born again, recreated in the new light. One might say that the chirping of birds is a fundamental ingredient of the beginning of a day; that all other aspects (including the visual) should be considered secondary, assuming that one is trying to relate the dawn to the birds in a distinctly perceptual way. Maybe this is correct, but I do not hear their song.

Lately I have been thinking of my explorations of the video arcades. Like the tiered open apartments of a Roman orgy hall, there were private peep booths arranged for the voyeur and his coins. The quadrangular plastic button changes the selection and yet another erotic scenario unfolds. Standing in the sweaty sarcophagus or sitting upon the hinged bench you switch the channel until a particular scene catches your fancy. The stinging ammonia smells lingered long after the booths were cleaned. I grew accustomed to this. Even after I had walked up and down in the rain, dashing into one place after another, I was never discouraged. I enjoyed the rain and, never having an umbrella, I did not look upon it as an inconvenience. Every scene caught my fancy. I viewed every scenario. No image escaped my attention.

I once had a memorable nocturnal pilgrimage during a raging summer deluge. It had been an extremely humid day, with steamy rain vapor fastened to my lungs. Clinging, visceral, it remained long after I entered the air-conditioned video centers. Drenched from head to foot, my shoes squeaked on the curling, stained linoleum. An ugly maintenance man sat on a stool opposite the booth of my choice. He was a fool, a moron; one of those flesh and blood ghosts destined to a lifetime of abuse, then a quiet, nameless death. And before he dies it is his job to swab the semen soaked floors of the booths with an ammonia-drenched mop.

Pleasant dreams each night, the joy of enclosure in the vision: always a chute, or a well, tumbling through a trapdoor. Likeness of this cell reinvented by the subconscious. Falling, plummeting downward, then side to side, or in spirals (no sense of natural gravity). Throughout this vertigo a panorama of things that should not be there.

I hid them. Every one. Many bodies, many objects. I worked in silence with a lantern set atop an antique Victrola. It shone behind me, casting deep silhouettes on the white sailcloth. I labored before this canvas that was very much like the material used to make old projection screens. The Victrola was from the Art-Deco period, made of smart two-toned woods: dark orange brown with darker, chocolate brown bands in thick vertical strips. I made no sound even though I shoveled dirt with a large, awkward farmer's shovel. My silhouettes were smooth, clean and black against the sail. Each time I tossed back a load of dirt I glanced at them and was reminded of the velvety wood. But the shovel constantly hit the floorboards. I made sounds. I will include what I choose. Imagery has painted every moment of my so-called "crimes" with unique grace, so it is my privilege to explain myself in an artful manner. After all, they ask me questions constantly. They are hungry for answers. There is no rule that says I must slice the bread one way or the other.

Exiting the booth (after bargaining in the dark for that special freedom, which only the screens can provide), I felt the abrupt, shocking chill of the air-conditioned video center. It contrasted so alarmingly with the subterranean heat of my recently sealed booth! A sensation of contrast reinforced not only by the lovely juxtaposition of humidity, cold rain, soaked clothes, fetid booth air, and stabbing refrigeration, but also by the steam rising from the soiled white cardboard container which the worker held in his filthy hands as he ate bits of grey and red meat. The steam in my nostrils only made my body that much more susceptible to the savage loss of its heat. As I exited the booth I saw the oil and sauce covered flesh (having already digested the last image of the girl bound and beaten). I watched the doltish worker smell the undercooked food before I turned towards the front of the arcade with its display of pink rubber objects wrapped in clear plastic.

From the cloud choked summer sky and its sauna-like air to the chilled slimy rain to my clothes wet and heavy to the cozy stifling heat of the tightly shut booth to the young girl's cries as her tenderest bound parts were struck to the delicate curls of vapor hovering above the container to the obscene ridges of ill prepared meat to the arctic attack of the air to those toys of the heart hanging like animal parts on display in a butcher shop sparkling with the play of neon light...throughout all of this is an exquisite thread that only I can pull.

It does not surprise me that the authorities could not understand. They wanted an explanation; they wanted a sequence of facts. But there has always been only a private logic for all of this, a logic surrounded by barbed wire and razors, protecting itself from scrutiny. In the little time left before my execution, I doubt they can gain access to this reasoning, I doubt they will find the bodies. I made it this way.

Supper bell. Six o'clock without fail it rings. Amazing mechanics of incarceration: first the left side, sliding metal frames release, opening the cells, hulking freight train sound, enormity of steel bulk. Same for the right side. Then the dead stop, all doors open, unnatural quiet. No one moves until the second bell. Then the silence on death row between the clanging of the doors opening and the piping of the second bell taunting, yes taunting you...for the second bell signals only that you may step outside, no farther.

As we stand in line outside our cells the guards pace up and down. They move so fluidly, relaxed, some with arms folded, aluminum Billy clubs idly swinging from their sides. Nothing to fear from this tribe of the condemned. They know we do not wrestle with the desire to escape or rebel. They are like big game hunters striding past carcasses after the kill, limp forms laid to waste in the twilight of a sprawling African landscape, soon to be gutted. The inference of their insouciance and composure is clear: they are walking among the dead. Yes, they walk past lifeless matter on this cellblock.

Sometimes the faintest sounds draw the most interest. Before my arrest, in my room at night, I could hear the tiniest movements of the house so effortlessly. I heard and saw the smallest things in my father's house. I suppose this gave me a temporary connection to the outside world, with my eyes closed and the thousands of images I had lifted from the screens chasing after and blending into one another.

I have never questioned the rituals of association that my mind performs. With the indestructible devotion of the pious, I believe in the predestined purpose of these associations. The swing and toss of ideas running through my mind is like a secret code: meaningless or foreign to the uninitiated, it reveals the truth to the cognoscenti. And at four o'clock in the morning, my moist ear pressed close to the floor, listening to the gentle ticking of the little wooden shade ring as the wind tilted it against the glass, with the pages of the lewd color magazines spread at random across my bed, I discovered the truth about the apartment below. I could hear muffled cries, just barely hear them. But I picked out these sounds so carefully, like the first ripe batch of fruit in an orchard, or like the time I struggled with a damaged speaker in one of the booths.

I never accepted the convenient explanation that downstairs someone must have been having a bad dream, that their moans expressed the loneliness or discomfort or fear of their nightmare. Before the trial, one of the defense psychiatrists offered this explanation but I refused to be comforted by it. My sense of perception is too all encompassing to be fooled. My mind has acquired the dimensions of a warehouse in its capacity to translate and interpret.

In a prison rumors spread like cancer. There are rules of silence but they cannot be unilaterally enforced. Inmates meet throughout the day, for work, for recreation, for sex. Many opportunities for furtive conversation present themselves, when stories of our crimes are circulated with enthusiasm, especially at mealtime. I must say I find this gossip most amusing, and even more so when a curtain of uncertainty obscures the facts, when imagination and sheer bravura intercede on behalf of an incomplete reality. Colorful nicknames arise from this, and one of my hobbies has become the documentation of the more striking figures.

Eating always in silence (one of my own alleged eccentricities is that I no longer communicate with anyone unless under the influence of a trance), I absorb every new detail, more portraiture for my collection of invisible images.

There was a convicted child killer who spent the past five years on death row. Electrocuted a month after my arrival, his reputation as a mesmerizing storyteller persists to this day. He was known as "Jelly

Man," a morbid appellation playfully coined in newspaper stories based on early police discoveries of his penchant for the post-mortem disfigurement of his tiny victims' buttocks. Usually the instrumentality for such acts was a household iron or, at times, a blowtorch. Before my little pocket tape recorder was confiscated, I managed to document some of "Jelly Man's" almost non-stop monologue. They thought I would narrate some of my own crimes, that I might supply them with clues to charge me further, or help them find the bodies. But I used the device simply for the archival purpose of creating a document or a gospel of the acts of those who, like me, found a new path:

"...click...sss...one night I killed a fat chinaman 'cause he belched in my face when I asked for directions...he had a gun...he was rattled, so I sapped him down, I didn't like his...click...sss...who knows for sure why I started killin'?...I don't know, docs couldn't figure it out or the lawyers neither...and I never killed a kid I didn't fuck...when you have sex with 'em you always got to have a desire for 'em too...and like I told the docs, does hate and desire...click...sss...one time I lured a ten year old girl away...her parents had nodded out, she was playin' in the sand...said I was the cotton candy man and she could have all the junk she wanted if she took a ride in my truck...walkin' her through the alleys and side streets I saw the clown faces and beach balls painted across the old wood of the boarded up food stands...sun was real hot and I could smell the stench of stagnant water, decayin' corn cobs...when I was finished I looked up…one of her stiff tilted feet was up against the window of my van…through her toes I glimpsed a stained blue merry-go-...click...sss...I had a Polaroid a before and after of every kid I ever did...taped 'em like tiles all over the walls and...click...sss...chinaman was a real asshole he shit himself sloppy as I held him down for the last fatal...click...sss...my old man turned my backside into bloody pus used a three inch strap while he jerked himself off with the other hand in-between sips of cheap gin...one night he shot a load into my eyes told the family doc I had an accident with...click...sss...and I give it all back ya hear me give the pain back to the world that's my philosophy and I don't call it hate neither 'cause like I says I make love to...click...sss...one night I had this tubercular Egyptian whore a real pig you could smell stale come the second she uncrossed her legs...thick mustache on her upper lip like some shriveled seventy-year old bag...paid her an extra $20 this night told her to hold one a my girls across her lap...had the kid's arms tied to the bedpost so's all the blow-job had to do was keep them legs down while I got the iron hot...with her free hand she picked infected scabs outta her nose eyes half shut in junkie sleep...pretty strong I gotta say 'cause she held the kid's legs with one hand and boy did she kick when I laid on the iron good thing the gag was perfect...I didn't feel like waitin' till after I killed her usually I liked the iron part when they was dead it was like sculpture no more...click...sss...then I had a Mexican dwarf named Hector liked to wear a black derby smoked little twisted anisette flavored wop cigars...helped me do a few playground jobs 'cause with a fist full of helium balloons he fit real smooth into the situation, I mean, a foreign dwarf with a fuckin' derby sellin' balloons to kids, what's more natural than that?...once we had this gorgeous kid long black hair endless curls stretching to her ass...Hector put fishing tackle through all his big opal rings (was a little guy but he had pipes for fingers)...I shot my last load and collapsed on top of her that's when he leaned over to cut her throat...tight milky white skin tiny throat split open like a toy drum long flashin' barber razor initials H.J.H. on the leather handle...blood jumped all across my chest and it was good, y'know, like havin' a pee in the water when the clouds cover the sun...I rolled off her, fell on the floor, watched her choke on her own blood, had that abstract gaze on my face like the guy in the fish market when he looks at the new catch twistin' on the cuttin' table...before I could give myself another shot Hector had already shoved his five or six rings thick as dradles all the way up her tight asshole...then he yanked them out with the tackle...tattoo on his arm said somethin' like *Long Live The Innocent* and he massaged his stunted pecker with the throat blood...I caught my jolt by then and that numb dream awake junk feeling blurred this last image of the dwarf puttin' the bloody rings back on his fingers as he finished the meat off the turkey bones, lettin' the dog lick both bones and blood from the rings...shiny rings black opal shiny black again with the blood licked off...click...sss...shiny black again with the blood licked off...click...sss...shiny black again with the blood licked off...click...sss...shiny black again with the blood licked off..."

Someone must have damaged the tape recorder. A lack of sensitivity for private property. I can think of no other explanation. Moral abuse comes in many forms.

Childhood shyness towards sharp edges (especially where my fingers are concerned) has dictated a lifelong habit of slicing meats or other solid foods in a most peculiar manner. I cannot allow my knife to come into contact with my other hand. Holding my food in place with my elbow (here in prison I am quite fastidious about having a steady supply of short sleeve shirts, to avoid staining my wardrobe), I make the necessary incision. Then I release the larger piece from the pinning grip of my elbow, exchange knife for fork with the same hand, and finally stab my morsel. Lately, though, this has begun to concern me. During the prolonged conviviality of story swapping that governs our meals, it is possible that another inmate, or worse still, one of the guards (they might be aloof but they are by no means inattentive), will note the incompatibility between my neurotic avoidance of the blade and the horrific manner in which my victims were allegedly dissected. I could not tolerate the aspersions cast by such an observation, that I could not have worked alone, that I could not have committed the murders.

At this stage, I would certainly jeopardize everything that matters most to me if I were to diminish, in even the remotest way, the voluminous body of evidence that secures my place in this arena of evil. My highly detailed, finely carved wooden sparrows are sufficient (if indirect) proof of my abilities with a knife. Thankfully no one has ever seen me do the actual carving.

That day in the booth, the soundtrack was indeed faint, and each time the brutal muscular man struck the girl's exposed buttocks, her squeals and cries could barely be heard. I was not supine on that occasion, with my ear glued to the circular metal speaker, like a spy listening by the wall that separates him from the Great Secret. Sometimes it is more comfortable to be lying on the floor, in the privacy of one's rooms, listening and transfixed. Then it is a floor that deprives you of a kind of food. The origin of the sound matters little; the only thing of importance is how the mind transforms it.

Have I changed in some enigmatic way? Or have I simply found my true path through a bizarre mixture of will and fate? The powers I command must derive from the unmistakable similarity between the video booths and my cell. Never underestimate the potency of the magic box. If you want to vivify what transpires in the imagination of a man, put him in a place where nothing is real. And so if I have changed, it must have been a slow, internal process.

All of my desires were admissible evidence, but it was difficult to find the appropriate defense. My cell cannot prevent me from remembering what pleases me, and I will not admit anything to anyone. Yet even now they ask me questions! Tomorrow morning they will separate my soul from my body, and still they seek answers to the questions that will not go away.

Did you really kill them? Were you just an accomplice? Maybe all you did was bury the bodies? Is there someone else? More than one? Are there more bodies? If you tell us, we can get a stay of execution, maybe a new trial...don't you want to live?...don't you want to live?...don't you want to live?

In the beginning I responded vigorously to the questioning with an endless supply of fictitious answers.

I remember cuddling against the blankets at night, laughing softly at the thought of vast search parties scouring moonlit fields. Nothing would be revealed when the earth was parted. Somehow my bedclothes and sheets were a part of the digging, and the more I entangled myself within them, the less likely it seemed that the loosened dirt would yield something. Suddenly, a search lantern casts a rectangular band of white light across the eyes of an anxious bloodhound, or the cries of "Over here!" are heard when a particular excavation crew makes a sickening discovery.

The dampness chills the bone; the salt air is too acrid to endure. Pictures follow one another so effortlessly. This was my pleasure in the early stages: lying in the dark, delighting in the fact that I had created these search party scenes, scenes I could enlarge with little details...like the eerie shock stare of a dog's illuminated face...the stab of early morning chill as a special agent rubs his numb fingers by the shore...orange ambulance lights reflected in a blurry haze across the silver of the command officer's badge...dry twigs snapping under heavy work boots...the sound invading the quiet of my cell.

This was a great freedom, even though I was and still am imprisoned. It was a freedom invisible to eyes that see only what is there, it was an escape through the door that is always locked, just as the motion picture screens (made out of taut canvas sheeting) or the glass video monitors (attached to a solid wall) were portals opening into another world. As long as there was something to see outside of myself, I could bypass the arid vacuity of my life. With special certainty, years before my arrest, I knew that my death would mean having to look inside my soul, like a jolt of vision suddenly, irrevocably erasing a heartbeat, but the drumming pulse does not resume. As a child I saw an enormous cobweb for the first time, its plethora of intersecting strands reaching in all directions. The mystery of the outline, the radiant delicacy of traps and compartments fascinated me. It was a universe unto itself, replete with all the drama of life and death, time and space. I sent them looking in so many places only because of that silken geography, the intricacies of line and the carefully shaped topography of the web demanded a convoluted search. So I told them to look for the bodies. They looked.

"The Teacher" was executed last month. Professor of English at a prestigious university, his specialty was the murder of retarded men. Something about the victims being a living example of the Professor's "philosophy." Many of my first months were spent in his splendid company and he discoursed constantly on the vicissitudes of life. Here too I managed to secure a memento, a record, a documentary object of some historical significance. I took advantage the week of his execution of my latrine duty, which gave me access to the cells on his block. He communicated only through writing, and kept extensive diaries. I stole a page from one of his notebooks. I always admired his florid, stylish penmanship:

"Everything is metaphor understand that and the human machine becomes less enigmatic life cycle death cycle birth death progression of seasons A B C D pattern of the elements pattern of the physical pattern of human life animal life insect life vegetal life why a pattern we use God for that we say anything that occurs in an intelligible sequence must be the result of a governing intelligence that is the hoax that is the secret of secrets that is the deception why not an accident why not a dream why not earth a work like a play or a film or a novel in perpetual sequence without end the ultimate metaphysical practical joke there is no afterlife there is no meeting of souls we are machinery with a conscience machinery without a conscience we are process occasion acts matter animated driven to reproduce driven to imitate our likeness hold up the mirror play back the tape mannequins robotics computers artificial intelligence invented by the invented why not an accident a dream the insects are nervous systems no brain no brain tissue but look at the ant colony look at the architecture look at the design for purpose and practicality why not an accident why not a dream the soul is the snake oil held up in the giant hand of the world religions slave to the belief in heaven and hell give us everything and salvation is yours so death is just another movement in the sequence it has no consequence good or evil and I killed without a

smile without a frown I was another ant doing my job carrying my pebble in the ranks of my brethren another soldier another piece of the machinery."

There is always a lesson to be learned. One must never settle into the dust of spiritual complacency. I have found that the gravest mistake is to believe in the rational.

The moonlight is a silver blanket moving across the floor of my cell. It is such a delicate light. Gentle folds and the smooth luminous persistence of flickering motion picture film. A foraging insect scuttles across the moldy cement. It lifts the grey veil as if it were a scurrying bump traversing the entire length of the bedspread, like a shark's fin protruding above the surface of light, making it three-dimensional. Now I can see the figures of the film screen.

I remember the blind windows in the abandoned building across from the bridge. I saw them often as a boy riding the train with my father when we went to the city to see a film. The brick surrounding the window frames exhibited the mark of filth and age, but clean, new stone was used to fill in these rectangular gaps. It was such a strange combination, the utter uselessness of the stifled openings, the fresh construction to achieve the occlusion. The windows were like ghosts: stripped of worldly function, a bizarre echo of what was.

The suggestion of a hidden world was exciting to me. I savored the duality of the permanently sealed exterior and the obscure space within, the dance of rooms and corridors dividing and stretching into nothingness, available to no scrutiny other than the imagination.

My father told me that the early experiments with cinema offered a similar mystique. One finds it in the hypnotic symbiosis of projection surface and spectator, as in the case of the train film. Often my father argued that the many reports of the startled reactions of the first viewers of primitive films, of audiences experiencing a profound shock, proved that their complacent acceptance of this new "imitation" of life was violently challenged.   The sacred bond, explained my father, hinged upon an unwritten law that the illusion of reality prohibits a certain boundary line from being crossed. And like the Egyptian cult of magic based upon the utterance of special words, this taboo and the psychological chicanery it produces fill us with awe. We worship the false, shallow character of the projected surface, easily challenged yet impossible to penetrate. It is supreme because it is impregnated with the narcotic excitement of the unreal presented as real.

My father told me that in a way, all creation, everything that is physical, is viewed in a mystical sense by religions of the world, ancient and modern, as a phantom, a mirage, a test more specifically, a veneer meant to somehow guide humanity towards a true understanding of the all important difference between body and spirit. And like the Christian prophet's warning, that to gain the world means losing your soul, there is a terrible danger that accompanies stubborn belief in the physical world. The fanatical, including my father, would even maintain that the invention of a powerful image system such as cinema is itself a reflection of this "sin," that is, to remain enslaved to a false god, to perpetuate belief in the unreal. Often I have wondered if subconsciously or not I have elevated my father to the status of a god. From him I received not only my human life but also a life of imagery. Through the years we must have seen hundreds of films together and through the brume of childhood I associate him with little else. In my days alone since his death nothing but images and memories have sustained me. And will I fail the test? Have I missed the point? Did I cling too long to the obscurations of life, ignoring the fire of life? Let the priest answer these questions tomorrow morning before they execute me. Unless I spit in his face before he has the chance to speak.

The illogical landscape of the imaginary, a devotion to the spell of falseness...sometimes the labyrinth is heaven, not hell. What difference does it make if I told them I have murdered? Does it matter how many, who, where, how, and when? If I spoke the truth? If it was the whole truth? What I have done was necessary, and what was necessary was the act of telling, the act of describing. My resultant death will simply be a by-product of the very motion of my words, like the bits of paper whisked away by the sudden, swift movement of that train long ago transporting a child who could not understand that some windows do not sponsor the light. They disown it.

One evening, the upper edge of a booth door left ajar cast a thick shadow that split the maintenance man's face. The peep chamber had been shut down due to mechanical problems. The door swung freely each time a prospective customer approached the video monitor and then chose another after noticing the "Out Of Order" sign pasted across the dusty screen. It was in this booth that I had encountered auditory difficulties, forcing me to press my ear against the little speaker. But look, see how the spy has escaped with the special sounds in his mind? The drama of his departure is highlighted by the menacing swing of the door creaking to and fro. Can you hear the bark of the silky, sturdy hound frozen for a snapshot instant by the isolating bright band of searchlight scanning its uncomfortably alert face surrounded by pitch black space? Can you see the discolored flesh of the female victim's nude foot, bruised and thick like the underbelly of a fish washed ashore, gashed by a predator's underwater attack? Can you smell the shore wind filled with salt air, fresh rain, and the perspiration-drenched trench coats of all the detectives hovering around a corpse? I can.

A life at sea, in a time when the nautical arts were primitive, that would have been soothing to me. Trireme ships, the nomadic search of the ancient travelers, unaware of the distant lands. Movement towards an unknown shore, the moment of disembarkation filled with a terrible mixture of excitement and anxiety: what will they find? Advance information simply does not exist, there are no records, communication occurs so slowly, and there is always the lethal danger of an unpleasant discovery,

The most impressive figure, the one who received most of my reflection and attention, was "The Grafter." 42, 5'11", approximately

175lbs., gentle blue eyes, blond hair, thin eyebrows flaked with dandruff. Embroidered with innumerable tattoos like a mad harlequin. On the left calf his favorite figure: a butcher at the block, raising a cleaver covered with the faces of screaming children, smiling at the instrument the way a dog becomes excited by the appearance of a new meal.

My resourcefulness came through once more in "The Grafter's" case. I managed to find a few pages of the trial transcript. Apparently he was questioned quite extensively when the Defense allowed him to take the stand. In this testimony he never admitted that the mutilations were dictated by a vision, by a voice, by some other-than-the-self message process, the way newborn Capistrano turtles, equipped with strategic genetic information, begin their journey towards the sea, laboring blindly across the hostile shore. I admire those secret voices. His conversations that made no sound. I worship that language. I envy that communication.

Little trapezoidal shapes of moonlight seeped through the tears in the sheet across the high recreational cell window during repairs done last month. Suspension of the frail geometry, the shapes gentle and dreamy, like a ship's sail or deck hatch golden in sunset. On the marble chessboard too, as we played during those evenings and I placed the grey-green marble Rook's solid round base on one of the floating moonlight sails, two squares away. "Nooo!" he would say repeatedly, addressing no one in particular, always afraid of being asked more questions, of being put back on the stand. Then "The Grafter" would grasp in his fitful hand a more green than grey marble pawn withdrawn from the danger of the open hatch, the missing swirls of grey replaced by his ashen cheeks.

For the most part our chess games calmed him, and he learned to trust me. He described his technique, and he kept returning to the last murder, the one just before his arrest, the one highlighted during his trial.

Mealtime tied very nicely into the macabre details of "The Grafter's" crimes.

He would take the head of a chicken and suture it to the body of a cat or a dog. Do a little series of the same kind, leave them in the death room with the victim's body, and sometimes arrange them throughout the entire murder scene.

He used a needle and threads most of the time. Occasionally it would be an industrial shipping stapler. Vulgar light of the glaring bulbs in the lower class apartment buildings he stalked. He was sitting yoga-style next to the toilet bowl; the strange, mean starkness of light struck his massive chest. There were flakes of sawdust stuck to his skin because of the sticky taxidermist fluids. He must have looked like a Santa Claus figure from a lumberyard, little wooden scraps covering his body like fresh, cream colored snow. Then up on the bathroom windowsill lined neatly in a row: three puppies forever stiffened into the begging position, three floppy chicken heads stitched to their necks. Weight of the fully-grown bird heads causing them to droop forward, like a heavy old man asleep on a bench, bowed crown completely relaxed. Incongruous pastoral green diamond patterns on the filthy blood streaked tile to the left and right of the grafted mummified objects. Medicine cabinet door ajar, halving the bulb glow distributed upon his nude, floridly tattooed form. Written inside the cabinet in excrement: *If Not Two Heads Better Than One, A New Head For Rover Means Extra Fun.* Necklace of dried blood caked around the double stitching which secured the pale yellow poultry masks to the rich brown dog fur. A shade of brown probably like the Victrola, only not as dark.

He killed only during the summer months. Pleasure of the colors and textures of these macabre tableaux in the thickest heat of an August day.

I learned that the detective in charge was a morbid, older man with enough time on the force to retire (there were those times when "The

Grafter" was remarkably lucid). At the scene of the final murder this detective stood stoically before the grotesque surgical horrors. A crust of chili sauce and mustard had formed across his dirty, dark grey mustache. It had a flaky texture not unlike the sawdust particles left on the toilet floor after "The Grafter" fled the apartment. Some of this desiccated food matter had alighted upon the shiny Chi Rho pin that the detective always wore on his label. The forensic team set up their fingerprinting equipment as the photographer wiped perspiration from his forehead, preparing to focus the shot. The detective smiled at the thought that although much evidence was recovered after each murder, the possibility of catching the killer was hampered by the lack of leading clues: they still had no idea of "The Grafter's" identity.

The defense attorney (well bred and used to a high standard of living even before the success of his very lucrative practice) must have experienced a twinge of disgust when listening to "The Grafter's" description of clumps of frog eggs slimily erupting during one of his boyhood vivisections. The lawyer may have made an unpleasant association with the many meals of shiny black Russian caviar that he loved to eat, even at lunches during recesses at the trial. Certainly if he had been present at one of the crime scenes, if his senses had absorbed the oppressive heat and stench of one of these pasty, smeared, nightmare museum displays of animal parts incongruously joined, he would have foregone these delicacies for the aristocrat's palate.

The photographer enjoyed a mouthful of cubic, thick, colorful candies as he set up his tripod for the windowsill shots of the dog-chicken figures. These sweet, delicious squares were smaller than the bloody panels of bathroom tile but the shine of their wet, sucked surface was greater than the glint of the metal scissors and comb lying on the medicine cabinet shelf. From time to time he rolled his tongue around his mouth and the reflective planes of the fat lozenges captured fragmented slivers of the scene. Inside this kaleidoscope the detective could be seen walking into the next room. A transcript page twirled within the candies' slick sheen:

1	PROSECUTION	Is your testimony that you were
2		delusional, that you heard voices
3		and commands to do certain things?
4		
5	DEFENDANT	Nooo! Nothing heard voices no more I.
6		Prevent can't haven't. Without pain.
7		Without pain. Big figure dark woods
8		vegetables told me to do it. I more no voices
10		heard nothing.
11	PROSECUTION	Your Honor, may we approach the bench
12		for a side bar?
13	DEFENSE	Your Honor, there's no need for this, the
14		Prosecution is merely trying to abuse
15		the defendant.
16	DEFENDANT	Shop visit did I go frogs Hoppy and Harry.
17		Hobby shop frogs in bottle dissect. Summer
18		vacation hot time with knife. Liked smell
19		knife cut good vegetables told me to do it.

20	DEFENSE	Your Honor, the Prosecution is preparing
21		Sgt. Jauntley's testimony for tomorrow
22		morning. As we all know, the detective is
23		not well. The Defense realizes that he
24		was deeply traumatized by what he saw at this
25		crime scene, that he suffers in particular from
26		an ulcer aggravated by a nervous condition.

His burning stomach air belched the last vapors of the undigested chilidog into his throat. He was on his way to inspect the bedroom. He wanted a good long look at the death scene before the photographer was ready to transfer the equipment there. And even Jauntley could not resist his stomach's demanding reflex, forcing its contents through his esophagus, forcing him to go quickly to a corner where he vomited sloppily, powerfully, as though the hot, viscous matter could dissolve the vision so intact and silent and serene and symmetrical. Jauntley who made no secret of his passionate desire to witness the aftermath of psychotic violence, even he could not look beyond that first moment of recognition of what "The Grafter" had done to the woman.

Not even Jauntley's charm could help him recover, his little talisman which ridiculed the moral lesson of the three monkeys who would not see, hear, or speak evil. A three figure plastic key ring with the familiar expressions of animals clasping hands to eyes, ears, and mouth, only behind them was the unexpected figure of a huge gorilla gleefully subjecting the smaller simians to the hardly miniscule discomfort of anal penetration.

The message of propriety and restraint, so mocked by Jauntley's key chain, would register its ironic impact today. In this bedroom, in this heat and fume of dried blood, sweat, stale food, and now fresh human puke, the joke was in reverse a second time, and the joke was on Jauntley.

The woman was crucified upon the wall above the bed. Not in the traditional manner, but with legs spread apart, almost parallel to the outstretched arms. Cracked leg bone protruded through the flesh at oblique angles. He had used construction bolts to secure the body, shot through a kind of gun used to penetrate wood or even metal. Suspended in front of the window was a stained glass ornament designed in a trefoil shape. Rays of lavender light covered the woman's fingers.

She had been decapitated and the head of a tiger cub was stitched along her neck. Pieces of her shredded shoulder and chest skin, uplifted and stretched around, appeared like a ragged muffler covering the tiger's jaw. How "The Grafter" managed to find a tiger cub head was beyond speculation, but nevertheless, there it was.

The woman's eyes were removed and, lids slashed away, they stared in blank lifelessness stuffed bloody and uneven into the baby tiger's sockets. A bulging eye effect ensued, like one of those gag heads in the back of a novelty store. Sewn to her nipples were the smaller tiger-eyes, tilting downward like little Christmas ornaments on a sagging tree. Deep bite marks over the entirety of both breasts gave the impression of ski tracks indented into the slope of a mountain.

Perched mischievously upon the tiger's head was a little nylon pointy blue clown hat. Attached to the hat was a balloon and on the balloon in purple lipstick was the message: *Come To The Circus Today!*

"The Grafter" had eviscerated the woman's stomach, inserting her head into the disemboweled cavity as though it was a clock face adorning the ceramic body of a swan or an owl.

The eyeless head was completely shaved. The woman's blood matted black hair had been stapled in myriad strands all along the ceiling, like foliage hanging in the Amazon forest. "The Grafter" had secured the long dried entrails to the ends of the twisted strings of hair. When he did this, steam arose from the still living tissue, but that was several days before Jauntley and the homicide crew arrived, and so it was impossible for Jauntley to make the easy visual association between the vivid changing shapes of steam released by the organs and the similar, less convoluted steam escaping from the chili dog he purchased before entering the house.

The vacuity of the woman's sockets was particularly arresting given that her own eyes had been so obviously misplaced within the head of the cub.

The entirety of the bathtub faucet was lodged very securely into the vagina, the spigot facing upwards in defiance of gravity. A reflection of Jauntley's key ring (which he wore on the side of his belt) appeared on the lustrous metal. The woman's toes had been severed and sutured to her face, in two vertical rows directly beneath the hollow sockets, to give the effect (one would assume) of escaping teardrops.

There was no evidence of semen anywhere in the apartment but Jauntley's vomity handkerchief stank even in the fresh air after they carried him outside. At that moment the frail old man was pushing his little hot dog stand away from the house. A greasy, stained rag hung from the back pocket of his overalls. No steam emanated from the cylindrical well in which the food was cooked because the gas burner had already been extinguished. A little boy scooted past the cart carrying a toy plastic trumpet. Jauntley thought he noticed a stain on the rag shaped something like a cross, but his concentration was hampered by another explosion from within his abdomen and at this instant when he almost positively identified the shape on the rag forensic technicians inside the house began the extremely delicate task of disengaging the woman's corpse from the wall.

Transatlantic Pictures

Interoffice Memorandum

From: J. Wakdjunkaga, screen-writer

To: C. Loki, Executive Producer

Re: Final White Draft of "The Confession "

[Autopsy Narrative]

Dear Mr. Loki,

Enclosed for your approval is the Final White draft of the Autopsy Narrative. As you recall, we discussed this scene in some detail over dinner last evening. I liked your suggestion that the camera, for the most part, be placed above the dissection table, so that the viewer sees the body from an aerial perspective, as well as the coroner as he leans over to make various observations during his examination and narrative. The viewer will also see the long attachment coming down from the fluorescent lights, to which a microphone is connected so that everything the coroner says is recorded in real time as he conducts the autopsy. We can avoid showing anything too explicit by letting the coroner's head and shoulders obscure certain parts of the woman's body. Also, there can be some interesting cutaways, with the coroner's narrative voiced-over, where we see only impersonal things: maybe the recording apparatus itself contained beyond a wall or something like that; the instruments being used; the rows of slabs elsewhere in the morgue; the coroner's office, etc.

We might want to establish elsewhere in the scenario that this is the body that is referred to during the Detective Dialogue, i.e. the woman's corpse that so upsets Detective Jauntley.

Please let me know if this meets with your approval. I wasn't sure if the use of repetition in the cutaway shots would stand up or not. We don't want to make everything too compartmentalized. I suppose there is the danger of the final result becoming too unnatural.

Best regards,

J. Wakdjunkaga

INTERIOR. NIGHT. AUTOPSY ROOM IN CITY MORGUE.

A woman's decapitated corpse is laid out upon a metal autopsy table. The camera, positioned above, shows the body and the coroner from an aerial perspective. We see the top of the coroner's head and shoulders as he leans over different parts of the body. There is also a long microphone cable extending down from the ceiling, descending at the center of the frame. The coroner speaks continuously into the microphone as he proceeds with the autopsy narrative.

CORONER:_The body of a murdered and mutilated woman was discovered in a shack near theshore of a small fishing village. The body had been found hanging by the heels from the rafters: decapitated and eviscerated. The head and viscera were in the same location; the vulva in a jar;the heart in a plastic receptacle. Before performing this autopsy, the above-mentioned location was visited to search for more forensic evidence.

SAME LOCATION. INNER WALL OF AUTOPSY ROOM.

The camera is placed inside the wall where the tape recording equipment is contained. Each autopsy table has its own microphone, shown in subsequent shots. These tape recorders are kept behind some recessed control panel and the soft hissing of the tape can be heard during a medium close-up of the machine. The coroner's voice, somewhat fainter, is heard as he continues.

CORONER: The body was that of a 25 year old, well shaped woman in a state of adequate nutrition. Decapitation was at shoulder level, achieved with a flawless spherical incision, which severed skin and most of the soft tissue. The intervertebral cartilage between the 5th and 6thcervical vertebrae had been cut with a sharp instrument.

There was no evidence of jagged edges indicating that an ax or comparable device had been used.

INTERIOR. NIGHT. AUTOPSY ROOM IN CITY MORGUE.

Return to aerial shot: same angle.

CORONER: The body had been opened by a median incision from the manubriumsterni, extending in the midline to the area just above the mons veneris. Here the cut

circles around the external genitalia for the complete removal of the vulva, lower vagina, and the anus with the lowest portion of the rectum. To accomplish this, the symphysispubis had been split and the pubic bones widely separated. From the appearance of the cut for evisceration, it was concluded that the incision was started from the lower end andterminated above the stomach pit. The reason for this was the somewhat jagged appearance of the cut skin near the chest, indicating hesitation in terminating the knife cut.

INTERIOR. NIGHT. AUTOPSY ROOM IN CITY MORGUE.

There is a slightly canted long-shot of the entire autopsy room. We see upwards of seven metal tables in a row, with the coroner at the middle table. He is illuminated because only the glaring fluorescent lights above the table where he works are on, so there is a good deal of shadow in this shot.

CORONER: The removed vulva and adjoining structures were presented in a *Play-DohHappy House Figure* carton, with preserved and dried other specimens of the same type.

The freshly removed vulva fitted well into the tissue defect of the body. Only a few pubic hairsremained on both sides of the removed organs and a portion of this hairy skin was removedremoved for purposes of identification. Examination of the outer genitalia revealed no evidence of trauma and no conclusion could be reached whether or not sexual intercourse had taken place.

SAME LOCATION. INNER WALL OF AUTOPSY ROOM.

Return to close-up of tape recorder: same angle.

CORONER: The body cavities had been completely eviscerated together with most of thediaphragm. Inspection of the trunk and extremities revealed how the body had been hoisted by the heels.

SAME LOCATION. MEDIUM SHOT OF CORONER'S OFFICE

In a slightly upward angle view, we see the coroner's desk. A large stack of files appears to the left, exaggerated by the angle. To the right is a photograph of a girl approximately ten years of age, presumably the coroner's daughter, leaning over a stone drinking fountain in a public park.

CORONER: There was a deep cut above the Achilles tendon of the right leg and a pointedcrossbar made from the metal, tubular base of a movie projection screen had been forced underneath the tendon. The other side of the crossbar had been tied to a cord, which was tightlyfastened to a cut of the leg above the heel. This cut had severed the Achilles tendon and hadnecessitated the tying with cord to hold the body securely to the crossbar. The length of the crossbar was estimated as about three feet. Both wrists had been tied with longer hemp ropesto the corresponding ends of the crossbar attached to the feet, thus holding the arms firmly when the body had been suspended by the heels.

SAME LOCATION. AERIAL VIEW OF AUTOPSY TABLE.

Return to initial aerial shot.

CORONER: Inspection of the skin surface of the body revealed dirt covering the shoulders,mostly the upper dorsal area, and the dirt resembled dry mud in thin scaly crusts. The skin of the back, both arms and legs, less of chest and abdomen, was somewhat discolored by dust whichshowed irregular smudgy areas of heavier covering. Rather striking was the amount of black dust covering both plantar surfaces, dust which appeared somewhat 'rubbed in,' as if from walking barefoot on a dirty, dusty floor.

SAME LOCATION. EXTREME CLOSE-UP: INSTRUMENTS.

An extreme close-up fills the entire screen with a metal tray containing all of the incision and dissection instruments used for the autopsy.

CORONER: Both breasts appeared good sized and well formed. They felt medium firm,mostly because the adipose tissue had hardened from the exposure to cold. The right nipple appeared normal, the left was somewhat inverted. Both breasts appeared to lean upward,apparently due to the long suspension by the heels. There was no evidence of mutilation of the breasts except for several minor V-shaped scratches, which might be the result of deliberate light probing with some kind of carving tool.

SAME LOCATION. CANTED SHOT.

Return to angled shot of rows of autopsy tables.

CORONER: Inspection of the body (trunk and extremities) revealed no evidence ofante mortem trauma. The exsanguination was complete, only fingernails showed moderate cyanosis. On the left ring finger was a cameo ring. The empty body cavities were glistening and free from blood. They appeared as if they had been washed. Nofractures of the trunk or extremities were found. The seventh vertebra was removedfor further examination.

SAME LOCATION. INNER WALL OF AUTOPSY ROOM.

Return to close-up of tape recorder: same angle.

CORONER: The thoracic and abdominal viscera had been separately kept, hidden in a bundle of old clothing behind a large stuffed tiger toy. These viscera consisted of both lungs with the trachea, the aorta from the base to the abdominal bifurcation, the esophagus, stomach, small and large intestines with mesentery and omentum to the lower rectum. En bloc with this were removed: the spleen, pancreas, adrenals, kidneys with the ureters, upper half of the urine bladder, and internal genital organs. Separately removed were:

1. Heart (without the pericardium). This had been kept in a plastic bag.

2. Liver.

SAME LOCATION. EXTREME CLOSE-UP: CORONER'S LIPS.

The camera is placed directly under the coroner's face so that only his lips appear in an extreme close-up. Volume of his voice highest in this shot.

CORONER: The head with the neck was submitted in a separate cardboard box.It fitted with the trunk of the body. The hair was medium short cut and somewhatcurly. It appeared soiled with dust and smeared with blood. The color of the hair was dark. A round hole in the scalp, which was difficult to find on outer inspection, measured, when moderately stretched, 0.76 cm. in diameter. The edgesof the defect revealed a narrow marginal abrasion. There was no tear in the contour of the opening and no evidence of burn, nor could any powder particles be grossly visualized. This skin defect, suggesting the entrance wound of a bullet, was located to the left of the midline and about 6 cm. above the neck hairline, 3.5 cm. laterally and 2 cm. above the outer occipital protuberantis.

SAME LOCATION. AERIAL VIEW OF AUTOPSY TABLE.

Return to initial aerial shot.

CORONER: The face appeared covered with dust in irregular distribution. There was no evidence of external trauma to the face. Both eyes were closed. The nose appeared intact on palpation, but there was blood in both nostrils. The left ear had a hooked spike inserted, the tip of which was at the time of examination 2 cm. deep in the external earcanal. There were slight, apparently post mortem excoriations, on the outer border of the ear canal. Blood oozed from this ear in larger quantities than the excoriations indicated.

<u>SAME LOCATION. MEDIUM SHOT OF CORONER'S OFFICE.</u>

Return to upward view of coroner's desk.

CORONER: Tied to the head of the hooked spike was a cord to which another hooked spikeof the same size had been attached. This right spike was at the time of examination not inserted in the right ear canal.

SAME LOCATION. EXTREME CLOSE-UP: INSTRUMENTS.

Return to same extreme close-up of instruments.

CORONER: The neck revealed no evidence of applied force, like from strangling, no finger or nail imprints, nor scratches. No blunt trauma, as from a chisel or crook. The trachea and larynx appeared normal. The portion of the lower medulla oblongata and the upper cervical spine had been ripped out. This portion of the spinal cord was not found.

SAME LOCATION. EXTREME CLOSE-UP: CORONER'S LIPS.

Return to same extreme close-up of coroner's lips. Volume of his voice highest here.

CORONER: Dissection of the brain showed hemorrhages in all ventricular spaces. The actual bullet track through the brain was difficult to visualize.It was evident that the bullet had traversed the brain beneath the corpus callosum passing through the ventricles, and struck the sphenoid bone. To facilitate the localization of the bullet, as there was no exit defect, x-ray pictures were taken and the bullet, apparently of .22 caliber, was located and found within the right orbita beneath the median portion of its roof without destruction to the eyeball.The extension skull fracture had been the cause for the bleedings from the nose and the right ear canal.

SAME LOCATION. INNER WALL OF AUTOPSY ROOM

Return to close-up of tape recorder: same angle. Volume of coroner's voice lowest level.

CORONER: Examination of the decapitated and eviscerated body revealed the only cause of death to be a bullet fired at the back of the head. The bullet had penetrated the brain anteriorly causing destruction of the vital areas and interventricular hemorrhage as well as extensive skull fractures and some subarachnoid hemorrhage. The bullet had lodged in the left orbit. It had apparently not been a contact nor a very close shot. Death had apparentlyoccurred shortly (seconds or minutes) after the shot had been fired. All the other mutilations of the body had been carried out after death. Most of this mutilation was inflicted upon surface regions, instantly visible to the naked eye.

The Son: Chapter II

No screams: the gag was perfect. Ball of hard rubber secured by strips of rawhide strictly tied behind the head. No saliva leakage either, although it is certain abject fear makes her throat totally dry.

Arms tied above the head, legs bound at the ankles. Suspended. Slight swaying like a weary pendulum, delicate, very slow, as if she were a tassel faintly disturbed by the tiniest breeze. Tears rolling mechanically without concomitant sniffling sounds. And in the clear water of the flowing drops the reflection of an impossibly huge man. He holds his arms together, implacable, sweating profusely, austere.

It is a basement room: ugly, desolate, cement walls and floor, clutter of entangled pipes chokes the ceiling, every surface caked with sediment and rust. A little wash sink in the corner, old porcelain smudged with grease, filled to the brim with bubbling filth: contaminated water, human hair, rodent droppings, sludge. Refuse from the inhabitants of an apartment building; in the corner some broken, filthy toys.

His mask the hackneyed Man-From-Space concept of the tubular helmet. Flecked with metal studs, it smells and shines the way only leather can smell and shine.

There should be a staircase leading into this subterranean parlor, at least for dramatic effect. Littered upon that staircase should be scraps of clothing: old, brittle, stained, torn. The condition of these pieces must be so disfigured and their arrangement upon the steps so haphazard that anyone descending the staircase must be immediately startled by their contrast to the bright, new, intact leather of the carefully stitched mask. Is this what remains of the girl's clothing? Clothing of other victims from the past?

The teller of a story would know that the screech of a speeding train becomes her plaintive cry after the gag is removed, that the public service poster inside the train (depicting the degradation of life in stark tenements) becomes a portent of the place her captor will drag her to, where she will be alone, helpless, doomed. But these are hollow portents, saving no one.

Chunky clang of steel as the hulking captor scrapes the concrete with his soles, moving closer to the girl.

This underground space is not so far removed from the sounds of everyday life as one might think: at least the blurry chaos of dense freeway traffic can be heard in the distance. It is not a distinct sound. There are interstices of silence between the paddle's impact, the muffled groans, the metallic footfalls. Through these cracks of quiet a wave of traffic noise suddenly spills forward, as though one were floating through a room insulated by the silent moments, then passing an open window beyond which the angry charged noise of a swarming bees' nest abruptly assaults the ears.

A passenger in one of the rushing freeway cars picks absentmindedly at a scab on her forefinger just as the nail studded paddle reaches its second stage of inflicted pain, breaking the skin and causing some initial blood flow. The man sitting next to her has been driving all night. He reaches nervously for yet another cigarette. His hand movement is not as quick or as pronounced and certainly not as vicious as the next descent of the captor's wrist again bringing the thick leather paddle down upon its long abused, totally helpless target.

The desiccated corpse of a small dog flattened against the highway railing betrays no trace of wet blood, yet the bound woman's buttocks and now her upper thighs have begun to bleed quite freely. The red liquid clings for several seconds to the black paddle and then streams away into rivulets, the way rain channels itself along a window pane over and over again, continually forming a new pattern and a slightly different angle of descent. Dozens of tiny brown ants scurry in and out of the dog's nostrils while a very large water bug remains stationary in a corner of the ceiling, not too far from where the woman is suspended.

Many years ago, when the deceased animal was a puppy and lived in a cage in a pet shop, the proprietor of the shop past by holding a clay bowl filled with water. The man's height, the angle of the bowl, the position and intensity of the available light, all combined in such a way that a shadow shaped something like a parenthesis appeared across the dog's bright face, its white and yellow fur displayed this parenthetical or crescent shadow which disappeared as quickly as the blinking of an eye or when Venetian blinds are shut.

As the man reached over to open the cage, he shifted his weight and his pocket change gently collided with his keys. A similar tinkling is heard as the woman in the car scrapes off the remains of her dry scab. She flings away the particles of dead skin and this gesture causes her charm bracelet to jangle slightly. This happens as the car passes the dog's carcass, but since the vehicle is moving so rapidly, she has no opportunity to notice the animal's body.

The past sound of the pocket change is like the present sound of the bracelet. There is an aural bridge that links them. It is in the basement room, where the man now unlocks the woman's handcuffs. He wants to shift her blood soaked unconscious body into a new, even more restrictive position. One cuff remains fastened to the woman's limp wrist while the other cuff falls unlocked, bouncing off its counterpart, jangling like the bracelet, like the coins. These sounds of metal suddenly cause the man to look over at the the ancient boiler in the other room. The man's scraping soles apparently disturb the water bug. It crawls along the ceiling toward the only light bulb in the large room. It travels slowly, as it has not been really frightened by the footsteps; it just cautiously removes itself from an area in which activity has been recorded. Approaching the light bulb, its antennae cast faintly waving, wire-thin shadows across the glossy red splatter of the woman's lower back.

At the moment that the pet shop owner placed the puppy's dish inside its cage, a young woman at the check out counter opened her purse to pay for some birdseed. The bright red leather shone vividly beneath the glaring florescent light. The purse was embossed with a large gold insect, possibly a beetle. Here the antennae were emphatically splayed across the smooth surface of the expensive handbag. But the beetle appeared to have been contorted into a very odd position for the sake of emblematic effect: instead of lying flush upon the bag in accordance with the laws of gravity, it had been forced into a double perspective, as though it was being made to look back upon its own body.

Inside the woman's purse was a letter she had recently received from her grandmother who lived in the country. For the last few summers the young woman had visited her grandmother and this letter was a kind of annual invitation and preamble to her stay. Her grandmother described some of the changes that had occurred on and around the property where her summer cottage was located. A pond had been constructed just behind the house, and she spoke of all the beautiful fish they had put there. Her husband, a retired carpenter, had been busy all spring making a dock as well as a little rowboat, which would be perfect for afternoon picnics on the water. He had hurt his thumb (though not too seriously) while working and this required a trip to the local town for some antiseptic ointment. Her grandmother commented jokingly that her husband was so preoccupied with sporting and recreational activities that he frequently overlooked basic supplies, sometimes even groceries. He had also recently completed a tree house for their younger grandchildren, and she commented that the woman's cousins were anxious to see her again, especially as one of them had just begun to do some paintings and he wanted the opinion of his older relation who was looked upon as something of a connoisseur of the art world. There was a sparrow's nest tucked under one of the higher branches near the tree house and the old woman complained lightheartedly that they would never be able to sleep late anymore because of the incessant chirping.

Nevertheless, she also spoke of the many crumbs she had been leaving for the little creatures, since her baking was prolific particularly during this period when they were enjoying their summer holiday. She even baked for an entire school field trip just before the end of the term. The schoolchildren were jogging in a deeper part of the surrounding forest and their teacher (a friend of her husband) brought all down to the cottage for a visit. Lastly she told her granddaughter of the perfect blooming of the apple trees, promising (should she prolong her visit into early fall) a bountiful harvest, plenty of apple cider and pie, and a lot of healthy exercise in the process.

The abducted girl's basement tormentor does in fact retie her with an agonizing disregard for the anatomical limitations of the human body. He knocks aside a can with brutish indifference and the shock of noise sends the water bug scurrying into a dark corner, yet the woman walked slowly out of the pet store, calmly placing the bird seed into a small plastic shopping bag and hailing a cab with a gentle motion of her palm.

Having turned his prisoner upside down, the abductor hoists her towards the ceiling by means of a pulley and rope. Removing the handcuffs altogether, he uses more rope to secure each wrist to the corresponding ankle, viciously pulling back on the rope until her arms describe a semi-circle behind her back, her elbows almost parallel to her calves. He steps back to admire the savage bondage he has imposed upon the girl, his sweat dripping in the unventilated basement, daubing his face with a filthy red handkerchief, smiling the utterly self-indulgent smile of one who is dangerously insane. The can spilled thousands of pieces of gravel across the floor, some of it rising into slowly flowing pools as water rains across the area, falling from the damaged ancient pipes. It was the end of summer but still very hot and the oppressive humidity is amplified by the enclosed underground space. The assailant is used to extremes of heat, he often exercises in this basement, developing his already muscular frame by breaking up pieces of old wooden furniture such as the bookcases, shelves, cabinets, and bureaus which litter the entire area.

The birdseed made a low rattling sound as the motion of the cab shook it mildly against the cardboard container. The woman closed her eyes for a while, trying to rest as she contemplated her earlier consideration of visiting the museum. She wondered if she was not too tired to go, and burdened by the pet shop purchases, she felt it would be a cumbersome expedition. She was eager to view the new exhibit of Surrealist paintings on display that month, especially one of her favorites, *The Human Condition* by Magritte. She wondered if it would not be better to stop at home first and take a nap. At least that way she could divest herself of her numerous parcels and go to the exhibit more comfortably.

Across the street from the pet shop was a little bookstore specializing in large black and white photography books. There was a short flight of steps leading down to the bookstore, then an extended anteroom filled with magazines and newspapers before one reached the bookstore proper. In the lower section, below several more flights of stairs were the photography books. As the woman entered the cab a man was leafing through a collection of photographs of the city taken many years ago. He was fascinated by one picture in particular. He was a physics student and deeply interested in the laws and composition of matter. It happened by coincidence that he was actually acquainted with the woman from the pet shop; at least she was familiar to him because he had noticed her many times at the university where she had been taking some art appreciation courses. On several occasions they had both stopped at the water-fountain at the same time but never spoke. The photograph reminded him of her in some curious way. He was completely engrossed by this picture of a stone drinking fountain, which beautifully captured every stage and nuance of the spraying water. Like a sequence of transparent sculptures, the invisible time of motion was depicted in all its minutiae, all the secret phases of moving matter were made visible to the unperceiving human eye through the technical intervention of customized photography. He was obsessed with this revelation of a kind of hidden time; that matter behaved on several planes at once. His studies had already shown him that matter and the perception of matter could be two very different things, and this photograph certainly intrigued him for that reason.

The shadow of the abductor falls across the white sink as he bends down to sprinkle water on his prisoner's face in the hope of restoring her to consciousness. In the past, there were many newspaper shreds on the bottom of the puppy's cage and in one corner were three strips previously forming the single image of the contents of a plumbing store sale. There were sinks, bathtubs, and fixtures in the photograph, but when the proprietor leaned in to give the dog its dish, no shadow was cast across the sink in the photograph. In fact, the puppy moved across the tiny cage even more vigorously after receiving its water, and the muddy tracks left by its filthy paws quickly blotted out the photograph in the newspaper advertisement. The abductor is still able to move adroitly past the sink in the basement.

He retrieves the can and goes to the sink to scoop out the rancid slop collected there. He tries to revive the bound girl by dousing her with this warm slime. Sprinkling droplets upon her face collected by handkerchief from the tiny pools on the floor has proven unsuccessful. As he breaks the curdled surface of the stagnant brew, all the congealed particles disperse, swiftly radiating in all directions like the elementary scientific experiment in which students "chase" away pepper floating upon water by inserting a bar of soap. Before being sucked into the whirlpool created by the water rushing into the empty submerged can, these crusty disparate particles resembled the stars in the night sky, their blanched edges bright against the inky water, in fact their outline is very similar to a particular constellation visible from the hill upon which the couple, driving past the dog's carcass, have just parked, thankful to be home after so long a journey.

A long series of stone steps leads from the couple's home down to a little rose garden beneath the hill. The shine of the moon plus a generous supply of security spotlights gives the grey stone a remarkable brightness, almost creating the impression of daylight. As the couple exits the vehicle a burst of wind whips through the valley, tilting an empty baby carriage past the foot of the steps. The carriage clears the first step and begins rolling down the inclined plane, gaining momentum as it clears each landing. The woman is the first to notice the runaway vacant carriage and, responding through sheer reflex, rushes towards it in a panic. At the base of the final flight, the woman's outstretched arms are about to grasp the hurtling vehicle just as the outraged captor raises his machete to inflict fatal injury upon his victim. In his derangement he is convinced that she has succumbed to unconsciousness only to thwart him in his pursuit of further sadistic pleasure.

The carriage comes to a dead stop, lying across the last step, caught in the woman's embrace. The front wheels expel their momentum by furiously spinning in mid-air and their blurry revolutions are echoed by torrents of the woman's spurting blood. It gushes across the gravel pebbles with such initial force that the little stones whirl about, as though being hosed away in a garden, forming little circles during these first moments of discharge. This blow is in fact a lethal blow, having burst the aorta. The captor steps back, murmuring obscenities, the shadow of the machete like an oversize ruler, a fat band of blackness leaking droplets. Very similar to the rectangular strip of newspaper with the porcelain fixture advertisement darkened by paw mud on the bottom of the puppy's cage. That dark band did not tremble, but the captor's hand shakes slightly. The thick blade vibrates in the air. Yet there were large water drops in the sink advertisement, almost as big as the dark blood specters leaking from the machete. In fact, a sink faucet dripped in the basement of the pet shop. Those water droplets descended at regular intervals in spite of the puppy's romping, animated muddy movements, which more and more obscured the faucet in the advertisement image. The machete droplets fall slowly and thickly, in vivid contrast to the animal's darting movements.

That very morning, the pet shop manager had changed all the animals' cages with fresh newspaper. There were several editions of different newspapers lying around, and then a stack of them from the past couple of weeks that the manager's assistant was instructed to save. The newspaper with the kitchen and bathroom advertisement was left behind by a man who had been to the store the previous day to purchase turtle food. He bought newspapers for one reason only: he was an avid racing fan and the only part of the publication that interested him was the daily race listings. Having browsed this section before getting to the pet shop, he had no further need of his newspaper. He had picked it up earlier that morning at a newsstand across the street from his apartment building. Next to the newsstand was a vacant lot littered with debris and the remnants of the demolished structure that occupied the site. The man was struck by a visual coincidence as he leafed through the paper to get to the races and in doing so passed a clothing advertisement that featured a beautiful model with long hair and a much-arched figure. Just ahead of him was a discarded mannequin with its wig still in place. It bore a striking resemblance to the woman in the newspaper. His attention was riveted by the similarity, which included a shock of perception: one of the plaster eyes was missing and a rat was burrowing into the vacuous head. The pose and posture of the woman and her inanimate counterpart were so much alike that the man half expected another rodent to pop its head through his newspaper. Of course he realized that this was impossible and he began to skim the listings of horses in order to choose his bets for the day.

Having rested with a long nap, the woman with the birdseed rode the escalator, which lead to the floor of the exhibit. She correctly foresaw that ridding herself of the bundles and catching a little sleep were the perfect ingredients for renewed vigor. Her strained faculties had regrouped, ready to continue their search for enjoyment. In the dream during her nap, emaciated sea gulls stood literally frozen upon a series of large rocks, an eerie incongruity given the unmistakable character of summer air. The gulls' staring eyes were like tar-black pellets and shined with disturbing clarity in the glaring sun. Each gull's webbed foot was imbedded in a block of ice, and next to one of these blocks was a detective novel from the 1940s, one of those books with melodramatic titles and lurid color illustrations of men in trench coats hiding blackjacks or syringes in the shadow of alleyways, silky buxom women smoking cigarettes with holders, covered in jewelry and fur. Just before she awoke, a jolt of wind violently ripped open the book, flipping back its pages in rapid succession. In the volley of skipping pages, little snatches of images made themselves miraculously distinct through the magic of dream logic: she saw two detectives with imposing, dark grey fedoras standing in front of a water fountain ablaze with the flames of a car explosion. They discussed whether or not someone's daughter would be brought to identify her father's body. Then a shaken detective being helped into a car, his expression totally shocked and traces of vomit on his shirt. Finally, a murderer fleeing the apartment of his midget victim; dried rose petals scatter during his exit.

There was a huge billboard in the background of the scene containing the detectives and the flame-strewn fountain, depicting a man coming into a new town and being greeted. It was a cigarette advertisement and below the huge caption *Welcome Stranger!* was a tired looking gentleman being offered a package of cigarettes in front of a drug store populated with smiling, pleasant townspeople. The traveler reaches for the pack with a relieved smile as he wipes his brow, the inference obviously that this brand of tobacco is both a sign of hospitality and comfort. Across from the man who is about to enjoy his smoke, sitting on a fountain stool in the store, is a jovial fellow wearing an enormous cowboy hat, a pack of the same brand of cigarettes protruding above his shirt pocket. The logo design of the package, a series of alternating black and white diamonds and squares, appears just above the rim of his pocket, standing out starkly against his light, cream-colored shirt. Because of the exaggeration of the perspective, the same diamonds and squares on the package handed to the man in the foreground appear as large as the fountain stool man himself who looks almost dizzy, with his squinting, broadly smiling face, as though he were about to faint. Behind him, on the other side of the counter, is an old brass cash register with a white marble top. Thin black lines run through the marble and the proprietor's eyeglasses rest (lenses facing up) on the cool stone surface. The newcomer wears official looking clothes and carries a professional attaché case, as though his arrival in this town signifies some kind of special task or mission that he and only he can perform. The townspeople might have requested his presence for this very purpose, and the warmth of their greeting and the general atmosphere has less to do with the benefits of the advertised product than the fulfillment of their plans and wishes.

The captor drops the machete as though in a trance, releasing the instrument with a mechanical gesture and shuffling away from the body in a somnambulistic manner. The succession of death throes has dwindled to a slow ticking of the rope shadow falling across the path of the plodding water bug. But the insect rushes away when the clang of the long knife echoes brashly upon the cement floor. The captor begins walking in circles upon the gravel, emulating the circumvolution performed by these pieces as a result of the blood flow moments earlier. He moves faster and faster, widening his circles and stepping more heavily and deliberately, trying to maximize the crunching effect produced by his heavy work boots, to make these sounds louder and louder. He begins panting from the exertion, running faster and faster, stomping more and more brutally, focusing more and more closely on the sound of crushed gravel, trying to make it louder and louder with each step.

I tried to adjust the speaker volume at this point but it was no use. The noise of ground gravel merged into the crackle of static, and I leaned close to the little amplifier in vain: now the captor ran about as though in a silent film, no trace whatsoever of natural, recorded sound. I began counting the rope knots as the corpse swayed more and more slowly, almost coming to a standstill. Suddenly the bullhorns called out my name, interrupting my inventory of knots.

The woman was dead. I could do nothing.

Transatlantic Pictures

Interoffice Memorandum

From: J. Wakdjunkaga, screen-writer

To: C. Loki, Executive Producer

Re: Final White Draft of "The Confession"

[Defense and Prosecution Psychiatrists]

Dear Mr. Loki,

Enclosed for your approval is the Final White draft of dialogue for the scene containing the Meeting of Defense & Prosecution Psychiatrists. After reviewing this dialogue, I thought we might try something a little adventurous. Perhaps there could be a camera on a swivel mount in the center of the table, a circular table at that, so as each doctor speaks and gives his opinion or objection or description, the camera can pan over to him, and then on to the next doctor, and so on. We could even make these "swish" pans, where the camera is moved very suddenly and causes a little blurring of the spatial interval between each doctor. The only problem with this idea is that there wouldn't be that much distance to cover, and to maximize the effect of the harsh or abrupt pan movement, we might cheat the normal distance between the characters, i.e. construct an extremely large, oversize table so that there is much more space between each person than would normally be the case, etc.

I think, or I should say I hope, that you will find the psychiatric comments interesting, insofar as the confusion and ambiguity that surrounds whether or not the protagonist has in fact committed murders is very much reinforced by what the doctors say. Based upon our prior discussions, it seems to me that we want the audience to remain unsure about our anti-hero's guilt or innocence.

Please let me know if you agree.

Best regards,

J. Wakdjunkaga

INTERIOR. DAY. JUDGE'S CHAMBERS.

A group of psychiatrists for the defense and the prosecution is assembled for preliminary discussion of the accused. Five doctors sit at a circular table, each with their own set of files and notes. The camera, positioned at the center of the table, is panned abruptly, in the manner of a "swish" pan, from one doctor to another as they take turns discussing the psychological characteristics and history of the defendant. The "swish" pan effect should create some visual blurring, as the doctors are seated several feet apart, thus the suddenly panned camera should create some distortion as it moves from doctor to doctor, establishing a medium close-up of each as they make their comments.

DR. ANDERSON: Not floridly psychotic at the time of the murders? Is that your conclusion?

DR. MURCHISON: First of all, I'm not happy with the premise that he's responsible for anyof the crimes he's been charged with. He may have been involved in some obscure way, butI don't think he actually participated in these murders. So any clinical conclusions we drawshould reflect—

DR. ANDERSON: Wait a minute, wait a minute, let's not confuse the priorities here, OK?He's been charged and he's about to stand trial for at least nine serial slayings. I'm not concerned with speculation on his culpability as charged, which is outside our sphere concerns.

DR. MURCHISON: I understand that. I'd like to add that it's refreshing to hear such an objection coming from the defense psychiatric team. My point is that I believe oneof the keys to an understanding of this particular personality disorder is to do some special research regarding the nature of his delusional psychosis, as I believe it applies not only to a distortion of reality but possibly to the legal issue of whether he is guilty of anything other than an obsession with death. We cannot neglect this avenue of approach.

DR. ANDERSON: You're trying to conduct a trial doctor, and as I said, this is not what we're here to do!

DR. DOYLE: Do you have any of the results of the *Multiphasic Personality Tests,*are the copies still with the attorneys or do we have our own here?

DR. RUTLAND: I'm not sure those tests were conducted yet, he's only been in custody about three weeks.

DR. ANDERSON: There's a lot of biographical information we can sort through, and I think a few of us have already had some preliminary personal interviews, is that right?

DR. O'CONNOR: I had him for about an hour on Tuesday. Besides a little stuff on the father, which I think you're all familiar with, all I got was a crash course on howto carve sparrows!

DR. ANDERSON: Yes, he covered that with me as well. He's rather talented, but I think his obsessional focus is a charade; I'm not convinced he has no choice in thedirection of thought patterns.

DR. RUTLAND: What about this account of the father's death, the fall, and his guilt,particularly the irrationality of the guilt, I can't quite put all that together. What about you, doctor, you spent almost three hours with him yesterday, do you have some kind of chronology here that might help us out?

DR. ANDERSON: Apparently the father fell down a flight of stairs in their home a long time ago, and he died. It seems that the accused was interested in a girl at that time, became quite obsessed with her. It was a classic case of unrequited love.

Certainly it's significant that the father's death occurred at the same time as the son's unrealized love affair, and shortly thereafter the son's preoccupation with pornographypreoccupation with pornography began. Here's where most of the symptomologybegins.

DR. DOYLE: That's right...irrational guilt concerning the father's death, obsessivethought patterns, anxiety, low self-esteem, displacement of normal sex drive with pornography, and finally the fixation on death, particularly violent forms of death exclusively involving women.

DR. ANDERSON: It's almost as though his phenomenological perceptions have been sabotaged in some way, I'm just not sure if it's a sabotage from within or fromwithout. Certainly there are schizophrenic tendencies here, but I haven't spent enough time with him to be sure.

DR. MURCHISON: I know the line of thought you're following, I've encountered it myself in the two interviews I've had. Cause and effect logic has undergone convoluted forms of distortion in his psyche, and it does affect perceptions of everyday reality. The paranoia is acute, certainly, but without further tests we can't be sure if it's an organicdisorder as extreme as some form of schizophrenia.

DR. RUTLAND: It does seem to follow some of the classic forms: the father's death becomes his fault since normal perceptions don't exist for him, or at best they existselectively, otherwise he could view this as an accidental, blameless death.

DR. ANDERSON: Exactly. The obsession with the sparrows is an even more extremeexample. He suffers from a highly irrational equation making process, which enables him to justify his guilt over his father's death, and the sparrows carry this one step further. Here, let me find my notes on this...

DR. MURCHISON: This is what I've been driving at when I suggest that we should spend a little time playing detective and look more closely at his involvement, real orimagined, in some of these crimes.

DR. ANDERSON: Yes, here it is: he described the paint on the steps where the father fell, saying it was splotchy and brown. There were sparrows sitting in a tree just beyondthe skylight overlooking the staircase. The loud noise of the father's fall frightened away the birds.

Since he had always observed that their feathers were similar to thedappled steps, he drew the conclusion that the sparrows' flight helped him to minimize the painful recollection of his father's accident.

DR. RUTLAND: He's either extremely disturbed or an excellent poet!

DR. O'CONNOR: Perhaps both!

DR. ANDERSON: Some of the pathology in this case, based at least on the patient history material that we have so far, is similar to a case I testified on several yearsago, and I believe you also were called in for the defense on that one, weren't you, doctor?

DR. MURCHISON: Do you mean the Steve Lieudonub case?

DR. ANDERSON: Yes, that's it. A critical difference here of course is that in this case there was savage hostility towards the father, whereas our patient has developedan opposite obsession with guilt and an almost religious reverence for a deceased parent whose death he obviously had nothing to do with.

DR. MURCHISON: Right. Lieudonub murdered his father during a hunting trip.

DR. ANDERSON: According to the FBI report, Lieudonub killed his father with a shotgun, emptying barrel after barrel until the man's entire body was riddled with holes. He then hoisted the body onto a tree branch and inserted a hose into the mouth, into which he pumped gallons of lake water. The behavioral science division came up with the preliminary profile, stating that, as a boy, Lieudonub's father would hold a colander in front of his penis and urinate on the child through the many holes.

DR. MURCHISON: That's right, that's right...the murder was a revenge ritual in which the child's abuse (his father's urination) was inverted, and this obviously wassymbolized by the manner of execution: the water (which becomes urine) runs through the man's corpse represents the instrument used to humiliate the boy.

DR. ANDERSON: Of course, this was a single killing and there could be no question as to Lieudonub's guilt. It was simply a matter of procedure in the determination of thevalidity of an insanity defense.

DR. DOYLE: And as I recall, that determination proved unnecessary because there wasno trial: Lieudonub pleaded guilty and the defense tried to have him committed to a mental institution.

DR. MURCHISON: That's right. Unfortunately, Lieudonub was sent to state prison and, needless to say, the isolation procedures were not strictly followed. He was murdered by another inmate after about a year.

DR. ANDERSON: I've been a clinical psychiatrist for almost twenty years, and it still fills me with the most tragic sense of waste and pity to see cases like the Lieudonub case. Here we see first hand the abject results of the victimization of the self, and the dire consequences it can have. Lieudonub was an innocent, a child systematically

abused by a monstrously disturbed parent, and in the final outcome, it is Lieudonub who receives the ultimate punishment by being killed in prison. These things never cease to disgust me. Excuse me. I simply reach a point where I'm infuriated by my own words; I can't stand to hear myself.

The Son: Chapter III

This cell is the projection booth of a palatial movie theatre. My mind is the projector. The wall is the screen. There are endless shadows here, like those from a Venetian blind, a row of vertical strips, like a ladder, like a stairway. A stairway, certainly. Like the staircase where my father fell to his death. No constraint is imposed by the cell. It does not inhibit my mind. It helps me conjure.

And on this day especially, as I wait to die, there is little to restrict my thoughts of him, of his death, my perceptions in the house where we lived. I know the truth. I would like to leave a record of it, while I still have the chance.

Above the sink on a little shelf my immobile tiny wooden sparrows are perched. They do not move, but my father's body tumbled rapidly down the steps. The psychiatric team spared no effort in its attempt to release me from the conviction that I held the blame for my father's fate in my hands, just as I held the carving tools which fashioned the sparrows out of nondescript chunks of wood, just as I held the monitor switch which shifted the video scenes...from the brown leather restraint cuff to the smacking of the paddle to the glistening rubber hood. The attempt was futile. The accidental nature of his fall was merely a charade, a costume of phenomenology meant to detour the attention of the spirit. Nothing suspends my guilt.

Imagery from the videos and screens stayed with me long into the night. Those were my years of preparation. And the images did indeed become a kind of food, an exotic food for which a special taste must be gradually and judiciously acquired. I chose to forever fast from the illusory happiness delivered by the bonds of love. I reached once for that love and I became the bewildered fool selected from the audience standing next to the laughing magician, hapless victim of the grand trick.

But I did not prepare my mind in vain. I have slowly traded places, and become the magician. Now there is no trick I cannot perform. Tiny coins drop with the smallest tinkle into the change chute on the bus, but their fall becomes the resounding impact of the severe paddle as it disciplines captive flesh; the delicate sweat bands of the whistling jogger really imprison her arms with the sensual authority of restraint cuffs; the child snugly stuffed into her winter hood is really wearing a ceremonial punishment garment, a foreboding symbol of the torture that is to come...

I remember long hours sitting quietly inside the little square vestibule at the front of our house. I enjoyed the solitude as well as the enclosure. Here I sharpened my talent for creating visions that went far beyond what I saw, the vision of things that were not there, the sacred plane where the new object lives.

Once I had listened to my father with the pure trust of a child. Once I could decipher the gestures of the soul. Like any sincere man, I cherished these glimpses into the goodness of humanity. But so long ago I learned the secret of my strange gift, and the terrain of the forbidden landscape became so much more compelling. At some point, I do not remember when, I stopped believing in my father's wisdom. Or rather, even more recklessly, I decided to adapt his words to my own self-indulgent ends. Finally the signature of spirit etched upon the faces of those around me mattered less and less. Beyond the lifting of a foot or the turning of a shoulder, there no longer was anything for me to see, except for what I might invent. It has taken a very long time, but I have finally abolished all traces of sadness from my thoughts. Now I must resist an unfathomable compulsion to watch the stalks being mercilessly ripped from the ground by the wild wind. They are sucked into nothingness by the invisible pockets of air, even though the window has been closed for some time, and I am quite safe from the storm.

But the new summer sky is clear and lustrous. The afternoon sun provides pleasant warmth. A small gust of wind calmly blows through the trees adjacent to the exercise yard. The leaves gently stir, quietly rustling in the distance, a ghostly sound similar to simmering water. One might be tempted to think of the smoothness of winding green fields. With this thought I must turn away from my mind's picture of the mailbox inside the vestibule. I cautiously rest my palm against my closed black cell door and quietly wait for dusk to approach.

Many years have passed since he fell down the steps. The nine steps of often treaded wood against which his bones violently collided. Splotches of dark brown stain covered every step. On a beach at night such details cannot be easily discerned. On that bright staircase they were unmistakably clear.

The bloodstains were removed from the tiled vestibule floor. This took several minutes. An old rag was used. It was not surprising that the blood flowed past the hallway and entered the vestibule. A persistent pooling of calmly seeping blood, clearing the narrow crevice beneath the door separating the vestibule from the chalky hallway walls.

The vestibule resembled a carrel: self-enclosed, it was perfectly foursquare. To the right of the front door, always reflecting the brilliance of the sun, was a gleaming silver mailbox. My father's blood crept through there, it moved across the geometric tiles, shining with the same sunlight as the mailbox. It was a very bright day. But now it is dusk and I see that the mailbox has been robbed of its shine, how each radiant line has receded into oblivion, how form is blurred by dimness, edges superimposed over the semblance of edges, surface blending with dimension. Even vistaed images suffer restrictions. The sunlight was caught in the blood, just as the mailbox escaped into darkness, just as I escaped into a marvelous capture.

I think I was arrested inside one of the video booths. Somewhere I remember bullhorns bellowing out my name just as I was about to count the number of knots in the rope used to secure the helpless victim. At least this is an image that my mind entertains. I never saw a bullhorn. I cannot tie knots.

It is not impossible that while preparing our breakfast on that day he somehow knew he would shatter his body by tumbling down the staircase. He was preoccupied with the slowly frying eggs and overlooked the top of the coffee pot. It was rising in the overflow of boiling water and naturally when out of the corner of an eye he glimpsed this impending disaster he suddenly reached for the top of the pot in an abrupt jerky manner. When falling (especially if one falls down a flight of steps) and overcome by the frenzy of such an unexpected, strangely self-inflicted, physical attack, one often blindly gropes about, at nearby bodies, at one's own body, at the object one is falling onto, in short at anything that may lend support and gravity. My father executed such a series of flailing, confused, snapping movements as he fatally toppled from the ninth to the first step.

Eventually the smell of coffee reached and filled the staircase. Its invisibly curling fumes cannot be satisfactorily compared with smoke, but while an extinguished cigarette lay smashed in an ashtray next to the bowl in which he beat the eggs, the lit cigarette held between the fingers of my father's hand continued to smolder when released from his grip after he fell down the staircase. He did not move after that. As I stepped out of the booth I was struck by the almost surreal stillness of the S.W.A.T. teams surrounding me with weapons fixed. No movement whatsoever, it was like a photograph, the misimpression betrayed only by the minute dangling of a few pairs of handcuffs or the slack of a buckle strap on a bullet-proof vest. I did not notice any cigarette smoke.

I remember that after I had eaten he would immediately brush the crumbs from the table. And at night, as I lay awake, I still heard those muffled scraping sounds. In the darkness and quiet of my room these sounds amplified in my mind until they were like waves, endless, monotonous waves.

When they searched my rooms they found dozens of tape recordings of the ocean. Much of this was recorded at very slow speeds, giving the reverberations of the crashing waves a monstrous enormity and an ethereal quality. I had transferred these recordings to little cassettes so they were portable and I might listen to them at will. I do not know what has become of them; probably they remain in cartons somewhere in the police basement among the other evidence. I would like to be able to listen to them tomorrow morning before I am executed. Maybe I will submit this as my last request.

Firmly walking towards the shore, his back spotted with brown moles, my father entered the water and swam out slowly, eventually becoming a head bobbing in the waves, a distant orb of flesh and muscle oscillating within the shimmering green sea. The hovering, investigative gulls might have mistaken the moles on his back for the blotchy skin of fish. At that moment a small school of seven fish was actually gliding past him a few feet away. On the shore were baskets filled to the brim with bait food and a multitude of human hunters preparing to compete with the gulls. My father circled around the minuscule fish party, ignoring his growing hunger as he continued his swim. His grey hair, faintly streaked with thin lines of white and black, was thrown back atop his head, wet and slick, almost sculpturally shaped as though it was pasted onto his skull.

The silver cement broke apart when he fell down the staircase. Strands of hair waved and twitched, like thin rectangular strips of cloth tied to the metal bars that house fans. The steps could be fleetingly glimpsed between the abruptly parted strands of hair. The air in the hallway was not particularly cool.

What thoughts pass through the mind and what sights pass through the eyes when the body is immersed in the chaos of falling down steps? I am certain that the blanched hallway walls reminded him of my pallid complexion because, upon hearing the sound of his fall, I grasped the white doorknob and ran out my room, but by the time I reached the stairway the palm of his hand already was flattened against the wall. It is also a certainty that my quick movements contributed to his distorted perception of the looming stairway wall, making him see it instead as an explosion of cascading fragments. At least once during his fall, maybe several times, his head must have been wrenched upward, forcing him to look directly at the skylight. The triangular skylight danced before his eyes, its thick layers of dirty glass eddied within his dizziness while remaining immobile above him. The brilliant sunbeams permitted him to discern even the blurry mass of growing leaves dangling over the opaque glass. He might have glimpsed the fleeing sparrows flying from their branch. The rag they later used to clean away the blood was slumped over a blender.

He might have counted the steps as he descended, adding one to another until the ineluctable loss of consciousness erased the clearly amassed total of nine. I am certain that if my arrest had occurred only a minute or so later, enabling me to finish counting the rope knots, he might not have fallen, or at least he might not have fallen down a staircase containing so many steps.

One of the inmates committed suicide last night. There is a section on death row reserved for extremely violent prisoners who have been restricted to special confinement for varying periods of time. Their cells contain nothing. They sleep on the concrete floor. Through a sliding panel in the door twice a day a toilet bucket and meal tray is passed. I heard some of the guards discussing the man's demise. Apparently, over the course of several days, he bit himself so deeply that he bled to death. One of the guards pointed out that whoever oversaw these amenities for toiletry and dining was to be reprimanded for not checking on the man each day by opening the little slat at the top of his cell.

Black, jagged steel bands supported and divided the sections of glass in the skylight. Night has fallen. Its darkness helps me remember that there were four of these bands. I used to sit in the boxy murky vestibule as I watched the moon illuminate the roofs of cars. Its beams penetrated my eyes with sharp points of cold light. The steps were rectangles of smoothly sanded wood and the bands of steel were scabrous reinforcements and the knowledge that there were nine steps penetrated his mind even as he fell, even as he faltered in his counting.

Our landlord may not have been aware of the jaggedness of these bands during the fall since upon hearing the loud crashing noise he reached for the coruscated brass doorknob he would have to turn in order to open the door that gave access to the vestibule. The room from which he emerged was not dark.

Love for another can be the inhalation of sand. You breathe deeply but there is suffocation. And the sweetness of her gestures is irrevocably gone. She was visible and invisible, palpable and impalpable, present and absent.

Sitting there watching I often saw someone appear across the street, a moving solid form, instantaneously raising and lowering his feet, walking. See how he advances, step after step? He is returning home, his wife's eyes will tell him she is happy he has returned. He had not traveled by train but he stumbled before entering their bedroom in which hang no paintings. Here comes another. Do you see how he hunches his shoulders to make the fit of his coat snugger? Soon he too will be home, and a yellow dog will be excited at his arrival. It will sniff the buttons dangling on his coat before merrily dashing around him again and again. Its heavy leaping body will send vibrations through several eggs in the nearby refrigerator but the kitchen carpet where it will romp possesses no design of any kind. A husband's entering footsteps sound good to his wife's ears. A lonely man in a coat is warmly greeted by his dog.

What have I manufactured? And for whose sake did I create it? These are the drowning man's last images, the amorphous veil of algae clogs the eyes and the unimaginable silence of the bottom of the sea gives the mind a last meal of the sound of the living. So I see nothing beyond the lifting of the foot and the turning of the shoulder. Nothing.

To see more than this is to adopt the gaze of Ugolino, staring at the sea through the bars in the one tiny window of his tower, envisioning the bulbous flesh of darting fish. The horizon is calm, straight with nerveless quiet. Groups of drifting clouds, diaphanous and delicate, float across the deep blue sky. Inside the tower the children scream and the very air radiates pain. At night, as it weaves the waves into twisted blankets, the cold wind howls with macabre sonority. In the tower all is still. But on one of the stone walls, next to the bony sleeping face of a starving child, numerous little scratches can be found, frenzied bloody markings left by the clawing nails of the children.

Occasionally I would come across some of my father's discarded grocery lists. His poor penmanship produced the same reckless markings as those left by Ugolino's desperate children. The red ink stood out boldly on the clean white paper.

Seated at my observation post within the vestibule, my all night vigils often brought me from the passage of night to a new dawn, just as this evening's vigil will bring a new dawn, a perfect dawn. And in those dawns of past visions the enormous cylindrical form of the tower glistened in the morning sun. The dog peacefully slept by a window, its golden fur gently reflecting the light. Without stumbling, quietly leaving for work, the husband's footsteps echoed softly in the hallway. His wife slowly shifted about, her movements thick with sleep. One of her arms lightly fell across the bed as her husband reached the end of the stairway and exited through the front door.

Often I would obliterate every trace of moonlight by covering the little rectangular window of the vestibule with my hand. Even moonlight can eventually burn one's eyes if it is gazed upon too long. Once the window was blocked, I surrendered to the heavy darkness of the vestibule, and with my vision temporarily weakened by the glare of the moon, I felt satisfactorily alone. Then the corral formed by the vestibule's four black walls became more pleasing. The moonlight disturbed my vision and limited my perception of dimension and scale, reinforcing the impression of confinement associated with the vestibule. On the other hand, when I occupied the vestibule in total darkness, it paradoxically gave me the total freedom of an abyss, rather like the private darkness and intimacy of a priest's confessional box, without the accompanying moral turpitude. The sectional pattern and of course the density of the glass in the skylight do not quite allow the same freedom.

To make room for new furniture he had to break apart an old wooden cabinet attached to the kitchen wall. It was the end of summer but still very hot. He sat in the midst of boards and tools, his face powdered with white dust, flecked with beads of sweat.

A pot of coffee rested over a ring of small blue flames. It is not impossible that some of these flames were reflected on the side of the silver rectangular hammer whenever he raised the tool because outside while he was working two men were sitting in a car and almost continuously one of them pushed the buttons of the car radio in and out creating a senseless collage of random snatches of blaring music. The man was neatly attired in some kind of uniform and, aside from his anxious handling of the radio, displayed a controlled, almost robotic manner. Many small pieces of splintered wood had fallen onto the dark blue floor. These light blond splinters were distinguishable from the white patches scattered about the carpet. Each time my father brought down the hammer, his legs slightly shook from the impact of the blow, they faintly twitched upon the kitchen floor and, that night before falling asleep, he coughed very loudly. He must have inhaled some dust while working.

He coughed while shopping in the crowded supermarkets, the bloodstained grocery list dictating his itinerary through rows of shelves and deep refrigerated bins filled with packages of bulbous fish.

Several doors down was the butcher shop owned by the little old man with several crosses tattooed upon his once muscular arms. A clutter of rags stuffed throughout his stained many-pocketed smock, he pointed gaily to the carcasses hanging from the various hooks at the front of the shop: pig, rabbit, pheasant, and lamb. I held my father's hand one day when we stopped to look at the dressed lamb, its face smeared with saliva. I was wearing a sweatshirt decorated with multicolored sails and flags. To the left of the butcher's shop was a vendor selling soup, a trio of yellow, red, and pink roses in his lapel.

Although still a boy, my mind was keen and to please my father I immediately spoke of the ancient significance of the sacrifice of the lamb. To hide without being hidden, to be hidden without hiding: this is the irresistible attraction of Christianity, said I. Without opposite poles of thought as its foundation, the Christian myth would have evaporated long ago. But through my intensive studies I became quite attached to its basic tenet that evil must be expressed through calculation, it must always possess a design. My father smiled. Good, however, emerges with a spontaneous formlessness, that is, without premeditation, refusing reward and unconcerned with opportunity. Hence the dramatic personal satisfaction when evil acts succeed, that forbidden delight enjoyed through the cause and effect nature of wrongdoing. On the other hand, goodness prevails as if by chance, as though it cannot be arranged in advance, and as if its strength comes without the attempt to be strong. On the dead glossy surface of the staring lamb eyes I could see a man hurrying past a corset store across the street.

In the high ceiling of the large market, ring-shaped panels aglow with cold florescent light blanketed the sonority of the shopper's weaving voices.

When I covered the small window in the vestibule with my hand, I could no longer see the row of blue radio buttons inside the car. That morning the impatient man entered the car and drove it to work. As he pressed one of the rectangular buttons, tinny music emerged from the diamond shaped speaker next to the radio. His figidity impatience overcame him once again and he immediately shifted the buttons in a manic survey of every possible selection.

Seated in a square dark booth at the radio station, the man playing the music was savoring a cup of hot coffee. Jets of thick steam flew from his cup. The broadcast might be interrupted suddenly, or some disorder might occur in the control room. Then he would have leapt from his seat, dashing through the room with great speed and alarm, the flowing coffee steam discreetly emphasizing the kinetic charge of his abrupt movements.

It was certain he moved abruptly because one morning long ago I awoke from a fitful sleep. I was dreaming of her and, troubled by my dream, I sprang from bed with convulsive fury just as my father poured into my cup the last black drop of bubbling steamy liquid. As he moved away from the table I saw the sharp gold of the wedding ring on his finger behind the shaking veil of pale steam. His hand did not shake. It steadily carried the coffeepot to the stove and replaced it over a flickering circle of compact flames. The miniscule torches had a uniform, consistent shape. Their curvature was controlled and regulated by the setting of the knob. My mother died during childbirth and my father never remarried. Oddly enough, this was the only occasion that I can recall noticing his wedding band.

On my father's nearly indecipherable grocery list streaming rays of sunlight formed a grid (like the diminutive speaker in the car and still more like the enormous circular speakers in the supermarket) of intersecting lines that symmetrically crossed the handwritten page he held in his hands. He heard metallic voices booming out of the bloodied golden page: agitated, resounding descriptions of discounts available on certain goods, comparisons to be made between size and price. But he could not hear the sound of the ocean and, as the dog energetically rose to its feet, a clump of scrambled egg fell from the edge of my plate onto the floor. The plate was directly between the kitchen chair and my room.

In sleep I sat with her. I saw her eyes and through my dream's eye saw us together. Only in dream is one's attention so artificially divided.

Only in dream are the particular and the general so deceptively superimposed. The setting was pastoral. There were many beautiful pink and grey windmills, like the lands of Zaandam, a pond, and the reassuring murmur of grazing sheep. There were roses in a lunch basket on the blanket between us. There was the echo of my words, merging with the aimless sheep, my vows, my plans, my devotions turning in the air like the windmill's hypnotic blades. On a white rowboat in the lake was a blue hand painted anchor. Water dripped from the oars in a slow, steady rhythm matched by the stubborn tread of an ant advancing from the blanket with a flake of bread. Glints of sun, caught in the oar water, reflected my open mouth as I spoke, and my stretched lips undulated like a rubber ghost. There was the smoothness of winding green fields and, in the distance, an incongruous component. It was a tall iron street lamp, surrounding us with a bright annular splotch of still silver light. This light made her eyes remarkably distinct but even in dream she turned away and the glow of the lamp increased until it woke me.

I tossed the blankets aside with the suddenness of ruptured air felt upon one's face when a large flock of birds flies from the ground.

Sand is a superfluous comparison. In those moments of terrible isolation, the very impulse to draw breath is itself suffocative. I should have prized silence. I should have been silent.

Last month one of the prisoners went on a hunger strike. I think he received some bad news: either his wife had left him or his mother had hanged herself. It might have been that his mother left and his wife hanged herself. In any case, suddenly he refused to eat. The medical office is near the cafeteria and I remember that the doctor's tie was loose and a cigarette hung from his lip. A long weightless barrel of ash did not dislodge even though the restraint cuffs were used and the man struggled strapped to the table. The doctor belched loudly and inserted the long feed tube into the prisoner's nostril. He gagged and shouted something vulgar. The heaping mound of pudding on my plate wobbled dizzily as I walked past. They had big mops for all the vomit and liquid on the dirty floor. There was an orange stain on the doctor's shoe.

The beach was nearly empty after six o'clock but we remained on the cool shore. Numerous cigarettes protruded through the beige sand. My father had inserted them after inhaling their smoke. There were no markings within these miniature cylinders, which remained within the shadow of the beach chair and did not glisten. The sea breeze was strong at this hour. As the white puffs left his mouth they were instantly whisked away, stretched into invisibility by a snapping lash of saline air. He did not blink his eyes and, when the clouds of smoke parted, the sky was fully and clearly revealed.

He was alert when he swam past the gulls perched upon the rocks; the moles on his back glanced across the surface of the green sea. When he swam he moved continuously without resting and because of this perpetual motion the blood could not conceal every splotch on every step. Yet when the blood reached the vestibule and reflected the sunlight, one could observe the brilliant union of deep red and piercing yellow.

On that day there were various letters inside the three separate compartments of the mailbox. I am irresistibly drawn to the design of objects that simultaneously perform an identical function for a number of persons. Fans slowly oscillating back and forth, cooling all those before them; escalators with their immutable, graceful ascensions and descensions, the passengers silent and still, unitedly transported in a kind of trance; the rows of video booths, the identical doors and moveable benches lifting on hinges, the thick glass monitors with the numbered selections.

After inserting the letters and turning the key in the lock, the mailman absentmindedly looked down at the bright tiles in the vestibule floor. He saw rows of pentagons, a geometric plane of porcelain tiles rigidly outlined by thin black lines. When he stepped outside and inhaled the spring air, a cluster of heavy grey clouds drifting past the afternoon sun or the speeding passage of a long black car suddenly obscuring the facade of a yellow house across the street would have told him (as they surely would have told me) that these tiles were soon to be covered with blood. No. More hollow portents. I did not see the clouds draw a curtain before the sun. I did not see the car block out the front of the house. Burdened by his heavy sack and depressed by the impending storm, the mailman could not have had enough presence of mind to notice such things. Impatient and tired he hurries from house to house with his letters, rarely looking up from his busy hands.

Often at night in the quiet of this prison that is like no other quiet on earth, the mutterings, the curses, the voices speaking in sleep, the screams, the ravings of all these men on death row mingle in a chant that is like a zoo of tortured, nameless animals left alone in their cages. The cries of madness and hunger twisting themselves around barbed wire; it is more desolate than utter hopelessness...it is humanity choking on its mirror.

My father walked through the crowded supermarkets where punctured gleaming fish and thick loaves of bread were momentarily recorded by his eyes housed in a head moving within the midst of many other heads. In the street, before entering the supermarket, he saw multicolored, plastic triangular flags hanging from the canopies of buildings and lined between telephone poles, fitfully flapping in the warm wind. Through a second story window a small child peered, his face smeared with saliva, gleefully but uncomprehendingly observing the bustling activity below. His right hand held a little pinwheel made of thin paper vanes. Like the bright storefront decorations, these pieces of paper were multicolored and triangular. They spun around slowly, revolving in the direction of the wind. Looking up from his grocery list, past the chaotic swarm of jerking flags, my father must have noticed the child and his toy. He must have seen the tiny flags inside the pinwheel warily mixing their colors with a gentle rotary motion. He must have perceived that the large flags in the street, so frenetic and disruptive, retained the brilliant purity of their colors: the blues, reds, and yellows remained distinct from one another, presenting in regalia a convulsive mass of lashing plastic tips.

In his mind this comparison must have been made because that night, after returning with groceries and cooking supper, his hand placed a dish of steaming soup on the table and on the face of this dish was a circular design. It was a floral pattern of small roses, with pinks, yellows and reds meshing and smearing into one another, turning around and around in the vibrant steam. The curtain by the kitchen window suddenly blew about when he returned the pot to the stove. A gust of wind had burst through the open window and the blue and yellow triangular tassels of the curtain spasmodically twitched in the cool night air. But by this time the child was asleep in a crib and the saliva on his face had dried. The pinwheel remained motionless in a corner of the room. Below in the streets were the closed stores and the flags appearing colorless in the dark.

Awkwardly entering his bed in the dimness, I heard his movements that night. He stumbled when he passed my room in which hung a rectangular painting. A room becomes so unfamiliar at night, as though space has changed its character, expanding or contracting in unexpected ways. One ventures forth with a caution that seems so strange in the daytime.

I could hear him turning in his sleep. One of his arms lightly fell across the bed. I was fully awake and, intimidated by the foreign terrain of my gloomy room, would not leave my bed, not even to get something to eat or to drink, as the soup did not sate me and I lay there hungry, the covers securely folded around me, listening, waiting for sleep. But sleep did not come easily because this was the night before he would die.

The following morning, after awaking from my dreams, I anxiously leapt from bed. The steam emanating from the coffee cup suggested that this leap might radiate with young romance, but the veiled movement of my father's sturdy hand proved that my energy and ambition would ultimately resound with hollowness, lost opportunity, and guilt.

The waves I had watched that day continued to spring forward as I lay in bed, unable to sleep. First the curled rising approach, then the reverberation of impact, and finally the flat hissing withdrawal from the shore. Gulls serenely glided over the black jagged rocks, white microscopic specks in the purple sky and the rocks were covered with a slimy film. Like the plates in the sink, soiled with food, the gulls were caked with layers of sand and feces, which increased their weight, making flight more difficult. Soaking in the warm water, the stains on the plates would eventually loosen their hold and wash away but the gulls flew above the ocean, frustrated by the darkness, unable to sight fish. Up along the shore, so far undisturbed by the widening reach of the tide, the ends of the cigarettes my father had smoked still protruded from the sand, randomly positioned like pegs in a board.

On that morning it was raining. A thin silver mist placidly suspended in the early summer air. My father glanced at this fine rain. He watched as it delicately sprayed its silence against the bumpy plaster wall opposite the kitchen window upon which faintly appeared the simulacrum of his hands washing the remaining dishes, while the gulls in respite sat upon the shore after their fruitless hunt. The pale dawn sky greatly contrasted with the heavy green sea. The rain had dampened the previously firm ends of the cigarettes and strands of tobacco now hung loose. The waves darkly and forcefully unfolded despite the earliness of the hour.

Someone on his way to work opened our front door just as a wave collapsed upon the shore. Before the door closed a sliver of light flitted across the bottom step of the staircase, a momentary flicker of white morning sun. The fleeting superimposition of this thin band of radiance for a moment made the brown splotchy step appear less ugly. The stained, dark wood seemed to frame the streak of light in much the same way that a small, cramped window becomes a vista through which limitless fields of yellow and green are laid open to the eye. Such moments are exquisite because of the fullness they bring and the bittersweet emptiness they leave. But the dull walls stationed on both sides of the staircase still towered above the skylight, tall churchly walls, which gloomily encased a deep, hollow space.

The gulls flew from the shore and scanned the surface of the water when my father turned the semicircular knob on the stove to ignite the gas. The sudden, startling emergence of the ring of bright flames catapulted them into flight and the hot, fully risen sun may have encouraged them to remain airborne. Now the darting oval fish were clearly visible and the gulls repeatedly thrust their beaks with force and precision. The kitchen became warmer immediately after the stove was lit, although the fully risen sun and the early summer air had already taken effect. The branches of a tree reached across the skylight and on that morning there actually was a mass of new leaves dangling over the glass. The sparrows had not yet perched on the branch. They were not too far away, in a neighboring tree gathering twigs. Occasionally they would cast their semblance on the leaves, tiny black trapdoors flashing against the bright angular green shapes.

The skylight, like the blender over which the dishtowel drooped, was made of thick, multilayered glass. But the leaves and the dishtowel were thin. The triangular edges of leaves, serenely hovering in the air, could be seen through the sunbeams streaming more and more steadily into the skylight. The dishtowel had worn so greatly that it had been reduced to nothing more than shredded pieces of dirty cloth. It was not possible to mistake these tips for the ends of leaves (despite the nearby presence of the radiant white plate upon which their swaying shadows appeared) because later that day this rag would be used to wipe my father's blood from the steps. Changed by the viscous fluid into a sopping bundle, no longer possessing sharp shredded points, and covered with an irremovable substance, the dishtowel would be rendered quite useless.

Myriad pebbles were scattered upon the roof of the house across the street, blond specks left after the construction of a chimney. Placidly reposing in the warm sun, the dawn rain previously shepherded them into running streams. These slowly bubbling rivulets flowed without distraction while my self-involved love remained trapped within the silver circle of lamplight shining with quiet mockery inside my dream. It is unfortunate that one dreams in spite of oneself. The subconscious desire to become another (as well as to omnipotently observe the transformation) always entails the richest of conceits. The return to the waking state is a great disappointment.

Many years ago, during the construction of the chimney, one of the workers took from the pocket of his overalls a red handkerchief and wiped his profusely perspiring brow. It was the end of summer but still very hot. He sat in the midst of bricks, mortarboard, and dusty bags of cement. The firm green leaves dangled overhead and the rapid accumulation of sweat did not render the handkerchief useless.

After the gas was ignited, my father placed a coffeepot filled with water over the flames. Then he adjusted the pot so that its base evenly rested on the grill and watched the water slowly begin to boil. Just then a gentle breeze calmly blew through the leaves of a tree. The clear, unbroken surface of the water gradually evolved into dancing curves. The stem of the basket containing the coffee was then lowered into the bubbling transparence, and finally the top of the pot was securely put into place. Almost immediately and in regular intervals the perking commenced, a jaunty, steady beating within the dome of the pot. The room would soon be filled with the heaviness of a rich aroma as the water eventually turned dark brown. Then it would be ready for consumption.

But a frightened fish, its brown blemished skin glistening in the sun, already was quite consumable as one of the gulls swallowed it in a spasm of muscles and hunger.

And the strands of tobacco, forced by the morning rain from their paper holders, had been so inundated by moisture that their brownness ultimately faded to a very light blond, making them almost indistinguishable from the grains of wet sand in which they were imbedded.

On the wall opposite my bed hung a landscape painting. I was always reminded of its frame whenever I looked at the rectangular shape of the silver mailbox. The dominant color of that painting was green. Within it sprawled an enormous field colored in many tints and shades of green. As I looked at the painting while in bed that morning I found it odd that I could be fully aware of the exact location of each object in my densely furnished room yet behold such an expansive space as the field in the painting. The sensation was very much like the video booths. In these enclosed chambers there was barely enough room to sit, yet the matrix of changing scenes produced endless space, endless expansion.

My father may have perceived a similar contrast because several times during his fall he was forced to look up and take fleeting glimpses at the skylight, glimpses which would momentarily replace the impression of enclosure created by the walls so narrowly bracketing the staircase with an impression of expanse created by the wide skylight, recessed so deeply into the roof, its bright glass free of the cluttered stains appearing everywhere on the steps.

But the cigarette was soon extinguished, it's dead black ashes had been rubbed into the bottom of an ashtray; the fork stood motionless in the bowl, its reflective surface submerged within the foamy yolk. My father's body would fall against the steps with a loud crashing sound despite the quiet stillness of the thoroughly beaten yolk.

I heard the man in the cell next to me vomiting early this morning. They came for him after that. His execution was scheduled for 8am. One of his slippers came off and I caught a glimpse of the guard's hand slapping his face because he was still vomiting and some of it spilled onto the guard's uniform. The prisoner cursed his mother and God and his job and the little boy he had murdered many years ago. I could not hear very much after that. Just a little faint cackling. Then another slap.

Later that day I traveled to the city in a thunderous train. The wheels screeched cacophonously and the fleeting objects I glimpsed beyond the rectangular train windows were barely discernible. I used to switch the selections of the video monitors with the rapidity of a Morse code operator, in an attempt to reproduce the blurred montage of that view from the speeding train. The mailman smelled the fresh coffee as he opened the front door and stepped into the vestibule. On one of the envelopes a smudged address evoked a conformation, a figure loosely recalling an object of some kind. It is not impossible that the gulls became frustrated by a fierce wind sweeping the shore, disrupting their casual inspection of the water's surface. The step blotches remained immobile despite the traffic of the fish now gleefully secure in the temporary safety they had won from the shore-bound gulls confusedly huddled in the thick wind. Strands of the wife's hair gently blew about as she slept, her husband having opened their bedroom window before he left for work. The train's metal body shook with the furious speed. I used to sit behind that doorway for hours, absentmindedly gazing at the night sky and occasionally, with close attention, observing the streaks of moonlight that clung to the mailbox. I could not see the staircase because a closed door with Venetian blinds separated the long hallway from the vestibule. Gradually the yolk solidified as the crackling pan oil transformed it into solid yellow bumps. Similar nodules appeared in a cluster of scarred tissue and hair on the back of the head of the video center mop man, the permanent reminder of a dog's attack. The train doors sprung open noisily and suddenly but the fork in my father's hand slowly and evenly separated the scrambled eggs. When I rose to leave through the open car doors I saw the hollow, circuitous train station. I walked through it very slowly. Dreams create false revelations. Her eyes were not her eyes and my hands were not my hands. The loudspeakers in the supermarket shuddered from the resounding, disembodied voice announcing the location and price of various goods. Fingering these goods, my father's hands were his hands; his eyes were his eyes as he read the print on the boxes. It is a pity that leather wrapping is folded over the eyes of the condemned that sits in the electric chair. I would like the witnesses to know that my eyes are my eyes when the current makes them pop and bleed, if that is in fact the method chosen for my demise. The child noisily lumbered through his room, searching for the paper toy and anxious to again look out of the window. He failed to understand that that hour of the morning provided very little to see. But beyond the train windows there was a great deal to see. I could not discern the plethora of posters and objects and grew tired from repeated unsuccessful attempts to focus them. Seated at the open window, the child watched his toy, expecting the wind to make the paper wedges rotate. But the wind had already subsided and the gulls regrouped with new vigor, ready to continue their search for food. Turning from the mailbox, I would look through the tiny vestibule window. Then the moonlight widened my eyes, filling them with harsh, burning light. If I looked away to avoid the glare of the moon, the hood of the uniformed man's car (always parked outside) reflected it into my vision. I had leapt from bed. I was seated at the kitchen table. My father returned the coffeepot to the stove. The yellow dog awoke. The line of my trousers was especially sharp that morning. They had been dry-cleaned and pressed the day before. I wore a fashionable silk tie and several pieces of bright jewelry. The air had grown chilly by the time I left but I chose not to wear a hat because I felt it would spoil my appearance. I dressed methodically, consulting with great satisfaction a large mirror hung behind my door. Its dull metal frame was cracked and dented. Later, after leaving the train and seeing the age worn columns, which lined the station, I would be reminded of that frame. Eventually the child grew impatient at the window. The street, though more populated than before, was far from active. Yet occasionally one or two people stepped out of doorways, entering cars or walking, and the wind did not blow. An odd looking man stooped over to pick up his hat but the wind had not knocked it off. The pinwheel's little flags remained motionless. The sunlight gave their distinct colors a beautiful radiance. Wearing his blue cap with the wide brim jutting forward, the conductor exited with enthusiasm from the right-angled, dim compartment of controls and switches, briefly glanced at me, and resumed his patrol of the train. In my dream the mounds of soft grass undulated like the folds of my blankets. But I was able to fling the blankets aside. I jumped from bed and sat down at the kitchen table with anticipation for the events of the day. There were many yellow lumps scattered across my plate. The mailman did not notice any conformation suggested by the smudged address, with his burdensome sack he had walked away incognizant of any similarity between this form and an everyday object. A silk tie, a thin, silk tie fastened by a round, jade stickpin. The train rocked with a weltering din. After its third catch, one of the gulls perched upon the rocks, dumbly waddling across them as it devoured the fish. Waves perpetually exploded against the rocks, making the bird shake its head, eyes irritated by the saline spray. I loved her as a mother loves her child: the same eternal, desperate clinging to that which is yourself. The pain still in sight reaches back for itself in the dark, where I wait, like a wounded thief, listening to the blood flow through her veins. Its warmth made her forehead so indescribably alive. I wanted to kiss that gentle forehead, just above and to the left of the temple, I pretended I already walked the steps that led me away, after my lips had touched her skin, having felt the mild heat of the red liquid I could not see, the way corpses cannot see the top of the coffin as it is mounted and screwed into place, oblivious to this last act and its unalterable finality. Inside the grating car, the conductor's amplified voice punctured the confused air, a metallic voice even harsher than the supermarket announcements calling out sales. The only moment of calm and silence occurred just after the train stopped, before the doors opened. While I hurriedly finished my breakfast very slow music began playing on the radio. The man in the booth at the radio station must have long since finished his cup of hot coffee. Comfortably seated and still, he could not know that I was rushing with feverish urgency, or that the train would produce a deafening noise. The hallway was steeped in darkness after we went to bed. I would lie awake, hungry and motionless. So many things occur to one, especially at night, when you do not move and it is quiet. That morning I watched my feet as I descended the staircase, deliberately placing each foot on one or another of the brown splotches, the way a child plays games with the cracks in the sidewalk. But there were so many of these blemishes that it took little effort to hit my target each time. The haze of dawn light thickened as I watched the morning begin from within the vestibule. When I finished my breakfast I was ready to leave, with my hand on the doorknob and my back to my father, I told him without looking up that I did not know when I would return. The night before, he had suggested that we go into the city together to see a film. We had not seen films for some time. I was a young man, no longer the child whose mind and heart were a tabula rasa upon which my father could inscribe his wisdom. I had come to know of the world in my own way and on my own terms. I knew that the senses and all their perceptions irretrievably complicated the simplicity of my father's distinctions between what was good and what was "evil." And above all else, I had fallen in love, strange fool that I was. Surely, I thought, romantic, idealized love must mean something special; it must validate the necessity, indeed the supremacy, of our senses. It did not occur to me until later that I had addressed my father without looking at him, a consequence I suppose of the carelessness of youth and the fact that I usually was in a great hurry, especially on that day. So I rushed away from my father, to see my beloved, to declare my love, to pronounce my devotion to her and her alone. It was the third time that day I failed to bestow upon my father the politeness one offers to strangers, choosing to ignore or deny his presence by arrogantly refusing to address him eye to eye. It was not until much later when I walked through the fish market and passed the slaughterhouse that it occurred to me, amid the cacophony of barkers and roosters' rude cackle. That was the day of my great foolishness, as I was about to reach for something I was never meant to have. But that blindness has been corrected. Now I see what is real. The gull's persistent hunger made it return to the pack, abandoning its perch on the slimy rock just before another wave crashed into it, avoiding the stinging assault of the sea. Before entering the next house on his route, the mailman lit a cigarette and glanced at the cloudy sky, not at all interested in the completion of this long day of monotonous work.

Through tedious, persistent labor they obtain twigs and other pieces of nature's housing. The two of them patiently struggle, feeble beaks shaping loose ends into the familiar round form. The surprising domesticity of the animal kingdom, the natural interdependence of the male and the female. When he toppled, when the empty hallway and his crashing body united to produce a resounding burst of noise, the startled sparrows jumped nervously from their nest, flying through the air with great speed. With the passage of the years, my memory impugnable, my death only hours away, I have finally understood that the sparrows were frightened hypnotists. With their dappled plumage, their flashing departure, they have tricked my mind, they have looted my thoughts: I can no longer see the blemished wooden staircase. When they flew away in unison the dignified poise of their brown heads was not diminished by fear and their movement was beautiful against the blue sky and the spread of their tiny wings was sharp and swift and their flight removed them from the sound of my father's fatal fall.

Transatlantic Pictures

Interoffice Memorandum

From: J. Wakdjunkaga, screen-writer

To: C. Loki, Executive Producer

Re: Final White Draft of "The Confession "

[Media Reports About the Killer]

Dear Mr. Loki,

Enclosed for your approval is the Final White draft of media announcements and commentary that will be used in the Montage Sequence of Various Media Reports about the Killer.

I liked your suggestion that we should take several different sources of news (television, radio, newspaper) and create a sort of mosaic of voices that follows the story from different angles and from varying points in time.

I tried to implement your idea by creating the kind of explanatory montage sequence that was in vogue in Hollywood during the 1940s, especially in films that dealt with World War II or crime, i.e. the opening of *Casablanca* or the surveillance sequence in *White Heat*. By using the media information about the serial killer that is available in three forms (radio, television, newspaper), I have made little bridges between elements in the text and, at times, included snippets of previous action, such as Sgt. Vargas having coffee and preparing to leave for work on the morning that the woman's crucified body is found.

I hope this creates some of the jumps in time that you seemed to be interested in, as for example when the anchorman on television ends one segment with "We go live now to our chief correspondent..." and doesn't complete the sentence until several shots later when he says "...already at the scene." I appreciate your fondness for *Citizen Kane* and what has been called its use of aural montage (i.e., Leland stating "Who entered this campaign..." and Kane finishing "...with one purpose in mind").

Best regards,

J. Wakdjunkaga

EXTERIOR. DAY. HOME ENTERTAINMENT STORE.

A large group of pedestrians is gathered in front of a store that sells home entertainment equipment. There is a bank of stacked televisions behind the huge, plate glass window. The pedestrians are watching the broadcast, visible on the more than twenty televisions, of a breaking news report concerning the latest victim of a serial killer that has been terrorizing the city. The anchorman begins talking after the *News Bulletin* sign scrolls across the televisions in red.

ANCHORMAN: In our top story tonight, the body of an unidentified woman was discovered in the same coastal area where just last month two other bodies were found. The police, though unwilling at this time to reveal key information, have now admitted that they believe the sameindividual (or individuals) committed these murders. No details or clues have so far been disclosed by anyone involved in the investigation. We go live now to our chief correspondent...

INTERIOR. NIGHT. NEWSPAPER OFFICE. EDITOR'S DESK.

Close-up of the computer screen of the City Editor for a major newspaper. He has been covering the serial killer story for some time. This shot occurs just as he's finishing his piece, on the words "...I urge you all..." He leans back in his chair to look at the article as the camera tracks in a little to give the viewer a chance to read this excerpt.

CITY EDITOR'S ARTICLE: 'I wouldn't rule out the possibility of a serial killer at this time,' commented the Chief of Detectives as he hurried from the scene surrounded by evidence technicians and state police. If this case continues to develop along these lines, I would like to remind all of my readers of our large piece on serial murder last year.

At that time we receivedmany helpful letters concerning missing person cases across the country. And so I urge you all to send any information you may have, care of this newspaper, as soon as possible.

INTERIOR. NIGHT. CONTROL ROOM OF LOCAL RADIO STATION.

Close-up of a panel board inside the control room of a radio station. There are many flashing lights amid a bay of digital and analog audio equipment. The camera pulls back from this area and pans upward to reveal the disc jockey sitting in his isolation booth, about to continue the radio program at the conclusion of the commercial that is playing on one of the tapes. There is a very large coffee mug in front of the disc jockey. Jets of thick steam arise from his cup.

DISC JOCKEY: '...now playing at theaters everywhere. Don't miss this critically acclaimedfilm which some reviewers are already hailing as a work of stark beauty and horror.' Just in time for Halloween, huh folks? Another chop 'em up flick. Well this one seems to be a little moresophisticated, but then, what do I know? I'm a DJ. Let's see now...the time is a little past 6am, and weather for all of our GUFF listeners is a mild 65 degrees, cloudy, and a little breezy. Astorm watch is in effect, however, particularly for the area near the state penitentiary where there is already a large group of relatives assembled for the execution of convicted serial killer J…

INTERIOR. NIGHT. OUTSIDE THE CONTROL ROOM BOOTH.

Two technical assistants, holding clipboards and wearing headphones, are checking the schedule and listening to the broadcast. We also see the DJ inside the booth, mouthing words that cannot be heard.

INTERIOR. NIGHT. CONTROL ROOM OF LOCAL RADIO STATION.

Back inside the control booth as the DJ continues.

DISC JOCKEY: ...T. Strong winds and hurricane like conditions are expected to develop within the next hour or two.

INTERIOR. DAY. KITCHEN IN SGT. VARGAS' HOME.

Sgt. Vargas is drinking coffee in his kitchen. He's watching a morning talk-show program as he prepares for work: finishes his tie, adjusts his holster, checks his notes, etc. He shakes his head in sarcastic disapproval of the conversation being broadcast between the show's host and a prominent sociologist who's written extensively on serial murder.

SOCIOLOGIST: It is estimated that there are approximately three dozen serial killers at largein this country today. Of course, that's an official estimate. The real total is probably much higher.

TALK SHOW HOST: Would you say that is this a uniquely modern phenomenon? Or could it be a form of pathological behavior that has existed throughout the centuries butis more visible today because of our technology that permits us to shrink the world, so to speak?

EXTERIOR. DAY. HOME ENTERTAINMENT STORE.

Return to medium long-shot of the store. Same crowd. The anchorman finishes the sentence begun in the previous shot and the image on the televisions switches to the field reporter.

ANCHORMAN: ...already at the scene.

FIELD REPORTER:_The mood is very grim at this pleasant ocean front community. There are stately homes just beyond those dunes, the splendor of the sea, and all the tranquility was shattered this morning when the coast guard discovered a young girl's body awash just about a mile and a half in that direction.

INTERIOR. DAY. KITCHEN IN SGT. VARGAS' HOME.

Seen from a slightly different angle, the television is in the foreground of the shot. In close-up, Sgt. Vargas hastily lays his coffee cup on the counter that is opposite the television set, moving his hand into the frame from the left. The program continues as Vargas is seen, through a large window in the room just beyond the kitchen, leaving the house, getting into his car, starting the ignition, and pulling away.

SOCIOLOGIST:_Well, the twentieth century certainly doesn't have a monopoly on psychotic or deranged personality structures. However, there does seem to be something fundamentally twisted or malignant in our spiritual fabric.

EXTERIOR. DAY. HOME ENTERTAINMENT STORE.

Return to medium long-shot of the store. Same crowd. The field reporter continues with his coverage.

FIELD REPORTER: ...near the town. Residents are shocked that evil and murder lurk right here in their midst. I spoke to the owner of some fishing boats nearby. He saw thedead girl only last night talking to a man by the bar on the pier. Then about midnight, according to this witness, there were gunshots, but at that time he thought it might have been someone doing a little target practice. He's behind me right now as you can see, giving his statement to the police.

INTERIOR. DAY. KITCHEN IN SGT. VARGAS' HOME.

Mrs. Vargas begins changing the channels, but discovers that other stations are presenting the same material. She switches to another channel where a serial killer broadcast is already in progress before turning back to the talk-show and yet another channel where a police inspector is being interviewed via satellite by another anchorman.

OTHER NEWS REPORT: ...with any changes in diplomatic relations. In local news tonight there appears to be a break in what has come to be known as the...

TALK SHOW HOST: ...we'll be back after these messages when we continue this special presentation on the psychological profile of the serial killer.

ANCHORMAN 2: But Inspector, isn't it true that this case has developed parallel suspects?Isn't the investigation also focusing on another man in the East?

EXTERIOR. DAY. HOME ENTERTAINMENT STORE.

Return to medium long-shot of the store. Same crowd. The field reporter continues with his coverage.

FIELD REPORTER: ...and other conflicting accounts. Some of the FBI people in charge of this case have already stated that they want to scrupulously avoid the dangersmisguided zealousness in attempting to eliminate the enormous backlog of unsolved murders. In light of this, they are carefully examining any further confessions made bythe present suspect.

INTERIOR. DAY. KITCHEN IN SGT. VARGAS' HOME.

Return to Mrs. Vargas, frustrated from trying many channels, returning to the original channel with the sociology professor interview.

SOCIOLOGIST: ...where that kind of mental profile is concerned. On the other hand, there have been cases where an individual has developed a terrible storehouse of irrational guilt. They create a private world complete with all the necessary ingredients to convict themselves, and to them this world is perfectly real and self-sufficient. But the horrible fact is that in most cases, these individuals have actually committed no crime. They know crime and the pathology of murder, but they are innocent of any wrong doing themselves.

INTERIOR. NIGHT. CONTROL ROOM OF LOCAL RADIO STATION.

Medium close-up of Disc Jockey as he reads another commercial.

DISC JOCKEY: ...with chemicals and stitching equipment included. That's right, boys and girls, be the first on your block to enjoy the rewarding hobby of taxidermy. That's just $99.99 for the complete kit.

INTERIOR. DAY. KITCHEN IN SGT. VARGAS' HOME.

Return to previous shot of Mrs. Vargas. She's resigned to the fact that all the stations are broadcasting the serial killer story and she begins feeding her child who sits in a high-chair next to the television.

ANCHORMAN 2: 'What about this newest victim, Inspector? Can you tell us anything about the young girl found behind the carnival?' Hello? Hello? Well, ladies and gentlemen, we apologize for this technical mishap. Apparently we've lost our live connection, if only temporarily. At least we hope so. We'll resume our studio coverage at this time.

INTERIOR. DAY. LOCAL BAR.

The owner of a bar, not open yet, begins to set up his stools after putting on the television. It is the same channel that Mrs. Vargas had just switched to, and the Inspector answers the question about the other suspect.

INSPECTOR: ...no no no, the suspect in the East is not necessarily a substitute for the present suspect. We are concerned about some of the apparent parallels between the individual already in custody and the man from the East, who is still at large. That doesn't mean we believe we have the wrong man. We've covered this case too carefully to makesuch a blunder.

INTERIOR. DAY. SOMEONE'S LIVING ROOM. ANOTHER CITY.

A man is watching an afternoon movie in another city in the same state. There is a medium-shot of the television taken from behind the man's shoulder. During a scene on a train where a woman is being questioned by some police officers, there is a sudden break and the serial killer news broadcast continues.

'You think perhaps he got off when you got on?' We interrupt today's movie with the following bulletin. Authorities announced today that they have positively identified the...

EXTERIOR. DAY. HOME ENTERTAINMENT STORE.

Same angle as before. The crowd has increased dramatically. In a previously taped sequence, the field reporter holds his microphone next to the witness who is telling a detective what he saw.

FIELD REPORTER: ...and that's about all I can tell you. Like I said, I was walking righthere along the pier and I heard shots. Then I saw that same man under the boardwalk.

But I didn't actually see him firing a gun and, since lots of folks do this around here, I just figured he was aiming at that old buoy opposite the abandoned lighthouse.

INTERIOR. NIGHT. CONTROL ROOM OF LOCAL RADIO STATION.

New angle: the camera shows the disc jockey in an overhead shot and the steam rises up from the oversize mug. Next to the studio microphone are some 8x10 photos of scrambled eggs and a man leaping out of bed (the disc jockey is an amateur photographer).

DISC JOCKEY: ...on the alert. The storm is expected to last until mid-day, unless prevailing winds increase its strength along the coastal regions. The execution has attracted hundreds of tourists as well as relatives and friends of the victims, now on their way to the penitentiary or already assembled outside the execution chamber. Switching to a lighter note, I'd like to play something I know you'll relax with, it'scalled...

INTERIOR. DAY. KITCHEN IN SGT. VARGAS' HOME.

Same angle. Mrs. Vargas is wiping baby food off of the television screen.

SOCIOLOGIST: ...the exchange of guilt. Certainly we've studied this particular psychosis in many cases, but the problem is in identifying the core issue: what bringsan individual to the point where the invention of reality is more important, in fact more essential, than the experience of what is real?

INTERIOR. NIGHT. CONTROL ROOM OF LOCAL RADIO STATION.

Original angle showing control board.

DISC JOCKEY: ...with that peppy, snappy flavor, you just can't beat the taste!

The Son: Chapter IV

At the end I lived in rented rooms. Desolate side streets. No elevator. Creaking steps. Paint chips in the water glass. Cockroaches in the bathtub. Bed by the wall. Dark convoluted mattress stains like an inkblot ghost. No hot water. Smell of old blood in the closet. Home for a week, home for a month. Then another city. Another room. Another name on the newspaper. Another set of identification letters for the television stations.

If he was in the South, I traveled south. When he ventured West, I followed west. The moonlight shines behind his fingers as he picks up the knife. The shadows unfold as I raise my hand. I wipe my forehead. I close my eyes.

I feel the wounds. I hear the screams.

Is this the room where the pregnant girl perspired during the hasty abortion that ruined the cheap bedspread? Is this the closet where the old watchman hanged himself, unable to hear the sound of his own voice? Maybe it is the place where the weary salesman raised the revolver to his temple. At that moment, a child sitting in a train on the elevated platform just beyond the salesman's window put into his mouth a hard candy shaped like a bullet. Or could this be the last room for a killer? A deranged man? A monster unable to refrain from the dark urge, deliriously craving the final peace of his own destruction? Every room has a death story. Every room is another museum filled with the irremovable or unnoticed traces of someone's fatal moments.

There was the vigorously applied razor blade left imbedded in the chunky soap bar. Dark flakes of hemoglobin were scattered across the white rectangle. They blew away as I raised the bathroom window with a bang. Three greasy fingerprints on the dull grey fuse box panel prefaced an outline of feet scorched on the shabby wood floor. Shards of a broken iodine bottle in the hallway leading to the toilet. Soiled grasp marks on the matrix of jaundiced damp sewage pipes. Nylons twisted into a noose lying like a coiled snake in a heap by the fire escape. An iridescent scabrous square of rat poison in the center of the loop. Crusts of rancid vomit in the Bible drawer. Maggots pinching through the Revelations.

A symbolic image, no doubt. The kind of thing that might appear in some controversial film about damnation, or the dissolution of religious belief. Dearest father, I did not forget your lessons. Everything I have seen throughout my life has been viewed within my own personal frame. Without really knowing why, the importance of a thing always depended on its visual content. I never understood the world, or its people, or its objects, unless I was making some kind of visual conclusion about the relationships between things. I could never resist what I must call a supreme demand, from somewhere within my nature, to establish and construe elaborate connections between all that my senses digested. It is as though my subconscious was engaged in some kind of esoteric archaeology, as though everything that could be depicted and suggested, especially all things that seemed *destined* to have a relationship, that somehow all this was already so, had been so, and now it was the duty of my mind's divination to uncover what was, to reconstruct and display it, like a great structure or artifacts uncovered in a dig. It was as though my imagination had inherited some kind of perverted obligation from the teachings of my father, or perhaps my imperfect soul had made it perverse. Now I feel a great shame in all this, I can see the great reluctance that prevented me from true communion with others, yet I cannot deny the great understanding that depended on the power of the imagination, the interiority of consciousness, the relativity of perception and cognition. Did I unwittingly turn your wisdom into a comedy of errors, dear father? Did I somehow turn your spiritual warnings about the dangers of illusion into a rationale for the processes of illusion? I know you were genuine in your heart. You never gave me a stone when I asked you for bread. You never gave me a serpent when I asked you for a fish. Somehow the light of my body depended upon an evil eye, the false camera eye that filled my body with light that is darkness.

Shotgun blast blood outline, contours like a hologram fixed upon the wall after the trigger was pulled. Here the body remained too long, and there was too much heat, too little maid service. Gas mask swinging on the knob of the cellar door, hollow eyes sunken deep like a desert bone animal face. Cracked plastic tube of the hair blower in the empty stained fish tank once filled with water. Eyelashes brittle next to the coral house on the bottom, evidence of a successful electrocution long ago. Hysterical suicide confessions scrawled in lipstick across the large pages of the telephone book still in place atop the decrepit wooden stand by the lobby desk. Stench of the manager's fingers as he flips through the book in search of a clean page. Monotony of his practiced gestures as he hands me the key, looks over the desk to be sure I have luggage, places the pen in the center of the decaying registration log, sits back on his stool, lighting another cigarette as he watches me ascend the stairs, wondering if I will become another suicide, another body carried out on the red rubber stretcher. A large cockroach does not escape the trained assault of his shoe. Its inner matter bursts with a gush as I turn the key to my room. Slowly the bent dusty blades of a fan turn about. The cockroach antennae twist a few times. I shut the door.

It is a curious thing to seek forgiveness for what has not happened. To want a reprieve from freedom, a pardon from oneself, permission for a life that was never lived. Like playing Russian Roulette with a ghost, and it is your flesh that is vulnerable, your bone that will shatter, then you see that the transparency before you is smiling, it is your smile, your face, you are the specter who has stacked the deck against you.

It was not difficult to align my mind with the one who did the killing. How did it work? Crystal Ball? Hocus Pocus? Abra Cadabra? Open Sesame? Take this bitter cup from my lips.

He used a hunting knife to make a deep cut and when he pulled back his hand in a violent abrupt manner I saw the thick blade shadow sweep the room like the broad pan of a searchlight scanning an embankment and the falling black droplets of blood were like a hail storm raining balls upon the earth.

I did not live the way others lived; I did not do the dance that thrived on sweet music, sweet light, sweet life turned away at the door like an uninvited guest.

I know he preferred strangulation (although he was by no means unfamiliar with the efficacy of the blade). How did I carve the sparrows? How did I acquire the materials? I suppose on death row they abandon fundamental security procedures and the ridiculous is allowed, like giving carving tools to a prisoner. Anyway, the psychiatrists liked the work, they enjoyed the detail of the wood, or so I was told.

Once in a stairwell of this hellishly filthy hotel I saw a cat choking on the rodent it tried too quickly to swallow. Scaly tail flipping madly like a gasping fish and the suffocation permeated the poorly lit landing. The shock and the eerie glow of the eyes of the gagging cat, the spastic mortal twitch of the rat's diseased tail, the imagined fish flailing in a desperate attempt to suck non-existent oxygen, and the neck of the girl under the grip of his hands, the gurgling, the gurgling, the little dead room at the bottom of the sea, sealed metal walls, silence without breath, silence without breath.

They make stories out of unrequited love, there is enough sorrow and passion to fill tens of thousands of pages, there is no shortage of legendary failure, of the torch carried to the grave, the morbid fixations of all the poor bastards like me who missed the boat, who got shoved aside so another could be happy, who turned their own lives into a nightmare. At least mine is ending soon, and I have tried to make the most of it. In a hefty plot, themes naturally emerge as you go along. That is where he comes in. With his knife. With his rope. Or with his strong paralyzing fingers wrapped around yet another throat.

But there is a conflict here. It is not as simple as it used to be. Maybe it is because my hours are numbered, but then I have always had a problem with counting, as in the case of the rope knots. I suppose in a way it is like a Peeping Tom who sees a woman being beaten, or worse, yet he keeps his shame and his thrill to himself, and does nothing. Or like a cannibal who comes to a specially arranged feast where a murdered human is devoured. He eats to satisfy his insane appetite, believing he is morally unconnected to the murder that made this forbidden meal possible. Or like this killer I know the way the philosopher knew his candle...in dream, in memory, in perception...the reality may be translated but it remains irreducible. He moves slowly and precisely and he wants to kill again. Now he is closer than ever before. What is sour in his dreams is twice as bitter for my lips, what is casually destroyed by his hand is an endless haunting of my soul. He strangles a girl in a remote spot behind the carnival. I see the act reflected on the lens of her fallen eyeglasses. An underwater image on the moonlit glass, wavery and indistinct. Slowly she sinks to the ground as he releases his fingers. I clench my fist. I hide my face as he steps into the glow of a streetlamp to light a cigarette. Our features blend. We dissolve into one another, face superimposed over face.

He goes back to check the body for items of identification. Even though it was a chance encounter and the girl has no personal connection to him, he goes out of his way to make her at least temporarily anonymous. His passion for meticulousness governs the aftermath of the killing as well. I can feel the little pieces of brittle dust as his fingers nervously scrape the inside of her dented pocketbook. Overhead, glowing in the cold moonlight, are wide staring owl eyes, a shade of yellow not unlike the bony tortoise shell cigarette holder used by the manager. Or was it a sparrow nestled quietly in the evening shadows, hiding its patchwork of stains from the moon? No, I am sure it was an owl, because a dot of shadow always fell across the yellow holder, the deep black "o" from the wooden *No Vacancies* sign hanging outside, a dark bead of pupil perforating an owl's iris.

Behind him the cloudy mixture of distant but familiar carnival sounds. Soft contours of vague noise blending with the hiss of the sea. The roller-coaster cart bursts the air, its descent punctuated by the clang of the strongman bell; both muffled like a dream of voices fading on a long stretch of beach. Popping of balloons in the dart game sounds like fire-crackers exploding underwater as he lets her limp form slip back arms akimbo flopping against the ground like broken kite sticks hitting the earth. The sick mixture of black and yellow is already evident on her skin where, like kneaded clay, his finger marks show dark and deep. The shade of her bruised flesh is not unlike the colored plastic eyes of the stuffed dogs staring trance-like in the shooting gallery. The clasp of his unbuttoned fly is a tiny rectangle of moist metal jangling in the scented air. Part of the owl's severe expression appears for a second on this wet tab before he turns around to cast a jittery glance at the carnival grounds below. Against the rough soil her creamy disheveled hair. Delirious revolving babble of the merry-go-round while he strips her. Wild swipes of the barker's stick snapping against a garish poster of *The Fat Lady* and the gleam of neon upon the flat woven grid of his straw hat.

In the rear of the opposite tent, a female fire-eater, *Sheila the Human Torch*, stares in drunken dismay at her sequined jumpsuit costume. On the floor of her dressing room lie the black shards of a 78rpm recording. One of the carnival managers, also her lover, had just smashed the record and beaten her up, disgusted that her drinking and antagonistic behavior have made it impossible for her to do the show, and not for the first time. Particles of wet vomit are indistinguishable from the garishly colored costume but one alarmingly reddish-pink spot of it stands out quite loudly on a piece of the fractured record. A black and white photograph of Sheila's father is taped to her slovenly-arranged vanity. He is seen in his youth as a carpenter, detaching a built-in cabinet from a wall, in the midst of boards and tools, his face powdered with white dust, flecked with beads of sweat. Before the manager had angrily entered Sheila's dressing room, the record spun in the old record player next to the whisky bottle and some lipsticks with smashed tips. The song, *It Can't Be Love*, an old blues tune, stopped in the middle of the title line when the phonograph needle skidded abruptly, making a sound like cloth being violently and quickly shredded, as the manager knocked it over in his hurry to strike Sheila. Wiping the evidence of both her abdominal discharge and blood from his knuckles before exiting the tent, the manager heard some screams not far away: possibly only the excitement of teenage girls rooting for their boyfriends at the shooting gallery, possibly something more ominous.

In the adjacent tent was *Hercules the Magnificent*, the carnival's strongman. Sitting in the nude on the edge of his cot, he had listened to the sounds of Sheila's beating with a mixture of revulsion and self-loathing. There were traces of dried semen on one of his massive barbells and dozens of Turkish cigarette butts squashed into the uneaten food on Hercules' dinner tray. A leopard skin tunic, similar to the one worn by Johnny Weissmuller in all of the *Tarzan* films, lay crumpled into a heap on the ground, half draped around a Kewpie doll. The doll's face had been burned and melted, forming a hideously disfigured expression. With a portion of the shoulder piece of the garment lying across the doll's head, it was as if some kind of fantastic shrinking process had taken place and the naked doll was formerly a full-sized adult. Perhaps Hercules regarded the macabre inanimate thing in this way. He gazed upon it with fixity and glowing admiration, then quickly held a hand mirror to his face and grimaced disapprovingly at himself, as if the doll were his alter-ego, but a diminutive version, shrunk to almost nothing, yet engulfed by the gaudy He-Man costume that Hercules so proudly wore during his weight-lifting shows. There was an interesting layering of irony in these parallels and contrasts of self-image and self-perception. Hercules was tormented by the beatings Sheila received from the carnival manager. This was not necessarily due to any empathy Hercules had for the abuse Sheila was subjected to, although, to a certain extent, he did feel sorry for her. It was more visceral. For the sound of the blows, and Sheila's sobs and pitiful cries of pain, always reminded Hercules of the childhood whippings he endured when his alcoholic mother vented her rage. She always made him strip, preferring to whip him while he was in the nude, striking every exposed part of his little body. This savage, prolonged punishment could befall him at any moment, for any disturbance or infraction, small or large, real or imagined. His father, who had abandoned them shortly after Hercules was born, left most of his clothes behind, including several very thick, very wide leather belts which were usually his mother's instrument of choice. Hercules could not resist a primal urge to play with his mother's cosmetics, and to try on her undergarments. He was always caught, and this, he found, produced the most vicious attacks. "Slut!" his mother would scream in-between stinging cracks of the belt upon his reddening buttocks, thighs, and back. "Little pig slut! Are you a slut-doll, huh?! A little Kewpie slut-doll burning with lust?!" Many times, when Hercules mesmerized the crowds with amazing feats of weight-lifting, he would stare at the female carnival-goers who were transfixed by the sight of his mammoth, muscular body and the enormous barbells which he so effortlessly hoisted above his head. But instead of a sea of young women cast into a sexual trance by his formidable male prowess, he saw his mother duplicated several hundred times, taking swigs of cheap gin with one hand, and swinging the long belt in her other hand, becoming drunker and angrier, ready to lash into him, to cause more pain and humiliation. His mother rarely left the apartment. Therefore, Hercules, who was almost never allowed to leave, rarely had any privacy. She supported them with prostitution; her husband went insane shortly after his departure and spent the remainder of his life in a state mental hospital. She was either passed out on the floor in a drunken stupor or having sex with men. Many of these men would look over at Hercules, urinating very loudly before they left. Hercules found a few moments for his "dress up" games only on Saturday evenings, when his mother went around the corner to the local liquor store to stock up on rancid libations in preparation for the long night of desperate men willing to pay for sex. Normally this errand took a little time because Hercules' mother usually performed sexual favors in exchange for several bottles.

Dragging the body into the woods, awkwardly pulling backwards this uncooperative weight, the killer produces the reverse motion of the little pushcart negotiated with similar struggle by the little man in the photograph in my cell. The cobblestones made it more arduous and the steam from his bulky stovepipe offered the aroma of cooked chestnuts. But the forest in the summer especially in the pitch of night makes the earth its slave and there is only the oppressive mixture of disturbed pungent soil, stagnant and thriving flora, the choking competition of the perfumes of the trees. A reluctant earth putting rocks in the way of this clay white corpse dragged like a sack of potatoes by a sweating man. Suddenly in agitation he stops midway and thrusts his long tiepin into her cheek. The muscles have not yet atrophied and rigor mortis is still about an hour away. The point of the tiepin finds its mark easily. Her blood volume, however, has begun to reroute towards the extremities, and only a hairline trickle emerges. I note its path as I watch the delicate fracture in the cheap plastering of my tiny room. A follicle of blood hair curving delicately across peeling white Spackle. A cockroach scurrying past the fissure in my wall's surface does not traverse the shadow of the post of the tiepin lying across her cheek, intersecting the stringy figure of leaking blood. The insect may continue this nocturnal pilgrimage until past inner walls and successive floors it too comes unfortunately under the lethal attack of the manager's shoe, joining the now dried particles of its fellow's crushed remains. Yet it might escape this fate if it chooses a more circuitous path within the building's layers of interior spaces, because the manager has a habit of dozing off around two a.m., the shadow slipping off his cigarette holder as sleep overtakes his body and his hand shifts into a new position.

The heads of the thrill-seeking masses file under a sign reading *Foolish House* as the murderer tosses the soggy bundle of the girl's clothing into a hastily dug hole. An excited boy clutches his father's hand while they cross the forbidden threshold of this exotic world and for now the child glimpses only the old pimply underside of the wooden lip of the ticket stand. Moonlight bathes the girl's dead white skin creating a peculiar glow rather like the phosphorescent long preserved flesh of *The Siamese Twins* floating in their large fluid filled container. The killer wipes the mud from his hands with a large plaid handkerchief. He feels better knowing the girl's clothing has been buried. Insects originally disturbed by the digging slowly burrow back to investigate the scents and stains on the garments. A cluster of slugs nestles within the protein rich bed of semen and blood on the underside of the cotton panties. The blanket of moonlight evenly distributed upon the girl's corpse transforms into shaking claws as a burst of wind bends the large branches of a tree making the radiant silver orb project jagged leaf shadows across the girl's nude form. A man wearing a plaid cowboy shirt wipes his filthy hands covered with mustard and grease from the hot dog he has just finished before turning to listen to the personal tragedies and special talents of *The Human Torso* and *The Geek*. The man exudes a foul body odor and he lights a large cigar releasing gelatinous circles of velvety smoke that slowly twist around the display cases filled with jars of deformed aborted fetuses.

In the room adjacent to mine the alcoholic retired detective breaks up ice chips with a long pick in preparation for his next round of cheap whiskey as *The Human Blockhead* removes a seven inch nail from his nostril with the ease and poise of fifty years of showmanship. Between the swift descent of the rusted ice pick and the slow withdrawal of the sleek shiny nail the girl's murderer dreamily waves his hand in mid-air as if in imitation of a conductor's self-absorbed direction of a particularly sensual passage suddenly changing tempo. The boy has wandered away from his father. He stares wide-eyed, transfixed by the joined twins suspended in their pool. They are like trapped lobsters on display at the front of a restaurant, too feeble to struggle, engulfed by drifting flaky particles of skin and seaweed. Like the percussive punctuation of a cymbal or kettle drum in the murderer's concert reverie, a clap of thunder shocks him back to awareness of his real surroundings. The crackle of electricity in the woods is complimented by the sharp bark of the boy's father reprimanding his son for leaving his side. The child scurries back to his annoyed parent as the murderer suddenly opens his eyes. Staring with surprise at the girl's corpse, the murderer for a moment reacts as if he actually were a sleepwalking maestro who lifts his head from the podium to discover that his music, in fact his entire orchestra has disappeared.

Screaming teenagers clutch one another forming a single body as the roller coaster descends a nearly vertical plane recalling the motion of the sled represented by a shiny red and yellow pin worn on the blouse of one of the girls. The quaint metal decoration vibrates uncontrollably like the leaves shaking from the storm's angry energy or like the spinning plates and gyrating birds that test the precision and skill of those trying their hand at the shooting gallery. The sticky skin of a jelly apple hangs from the boy's face as he chomps his treat waiting for his father to buy new tickets. At the same moment a red flake of paint flies off the girl's medallion whisked into oblivion as the cart plummets towards the ground and trunks of air fall backwards pushing against the huddled adventurers with a rude groping onslaught.

The claustrophobic hold of the woods is intoxicating, and the girl's body is certainly out of sight by now: he wants sleep, he wants the escape of sleep, his muscles ache with an ancient fatigue echoed by my face hollow, pale, and silver, staring back from the stark bathroom mirror. Can I rest through his sleep? Is he tormented by my enervation? In this morbid symbiosis I have created, there is a synthesis that helps nothing, cures everything, and searches for something that cannot exist.

The corpse concealed torso to feet by the fat oak tree shadow and head to torso by fallen moist leaves, he exits this scene of lurid melodrama, passing in haste the streetlamp glow which hurts my eyes until I have raised as a shield the heavy bed covers, causing my breath to become slightly labored. It is a relief that the Ferris wheel is near the shore, and he breathes deeply the brisk saline as he pauses to watch the colored lights that adorn each circling car in the enormous ride. A young girl passes him licking with cat like agility the soft curves of her vanilla ice cream cone, sending a shiver of sexual arousal through his formerly limp body. A purple quarter circle of light flickers upon the slick surface of her spongy tongue. His satisfaction of two hours ago is a calmative, yet not to the point of suppressing these new tingles of anticipation. But not this evening. He cannot act again so quickly. This evening he will sleep, and if the need for another release overcomes him there are of course the magazines that litter every inch of his room. The right angles formed ad infinitum by the stacks piled throughout the floor are as much a part of the latticework of the garden wall partition as I wish them to be. Viewing this back alley structure of intersecting lines, I see the angles of the forbidden publications, I know the way they overlap on the floor during his nights of feverish sexual imaginings.

Work boots make sloshing sounds, a heavy rain has fallen since the murder and the elapsed hours leave their mark in the changed soil, so mushy and irregular. Flashlight beams drive sharp white cylinders into the frightened owl's vision. It flaps away from the branch with heavy grace as the cigarette holder rolls from the desk onto the dim floor behind. But the owl does not go too far away, it is comforted by the omniscience of the cricket noise, since the pendulum clock beating next to the manager's desk flavors the lobby with a cricket's rhythmic arid accent, that steady beat of the insect's world, of the woods itself. A search party fatigued and wet with rubber trench coats slick from the rain. The professional men who do more of this work than they would like sweat in the humidity raised by rain and damp air after rain. A trailer has been arranged just outside the now cordoned woods so that the dead girl's parents may wait unmolested by the steadily gathering crowds and pressing media crews. The men in the trench coats know they will find a corpse. The father of the girl with the ice cream had not failed to observe the lecherous gaze of the strange man by the Ferris wheel. Provided with this information, the authorities concluded that such a setting plus the long butcher knife already discovered all point in the direction of the man they have been after for so long. Asleep now in his farmhouse far away, he dreams of the very scene they walk through, producing real mud splashes and real sweat and real shadows. This dream is as real as my knowledge of the gentle ripples of bark-brown coffee, which in the faintly trembling hands of the victim's mother, resembles a little pool by the tree selected as camouflage for the body. A startled squirrel drenched like a dishcloth rushes directly upward from the trunk to the branches. Its fur soaked with blood, it was sniffing around the mud immediately surrounding the body. Paws splayed across the tree one of the hounds confuses for only a moment the mixed scents of fellow animal and the human it was charged to find. *Over...* is heard with the muffled echo of a raised voice pushed through wet foliage, and the buzzing quality of an electronic transmission is produced as *...here*! comes across the make shift communications gear they have set up in the trailer. The coffee spills to the floor as a burly state trooper tries to revive the grief stricken parent and the rain furrowed mud pool next to the murdered girl's staring eye is suddenly hot white under the numerous combined flashlights.

Morgue personnel rush about as this case receives the highest priority. The squeak of thick rubber soles briskly treading smooth clean tile is a feeble sound, a hush behind stern metallic brashness as the coroner's assistant reaches for the next needed dissection instrument. The echo of metal rings eerily within the long hall of slabs, also metal, also cold. Thickness of the coroner's glasses so extreme that he seems eyeless, a bowing head directed by instinct without the benefit of vision. Coffee stains on the trooper's hat appear like a brown inverted lake on the dense lenses. He swipes at the wall with the large official felt headgear, angered by this new atrocity and the pitiful sight of the helpless mother. The rich thick ice cream reappears intact within the murderer's dream in spite of the burst of burning steam arising each time the assistant places a discarded instrument into the disinfectant tank. And in further contrast to the vapors of cold emanating from the white frozen substance, a minor residue of heat escapes from the last inner organs revealed after the initial exploratory incisions. The coroner speaks quickly yet voluminously into the rigid overhead microphone, tilting his head upward from time to time because the position of the recording device is not suitable for his height. Behind some recessed control panel the soft hissing of the tape can be heard, like sheets of paper lightly but continuously rubbing together, the way just now the arms of a little paper doll rustle against the wall disturbed so delicately by a thin breeze coming into the killer's open window. He dreams of the streetlamp not far from the tree and the girl now very far from the Ferris wheel, creating new geography as the two unite in an invented space. Here she is alone and much younger, playing with a rubber ball in front of the tall iron lamp. A large public bulletin (describing a child killer at large) is secured against the center of the lamp where she innocently tosses her ball. He sees his shadow loom across the poster warning, the ball hammering at the shadow, and it is here that he speaks admiringly of the pretty red and blue ball, asking her name. She answers innocently. The shadow takes her by the hand and leads her away.

Few if any shadows appear under the harsh desert like glare of the post-mortem facility. Glint of metal strikes the eye starkly without relief of contrast. Inside the cavernous trooper hat is the gentle quiet of darker space, and along its outer rim a decorative band of alternating diamonds and squares, identical to the band of black and white tile piping which lines the walls of the morgue. A friend or relative made faint from grief would see this strip of geometric shapes rising and falling before their blurred vision reached the dizzy climax of unconsciousness, if there were allowances for such a visitation, which of course is forbidden. Yet this sway of the diamonds, the sway of the squares occurs regardless of the anxiety of a shocked family member, as the trooper waves the thick hat back and forth, arms folded behind his back, impatiently waiting to learn the cause of death, and more importantly, the time of the murder.

There is no one to notice the movement of these shapes rocking up and down, from side to side. Just as no one notices the floating balloon as it drifts away from this new scene of murder, the dream murder of the child who made the fatal mistake of accepting a killer's gift. Before altitude carries the balloon beyond reach, the last shadow of the murder weapon flickers upon it. The ball rolls into a clump of bushes. The butcher knife shadow flashes across the floating orb like a lighthouse beacon giving a momentary caress to a drifting ship. The rush of sink water in the morgue awakens the sleeping madman who made this happen. He is frightened of the rain. He is reassured in his dumb sleepiness by the clear night sky beyond the window, and the stillness of the room. The paper doll has been twisted by increased wind into an obscene position. He smiles, reminded of the body of the young girl.

The old service elevator at the rear of the morgue makes a muffled fluttering sound like a large winged insect trapped inside a milk bottle. Smoke from the coroner's cigarette rises in gauzy bundles, slowly mingling with the skeletal lift cage. Spots of dim shaft light slowly daub the sutured flesh of the dead girl. They will think of decency just before reaching their destination, the twelfth floor where bodies are readied for the mortuary. For now the sheet hangs sloppily across her feet, trailing the splintered wood floor of the ancient lift. A slightly wider piece of shredded wood resembles the coffee stirrer that dropped to the floor of the surveillance van during the mother's fainting spell. The murderer (unable to fall asleep again) stirs his coffee with a spoon that captures the lewd posture of the paper doll each time it is lifted above the steamy liquid. The heavy castors of the gurney wheels will splinter the blade of wood just as busy feet will dislodge and crack the stirrer stuck for now to the linoleum floor of the vacant dark police vehicle.

The crooked bristles on the toothbrush (caked with blood dust from my futile attempts to clean the bathtub) resemble the shreds of tobacco that under the coroner's pressing foot unfold in wild brown disarray. The killer must know that they are about to reach the final floor and wheel the body towards the little room where the parents have been kept. He flings himself upon the bed and buries his face in the pillow, out of shame. Submerged within the remaining coffee he did not finish, the spoon no longer bears the likeness of the disarranged paper doll. Yet the silver content plate on the wooden filing cabinet inside the waiting room displays the haggard image of the mother's fatigue and sorrow filled visage. She has not slept one second since the previous evening. A very mild flicker of wind causes the doll's arms to reach forward in a gesture of solace, as though to embrace someone or something. Ironically at this very moment the administrator actually reaches towards the mother, in fact towards both parents. But it is with a clipboard containing a release form that must be signed. He pats them both on the back, however, bestowing at least some formal consolation.

Squeaking of the gurney wheels not unlike the tiny caws of crows within the field just beyond the murderer's house. Grotesque and forlorn a neglected scarecrow lunges robotically its torso shaken by a nudging breeze. Inanimate imitation of human form made more macabre by the senseless movement, the ridiculous clothing, the tortuous incomplete mouth mindlessly grinning at nothing. One strand of tobacco stuck to a wheel flutters away as a crow flies suddenly from a stalk. Crusty patches of the cracked shaft wall float by, their broken geometry forming a series of mutilated triangles and squares slowly sucked out of sight by the ever-ascending lift. Tick of the administrator's watch in the vacuum quiet of the office complimented by a tiny chip of shaft plaster knocked aside by the tap of a mouse's foot. Falling from the bird's body a piece of straw identical to the tobacco strand, just as minuscule, just as light, but on the field now buffeted by wind. Across from this field on the main highway the thick arm of a sweating truck driver distorts the anatomy of a risqué tattoo and on the cup of coffee he grasps the words *It's Our Pleasure To Serve You* are smudged by engine grease from his hand. On the floor of the murderer's bedroom moved also by wind the doll in its final position: supine, arms and legs at rest, still. Far above in a locked attic without ventilation the chunky smells of blood caked bandages, surgical instruments stuck together, children's pajamas, moldy dust imbedded toys, crusty droppings both human and animal. Sheeting flipped across the body as quickly they cover her. Discoloration of the coroner's nicotine stained fingertips similar to the paint stripped floor buttons of the vibrating lift. Last knot of the killer's tie the flapping silk looped around. Last tear from my eye as I pass by the mirror. First whisper of this child's name as her parents say good-bye.

Transatlantic Pictures

Interoffice Memorandum

From: J. Wakdjunkaga, screen-writer

To: C. Loki, Executive Producer

Re: Final White Draft of "The Confession "

[Victims' Families On Morning Of Execution]

Dear Mr. Loki,

Enclosed for your approval is the Final White draft of Commentary from Victims' Families that occurs outside the prison shortly before the execution.

For this sequence, I thought that we would achieve an interesting effect if we employed an extremely slow lap-dissolve as the scene moves from the comments of one individual to the comments of another. We can multi-track the statements so that as one individual is almost finished with their remarks, the next individual is heard speaking their lines before the dissolve is completed and the new face emerges out of the previous face. We can even go so far as to dramatize the results with morphing techniques, a la the Michael Jackson video "Black or White." While the purpose of the video was to show how multi-ethnic characteristics could be blended, we can use this device to suggest that the killer, in a sense, has "one victim," i.e. society itself, and that while the victims' relations and friends are all unique individuals, the murders have caused the same suffering for everyone.

Best regards,

J. Wakdjunkaga

EXTERIOR. DAY. VICTIMS' FAMILIES OUTSIDE THE PRISON.

It is early in the morning, around 6am. Today is the scheduled execution of the killer. There are hundreds of people in front of the prison, mostly relatives of the victims but many media people as well. Everyone who speaks appears to be addressing a camera, i.e. they look directly into the lens and volunteer their reaction as though they have been asked. Each person is shown in close-up. There are so many people standing shoulder to shoulder that the background of each shot is a blurred mass of faces. A continuous lap-dissolve is used, so that as one person finishes talking, their face slowly blends into the next person's face in the next shot, and so on, with a word or two of the last person's statement overlapping the first word or two of the next person's statement. The effect should be a kind of dream-like or subconscious continuity, as though this were one person transforming or "morphing" into many, saying the same thing a little differently each time. Numbers are used (Female Onlooker 1; Male Onlooker 2) to denote that we are looking at different people who are not otherwise identified.

FEMALE ONLOOKER (1): I don't think the system should take care of him. I think they need to string him up by his balls and torture him, slowly!

MALE ONLOOKER (1):_They don't even know for sure what happened, I mean, all these weird killer cases these days, and the media, the films they make, the books, some people justget so confused, and there's another guy, isn't there? They were looking for someone else too, weren't they?

MALE ONLOOKER (2): I don't believe in takin' a life for a life.

MOTHER OF VICTIM (1):_Where does all his pain come from? Why ask me? I had to put my little one into a coffin. What about my pain? What do I do with my pain?

MALE ONLOOKER (3): If the person got chopped up then we want 'em to chop him up, chop him up too and eat him like cannibals.

MALE ONLOOKER (4): It's not about revenge, no, I don't feel that way, it's from the Bible in a way, you know, an eye for an eye...if you take a life, you should lose your own.

FEMALE ONLOOKER (2): I believe in an eye for an eye tooth for a tooth.

MALE ONLOOKER (5): There is no price that you could put on any person's suffering. I think that person needs to be put into a cell with yourself and, commit…I don't believe incapital punishment.

MALE ONLOOKER (6): When I was a kid, my younger brother got run over and killed. It broke my mom's heart. Now I'm a grandfather and my mom happens to be alive, God blessher, and as old as she is, there isn't a day goes by that she doesn't think about her little boy…There's just no way to sum up the kind of hurt a parent feels when they lose a child. It's sucha terrible shame.

MALE ONLOOKER (7): Yeah…uhhh…actually, it's kinda hard 'cause it's hypothetical I'm not in that situation but I'm sure I would like agree with most people the person shouldsuffer but at the same time I'm over here thinkin' a person like that should be studied and if you kill them how are you gonna possibly in the future prevent somewhere along the linethis guy became who he became he wasn't born this thing happened to make him...

FEMALE ONLOOKER (3): I think justice is being served, but I get disgusted by the way the media turns these things into a circus, I mean, just look around here right now: six-thirtyin the morning, hundreds of people standing outside the prison, another 30 or 40 television, cable, and newspaper reporters, it's insanity piled on top of lunacy!

PROFESSOR: I teach a course on serial murder at the University here. There are timeswhen I believe that popular culture is a mirror for the collective subconscious. The morecollective subconscious. The more chaos and evil we create in cultural scripts, such as wewe find in movies or video and computer games that rely so heavily on the impact of violent images, the more we're becoming enslaved to a kind of self-fulfilling prophecy.Just look at all of the school shootings over the past twenty years, since that tragedy atColumbine. Unfortunately I think modern society has forgotten its divine ingredients: often we're too human for our own good.

FATHER OF VICTIM (1): I don't care what anybody says, giving him some go-to-sleep needle or whatever it is they do...hey, why does he get to die so peacefully when he causedso much physical pain?

MOTHER OF VICTIM (2): I'll never see my child again, I'll never hold her or hear her voice or see her do any of the things she could have done, they should tear him apart pieceby piece!! I just don't give a damn about his sickness or whatever else these smart ass lawyers want to call it, he's evil and that's all there is to it!

MALE ONLOOKER (8): I'm here out of respect for the families. I didn't lose a child or a relative, but I've seen some of those pictures of what was done to them. I still have nightmares about it. It just doesn't make any kind of sense.

MALE ONLOOKER (9): No matter what happened, taking another life isn't going to solve the problem, I mean it's just revenge, it's blood lust. He's being sacrificed so we canall feel less guilty about the world.

MALE ONLOOKER (10): I read that article, and I heard it on TV too. Where do these defense psychiatrists get off with their ideas? Saying he was delusional and that he wanted to punish himself? I don't buy any of that crap. What about the bodies? What about the evidence? Doesn't simple reality count anymore?

FATHER OF VICTIM (2):_They should leave the bastard in a room with the parents and let them torture him with those same knives he used!

FATHER OF VICTIM (3): I just want to see it, hear me? I wanna see this bag of human filth die with my own eyes! He killed my daughter! He killed my daughter!

FEMALE ONLOOKER (3): That's what I mean about the way the media gets some kind of thrill out of this stuff, I mean...well, maybe we all do in a sick kind of way. I mean, he'snot even dead yet and I heard just yesterday that they're already working on some kind of script for a movie about what he did.

PRIEST: I've come from the church because I requested to hear this man's last confession and to pray for his soul.

FATHER OF VICTIM (4):_What are you gonna do, Father, write a book about him like that nun did? You want to pray for somebody? You want to grant salvation? Why don'tyou go cry for the souls of all the dead children he tortured?

MOTHER OF VICTIM (3):_It's taken years for this day to come, do you understand?

Years! My little girl was only thirteen and she died in a few minutes. That was almost nine years ago. I've lived a waking nightmare for nine years waiting for this day and his monster has eaten, slept, read books, written, and relaxed all this time. Where's the justice in that? Can anyone explain this to me?

MALE ONLOOKER (11): They should do it the way they used to in ancient times...They should cut off his arms and legs and scatter them to the four corners of the earth and thenleave his head on a post for the birds to pick!

MALE ONLOOKER (12):_How much sex was involved in the crimes, does anybody know

for sure? Not that I'm excited by it or anything like that...I just want to know...I'm justcurious about it...I...

PROFESSOR:_In fact the conclusion of my lectures in this series touches upon some ofthe issues that have been raised by this case. I was permitted to interview this man, and to hear him speak you'd think you were talking to a prophet who is assuming the symbolic role of the sacrificial lamb. It's convenient, of course, in popular psychoanalytic jargon,to dismiss this as the typical "persecution complex," but with this man you couldn't be entirely sure. I know it sounds bizarre, but part of my thesis is that every age spawns a figure that is somehow an incarnation, negative or positive, of its spiritual destiny. Some-times I feel our society is a classic example of lost love, and the uncanny feeling I had when I spoke to him was that he is the perfect embodiment of that human malady.

FATHER OF VICTIM (5): They should have used a firing squad to get rid of the fucking bastard! I was a marksman in the service! I would have volunteered for the job! I wouldhave shot him into pulp with an automatic weapon if they'd let me! I hate his guts, I hate his motherfucking guts!

MOTHER OF VICTIM (4):_I hope he's tormented in Hell by every damned soul that ever lived the kind of evil and destructive life that he did! I hope he's tortured until the end oftime, and then have it start all over again!

MOTHER OF VICTIM (5): I'm wearing this T-shirt with a picture of my daughter because I want everyone to know that she's still alive in our hearts, and that she's remembered by every-one who knew her and loved her.

FATHER OF VICTIM (4): Huh, Father, what about that! You're a hypocrite with your forgiveness, there's no such thing as mercy for a creature like this!

MALE ONLOOKER (13): All right, all right, that's enough now! I don't think you or anybody else has the right to question the motives of this man. He's a representative ofthe church and of the

Christian way, and I happen to be a Catholic and even though I'm not a perfect Christian I believe in the principle of salvation and forgiveness. That's the whole point, really. There's no message in the lesson of forgiveness when it's easy, Ithink that's what the Father is saying now: the real test is when you have forgiveness for your enemies, for those who have hurt you the most.

FATHER OF VICTIM (5): I'm sorry, but I agree with this man. I don't feel that because he's a priest his judgment is unassailable. This bastard hung my daughter from the rafters of a shack and gutted her like a dressed lamb! Do you hear me! I want him to die like an insect! No forgiveness! No mercy! Nothing!

MALE ONLOOKER (14): I heard this psycho wrote some kind of diary or journal all these years while he was on death row, now I mean he's gonna sell this thing, is that what they're using for the movie they're supposed to make?

MALE ONLOOKER (15):_There's laws...

MALE ONLOOKER (14): His family or whoever is gonna make money off this thing and we're left with broken hearts and murdered children, is that what's going on now?!

MALE ONLOOKER (15): There's laws to prevent it. Whatever they do with his book nobody connected to him can receive any profit from it. They'll probsbly use the moneyfor a support group for victims' relatives or something like that.

MALE ONLOOKER (14): And what's this supposed to be, huh? His big confession, his filthy diary, his justification for ruining the lives of so many families and taking the livesof so many kids? Huh? What's this book supposed to be?

MALE ONLOOKER (16):_What if he is crazy? Maybe he didn't do anything. I know he never tried to deny any of it, from what I heard he stopped saying much of anything afterthe beginning. I just don't get it. A sane person wouldn't let himself be put to death if he knew he was innocent.

MALE ONLOOKER (17):_Can't you just feel the hate? It's like it's in the air, y'know?

Feel it? Can't you just reach it and touch it?

The Son: Chapter V

I hear the stretcher wheels. The rolling empty platform is coming closer and closer, shuttling noisily through the long prison corridors, straps dangling, snapping blindly at the empty air. Like the whipping tentacles of a predatory mechanical beast, the strap tips slap the walls as the gurney speeds voraciously towards me. A guard sits quietly reading a newspaper at the end of a hallway. His glistening Billy club reflects the flurry of flapping black leather strips, a shrunken silver image like a miniature explosion of branches thrust forward in a blast of hurricane wind.   Or conversely, like a giant spider convulsively flexing its innumerable legs in the moment of attack. Am I in *Foolish House*? Am I one of the exhibits, a carefully preserved freak of nature, a distillation of all that is bizarre and irrational? There is an interminable chain of chutes punctuated by garish clown faces. The clang of the spinning wheels becomes metallic laughter echoing from clown mouth to clown mouth. The gurney becomes a speeding train careening maniacally through the infinite stretch of cackling chute tongues. The wet red flesh twists crazily like smacking sails far at sea, splashing me with hot saliva. I feel the vibrations of the jaws of the clowns, churning like a massive diesel engine. Their eyes gigantic as a volcano, blinking like the sting of electricity in a lightning storm. Wildly painted gaping mouths are cavernous endless tunnels through which the steaming locomotive cart charges, rushing through the mocking laughter which travels in peals compounding in resonance and volume from face to face.

In keeping with the Egyptian concept of the after-life, according to which the dead must be equipped with those necessary and fundamental objects of everyday life (not to mention food and clothing) so that their journey through the land of the spirit will be more comfortable and safe, I thought it might be interesting if I were surrounded after my death with some of the things that have mattered most to me in life. A most peculiar looking funerary room would have to be arranged, filled with dozens of wooden sparrows, hundreds of little cassette tapes, the faulty tape-recorder, and several thousand reels of film. I suppose they could make room for my corpse if they tried.

The priest just left. Strange how the sound of the gurney began at the moment of his departure. Does everything happen on cue? I watched his crucifix dwindle, framed by the oviform keyhole, as he walked from my cell. I could not hear his footsteps. I suddenly remembered the footsteps of all of the supplicants who had walked away unburdened from the confessional box. In one great epiphany of recall I heard the multiplied footfalls and echoes of steps, all those who had come to me for guidance, forgiveness, penance. It was the aural equivalent of a scene from a war film, a montage of thousands of soldiers preparing for battle, marching, marching forward, the sound of their footsteps blending and enlarging like stones poured onto steel from a thousand directions. Not one body among the steps, not one face or soul or recollection of a person who had suffered some sin, some crisis of faith, and had come to me sorrowful, guilty, anxious. I could not summon even the slightest impression of any of the thousands of conversations I had with these pathetic figures. It seemed to me as though my sole purpose in all of this was being fulfilled only now, to remember the steps that led them away, the steps that brought them out of the set of double boxes connected by a little screen, the steps that resounded loudly on the marble church floor, the steps that brought them out of the enormous vaulted entrance. Dearest father, are disembodied footsteps somehow a signature for the soul? Are we finally no more or less than the trace or the record of where we've gone all through life? Remembering sounds, sounds that, like shadows, are simply and purely a conclusion, a summary, an indicator for what was. Yes, the gaze of Ugolino may let you see more than that, but the visualization of all the feasts of the centuries will not keep you from starving.

The priest fingered a clear tiny ampoule of holy water as he spoke softly to me. Certainly at that moment far below us in the execution chamber behind an exhaled sheet of thick cigarette smoke the man with the syringe must have been mixing the deadly fluids. I wonder if the hooded executioner's costume is employed, as in the case of the guillotine? It is almost as if the mask of anonymity is a therapy for the inflictor of the punishment, and not for the sake of the condemned at all. As in the case of the firing squad, where one marksman is given a blank cartridge, but no one knows who has it. That way the guilt is mitigated for all who pull the trigger since there is the equal possibility that any one of them has not fired a live round. A procedure that would be difficult to reproduce in this case, unless they were to multiply the syringes as well as the number of people administering the injections, keeping one placebo solution a secret. If they were to film the execution they could save the footage, project it against the next execution, film that execution coupled with its projected double, film that, and so on until a cancer of images grew into one enormous mass of image-tissue, so to speak. They could use the final product as a training film for amateur executioners. The trainee would reach for the two-dimensional canvas arm of the long dead condemned, like children playing pin the tail on the donkey. The priest clasped and unclasped his hands many times while he spoke and the rapidity of this nervous gesture made me disassociate his limbs from his body. For an instant all I could see were the wringing hands suspended in empty space, but the emotional inference of the behavior was unclear: were the hands wrung in worry? Compassion? Impatience? Muscular fatigue? I could not be sure.

Earlier I was on my hands and knees, toothbrush to the cell floor, scouring between the large stones to remove all the wood shavings from my carving. I did not want to leave things in disarray. Like Joan assisting her persecutors as she lifts the fallen rope to help them secure her to the stake, I wanted my surrender to be pure of human flaws.

I scrubbed every surface with the blind diligence of Sisyphus. The task performed with total thoroughness by the one who must totally fail. The bloodstains could not be removed. Not from the staircase where my father died, not from the basement where the captive woman was slaughtered, not from the carnival back lot where the young girl was strangled. The sanctuary of dream provides no immunity from horror, for the blood remains on the rubber ball, splattered across the killer's streetlamp duplicated in my pastoral reverie where I longed for lost love.

Even on the poet's vase there was at least the eternal promise of love fulfilled, an ideal achieved. Forever suspended in the moment before, there was joy at least in the approach towards happiness, something kept perpetually real in an imagined future. Where is she now? Where are the moments we might have shared?

Did I kill life with my bitterness? Did I waste the gifts of the spirit? My beloved unknown to me forever, in brutal loneliness I discarded life's feast, relishing debris instead.

But I am alive. I do not want to die without knowledge of love...I want to hear the sparrows.

There is the luster of all surfaces after I anaesthetized my pain with visions, but the shine does not hide the traces of death. The bathtub, the windowsill, the staircase, the floor, the vestibule, the amusement park, inside the closet, inside my soul...the mirror.

Somewhere he prepares to do it again. Somewhere he is ready to satisfy that hunger. He picks up the razor. My skin feels new wounds. Punishment comes for the crime of allowing the image to live a life of its own. Yes, it is true that the sinning soul brings it own punishment upon itself.

I have been given the injection. They transferred me to a cross-shaped table designed for the execution: left and right restraints at the bottom for the condemned's ankles; at the top left and right for the wrists. Everything is white: the little room I am in (less than a room, more like a hollow cube), the walls, floor, ceiling, and door. There is a plate glass window; actually it is the fourth wall, for the glass extends from floor to ceiling. The witnesses must be on the other side. Naturally this is a two-way mirror; my side is only the counterpart of the scene I am in, the full-length screen projecting the life size picture. If I turn my head to the left I can see myself strapped to the white table, wearing the white prison shoes, slacks, and shirt (short sleeves). The needle puncture is still sore.

The syringe and my father's cigarettes have an identical shape because he often smoked when he prepared food, cutting into vegetables or meats with a pointy...the syringe stopper...it is a...

...it is a cylinder, nothing more...it is like a cigarette...nothing more...he suffers from a highly irrational equation making process...

...sitting in the theatre next to my father I waited anxiously for the thrill of the house lights suddenly dimming, the undulating curtain parting with one silent broad gesture...then the screen permeated with that unnatural light...and the shadows, the ominous shadows of the haunted house, the dark cave, the deserted cemetery, the sinister laboratory...the fiend comes closer, he leans...he...

...he...

...no...but...the man who administered the injection...his dream last night included black shadows passing over a cloud, because he knew he would lean over me, in order to inject me...his dream...there is nothing...

...nothing...dreams...the executioner's dreams...what can I know of another man's dreams?...what shadows...across my chest...birds flying...away...the plastic security badge he wore...it was rectangular because they will put my body into a coffin...it bore a reflection of my face...the murdered girl's parents were there...crying...no...it is a shape...a shape...

...he leans over his victim with the howling wind at the door and the moon floating pale above the misty moors...then the scene changes to a romantic quarrel in a tawdry living room...a jealous husband shoots his wife's lover, the smoke from the gun seems to drift through her screaming mouth…but it is a film showing an audience watching this scene in a film...the real characters are on the stage in front of the screen...a man fires a real gun...someone in the first row is shot...the entire audience heaves a startled gasp when he slumps over in his seat...there is a...a...

...a shape...a coffin is simply a shape...no more than the booths, the vestibule, my cell, this room...the confessional with the little window...forgive me, forgive me...became quite obsessed with her...

...it was a classic case of unrequited love...the day my father died was the day I went to see her, to tell her how I loved her...how I loved her...but there was no solace for me, no comfort, she did not love me in return...a classic case...now the lights...the...

...lights are spinning, like a top, like the stretcher wheels, like a cyclone, blurry and fast...like the poster advertisements sweeping past the train window on my journey to her that day...Hey Browser, Browser!...What did you find?...What are you gonna do with that?...

...there is a man standing on what appears to be a mound or a little hill...behind him are changing backgrounds, shifting scenery which plunges him into ever changing locations and predicaments: he is in the path of a locomotive, being charged by Indians, about to go over a waterfall, underneath a massive rock slide…I was fascinated, I could not take my eyes off the screen, I...I could not...

...I could not let go of the pain...I did not want another...I closed my eyes...the betrayal, the betrayal of the gift...the bitterness won...until now...this is the way...this is the only way to defeat it...forgive me Father, for I have sinned...weird way to die, weird way to die...should I say that the monogrammed shirt of one of the witnesses on the other side of the glass has loops that are similar to the pattern of my shoelace?...say that the slender fire-extinguisher tube outside the sealed door of the execution cell is very much like the manager's cigarette holder?...

...will another owl flap away?...another beating clock create a cricket's sound?...another forest become the setting for the death of a new child?...

...and the wheels spin...grinding train wheels shooting sparks into the winking eyes of the hysterical clowns...spiraling webs spitting down from the *Foolish House* ceiling...trap doors pop open to reveal taunting messages as I rush past on the pontoon of chutes...*Now You've Gone Too Far...Never Put Off Till Tomorrow What You Can Do Today...O What A Tangled Web We Weave*...like the boulders rolling down the hill in the film...bicycle spokes...halos of ascending smoke...when my father smoked...an angry crowd follows him...they take pity because he stands there ashamed in front of his weeping son...the child takes his father by the hand, looks up at him with an adult's understanding...

...I killed no one...I took no one's life...no life but my own...I wasted my chance to live...my priesthood was a bitter refuge from the pain of lost love...an empty vocation designed to somehow recreate the lost connection to my Father...year after year my diminished faith bled itself dry, like Martin Luther's ever increasing contempt for a God that seemed to mock him...

...why did I pretend?...why did I lie?...I hid within the words, the reflections...buried myself with images...technology which permits us to shrink the world...but I hid the bodies...I...no...there were no bodies...I followed the real killer the way a puppeteer manipulates his little figures...the way a ventriloquist converses with himself through the illusion of his dummy...the way a magician deceives his audience with personal charm and sleight of hand...but I became the slave, I became the puppet, I became a prisoner of my own words...take the words away...peel away the semblance so I can be what I have denied...die without the mask, without the game of words...I was the one who denied myself...my beloved...my...

...my ideal...the glorification of sacred love...my arrogance was a mist...eye for an eye tooth for a tooth...another could have loved me, another could have saved me...I enshrined my love...if I could not have her I would deny another, deny the world, deny myself...hate vision, hate potential, hate ambition of the spirit...like the deranged soul lost in the Congo...raise the hand in a desire to heal but the fingers grasp a dagger...thirty years, thirty years of dirt...

...are they all there?...are they all bearing witness on the other side of the glass?...are they watching the hunger artist perform his last act?...

...*Jelly Man, Pumpkin Puss, The Grafter, Sam, The Coroner, Neon Noodle, Wong Dong, The Teacher, The Girl In The Basement, The Muscular Tormentor, Jauntley, The Girl From The Carnival*...what's the matter Jonesy, ain't you ever seen a gun before?...where's the girl?!...

...listen!...you want me to count three or somethin' like a movie?...*The Watchman, The Salesman, The Pregnant Girl, The Manager, The Psychiatrists, Hank, Jake, Manny, Becker*...are they watching, waiting for the moment of my transfiguration?...will you throw a little of that damn light over here!...I had a...

...a toy...a special toy when I was a child...one of those wooden puzzle boxes...you had to find the box within the box within the box...like the hidden book of magic promised to the priest of Ptah...it fascinated me...I kept it throughout my life...hiding, not hiding...appearance, reality...surface, interior...always a dichotomy, a paradox...the emblem of my existence, the terrain of my mental landscape...

...I remember...I remember...

...her hair, the black curls, the child like beauty of her eyes...I remember the cafe we sat in, when I told her of my love for her...the spring air...purls of marble in the coffee table...rose and white tentacular veins like strands of seaweed draped across the rocks...

...I don't love you, she said...you can see it in my eyes, in my gestures...I can't love you, she said...the smell of cowhide, rich, sweet, a little musty, the old jacket she usually wore...the fluted pipes of the large copper espresso machines...gnarled protrusions like on a very old tree...scents of tobacco, pastry, balmy air, her hair, her skin...the long hair across her shoulders...girlish hands...deep ebony pupils...hold me...

...caress me...

...give me comfort and rest...my beloved...it cannot be...obsessive thought...

...thought patterns...displacement of normal sex drive with pornography...the fixation on death...fixation on death...violent forms of death exclusively involving women...shadows...

...shadows crisscrossed upon our table because our journey towards one another would be circuitous...it was a sign of hope...we would struggle to find our love...we...

...we...there was nothing to hope for...there was no love to find...the jumble of shadows was the inevitable result of moonlight shining against the wrought iron gate...our table lay in its path...she left me sitting alone, she wanted no more of my pain, it was the last time I saw her...

...the dishrag was soaked with blood when I stepped outside the cafe...my father had already fallen...a squirrel darted past me near the curb...I was not in the house when it happened...I did not reach for the doorknob...my complexion had nothing to do with the appearance of the stairway walls...if my father's hand flattened itself palm against wall, it was the result of the fall...a lyrical veneer...to protect me from real sorrow, real pain...

...the body of a murdered and mutilated woman was discovered...my life became a record of disbelief...hollow...defiance of substance...refusal to acknowledge good...howl with laughter at the sacrifice of life, watch the blood drip down the gutted lamb...swaying of its legs like the playground swing, those children will be followed by a new murderer...shadows in the park...butcher knife gleam...balloons floating the strings loose no hands to hold them...and the shame of it, the utter shame...the sorrow of the families, the loss of innocent life...I glorified evil for the sake of my pain...I was a malignant voyeur fascinated by the powers of destruction...I presume you think that if you murder me here your sailor friend will get the blame and you'll be free to spend my money...the mirror is dividing, multiplying, turning inside out...I am a witness, I am every witness, I am watching myself die from a thousand perspectives...do not despair, one thief was saved...do not rejoice, one thief was damned...framed?!...who's been framed?!...the lamb is white, the field where it grazes is white, the sky is white...only the eyes, the staring black eyes...the gentle love of these eyes that know...Jauntley had to have his look...he loves to gaze at the gruesome...he was some kind of a man...what does it matter what you say about people?...press the button again, change the selection...another scene within the scene... you indicated that you wanted a long, convoluted tracking shot... the screen is the hallucination...yet it is a doorway...a surface painted with the spell of the unreal...what cannot happen *can* happen...what is impossible *is* possible...duck season, wabbit season...over here, Canino!...clever bastard...was a building maintenance man, did some handiwork stuff, painted...killed...raped every child he could find...who is to blame for this?...Damfino!...let us get into the balloon, let us float away from here...let us have some of that magic lantern stuff, a little kinescope madness...another racing train, or a charging bull, a house on fire, maybe an elephant getting the juice...poof!...thousands of volts...I told ya I brought you up here for a reason...give me the receiver, give me the damn...I wanted to love her, I could not love her...the fault lies not in the stars but...to hell with that!...trunks of lies made out of the tricks of poetry...tricks!...all you know are tricks!...no matter what happens now, tricks won't do you any good!...my voice is like an old wall eaten into hundreds of worm infested pockets...speak something true, something real, something for the pain, for the loss, for the misery of finally being nothing, nothing but a wretched fool who let his pride devour his soul...what is the mystery of sacrifice?...why is it so haunting, so powerful, so cleansing?...is there an answer I am obliged to give?...is there a question I have failed to ask?...back to the same old song again...who is it that is not your brother but is your mother's son?...no...what is the use of a game with ideas, another rabbit out of the hat, another skillful throw of the voice as the ventriloquist gulps down his glass of water, another badge of illusion so there is no further analysis, no further inquiry?...No...let me stay...I wanna watch!...I am going along my merry way but I would like to evict the lice before I die...so afraid...I was always so afraid to live...what do they say?...silly expression: come smell the roses...falling in love again, never wanted to...I hear the clowns...I am speeding along now a blur like a humming bird's wings...laughter gurgling a syrup of voices pours down greasing the wheels of the cart...here comes the fool, all dressed in drool...my Father...did I abandon you?...at least they came for me after you died...when I was arrested, that day so long ago...when they came for...did you not know that I would be in my Father's house?...please forgive me, Father...my ignorance...my vanity...my pride...a world of things, of images, of illusions...the senses are a house made of air...but I have tried to live there...breathing poison, the noxious fumes of deception...Oh Madeleine I loved you so!...feeling a little dizzy?...want to go outside so you can finish throwing up?...y'know, Jaunty, you better lay off them chili dogs...it's either the candy or the hooch…I'm your lawyer for God sake, if you don't tell me what the fuck really went on, I can't help you!…they've got positive ID on you, there's this business with the carving tools, that trunk full of damn birds you made, the shavings, the bloodstains, the picture of you lurking around the Ferris wheel the night of the last murder…I mean, what do you think I am, a miracle worker? …what the hell is going on?!...Who's life is it, anyway?…I am not paralyzed, no I am going into a release from paralysis now…fly away…spirit to tower, spirit to tower, ceiling unlimited, ready for take-off…I remember having caught a cold one summer…my father brought me to a theatre to see a new film…by the water fountain I felt that familiar tickle in my throat…the sudden alarm of a child who dreaded having a cold and especially one before the end of summer…such a large movie house, gigantic wall separating the seats from the refreshment area…the little fountain over in the corner…that feeling of modest independence, being away from our seats, on my own to get a drink…cozy in the embrace of darkness…small torch lights illuminating the old wood and marble…smell of popcorn…shredded seat material…dankness of the fountain pipes…bitter drip in the back of my throat…I feel it now…probably a side-effect of the shots…surprised I can feel anything within my body…before the tips of my fingers floated away…they became ten little white boats…rowboats actually but armed with the kind of guns you see on battleships…on that lake they sailed, where the picnic was, when I thought I would have her love…they all exploded suddenly like a confetti snowstorm…the lake boiled over and drowned me…she appeared in the seat of the Ferris wheel…immobile eyes staring forward…angelic and still…white silk nightgown flowing so slowly against the night sky…folds of phosphorescent silk undulating across the pin points of distant stars…the dark waves across from the wheel answered in kind with the rhythm of their curves…reflected across the swaying waters the same pattern of stars that hid behind the material of her gown…miles below on the seabed my choking face freckled by the mocking starlight…coral shackles held my restless body in place…an endless parade of sea creatures advanced before me…their rainbow of colors mixed into lines which became nets fastening me to the sandy dungeon floor…are my eyes melting?…there are swirls of black ink issuing from my sockets…iris and pupil mixing into the curling letters of *The Professor's* letter…they stream across me like an electronic scroll on the side of a building…I hope I am performing my function…performing my duty like *The Professor's* industrious ants…sacrificing my individuality for the sake of the whole…carrying my pebble for the good of the cause…suddenly the matrix of script letters transforms into the spider web I found when I was a boy…my father is the trapped victim within the web…he twists and writhes against the taut trembling structure...now the strands twist into unwinding strips of film…the hundreds of little pockets formed by the intersections become images from the films we saw together, alternately appearing and disappearing, where one fades another emerges in a different spot…like search lights beaming and extinguishing in a fog…

I...I see something...it is not very far...I am coming closer...I can almost touch it now...so pale...so delicate...so beautiful...such a sweet smell...like roses...there is a softness like roses...like velvet...click...sss...click...sss...what gentle music...like little bells...caress of delicate wind...I am coming closer...so close...so beautiful...click…sss…I would like to speak to it...so....so...I am com-ing closer…so close…so beautiful…click…sss…click…sss…there is something there…I know it is not impossible…what sweet music…such a sweet smell…there is a softness like roses…there is something…click…sss…there is a sweetness like music…click…sss…there is something…there is a soothing like whispers…something …click…sss…click…sss…something…some…click…sss…thing… click…sss…click…sss…some…click…sss…click…sss… d a m a g e d … c l i c k … s s s … m u s t have…click…sss…someone…click…sss…the …click…sss…taperecorder…must…have…some…one… one…thing…thing…click…sss…someone…click… sss…someone…click…sss…someone…click…sss…someone

The Father: Chapter Six

Today was a good day. The sparrows were hungry. Their beaks twitched vigorously. Last night's storm was violent. It greatly disturbed the nest. This morning I reconstructed it. I worked slowly and carefully. Today there was much sunshine. The sky was uniformly blue. It was beautiful. I could smell the salt air. I could see the hovering gulls. I could hear the repeating echo of the crashing sea. The rhythm of the waves is like a physiological clock. It gives the pleasure of consistency and reassurance. Somehow it makes the endless soul a little fonder of its restrictive body. I found some hay and twigs for the nest. A little mud helped to patch everything together. I worked carefully. I fed the sparrows. They ate quickly and did not overlook even a spec of food. There was a can of breadcrumbs in the cupboard. The tree bark smelled fresh and alive. All the rain and the morning sunshine gave a wonderful palpability to the skin of the tree. It is important to note the simple presence of God within the moments of one's everyday life. I have found that the misdirected energy of the garrulous atheist is perfectly counterbalanced by the pure radiance of every believer's faith. To believe in spite of empirical insufficiencies. To believe with the trust of a child. This is a good rule of mind. It is like the needs of the sparrows. It is like the delicate grace of the morning sun. These are the things I must teach to my son. He lays here in his crib in the first weeks of life. Sadly I can already see the tell-tale banner of mortal doubt imprinted across his tiny forehead. We are born unknowing yet instinctively suspicious. The great incredulity of all humans consumed by need and want who walk back and forth upon the earth. Only great wealth protects those very few from the harshness of life and it is harshness and illogic that compel us to despair. Self-awareness is always the first step towards cynicism. How can we be a rational part of an irrational whole? Why is life constantly beleaguered by illness and tragedy? What is the mysterious reason for the inevitability of suffering and death? The sparrows do not suffer from such meditations. Neither does the tree. There is no such metaphysical malady in nature. Such contrariness is singularly human. That is part of the divine plan. It is the glorious contradiction of being simultaneously released and reclaimed. I must show my son that the senses engineered by flesh and enslaved by time constitute an ancient test administered by God to all mankind. I must be flawlessly consistent in my teaching. I must omit nothing. As I reached up to the nest with my breadcrumbs I noticed the lovely matrix of leaf shadows against the branches and the upper parts of the tree trunk. The crispness and clarity of morning sunlight made the black and white swarming umbra of leaves so animated and precise. Shadows, however mundane, are important to a pious man. The tiniest index of the movement of humans or objects offers many possibilities for higher contemplation. The concept of the indexical plays a central role in all of this. It is the reflection of things in the world that makes man's attempt to relate him to a divine being less strange and more natural. I saw the shadows of my hands fluttering across the bark as I repaired the nest. The duality of the material object and its immaterial shadow is the key. Between object and shadow there is a perfect timeless paradox of inescapable connection and irrefutable difference. On a sunny day you may watch your steps seamlessly translated into accompanying shadows without realizing that you as the corporeal thing and the shadows as the ethereal phantom cannot escape one another. Have you ever felt yourself gently compelled into mystification when you consider the duality of shadows and things? It is so odd that as humans our attention is fixed upon the practical and the functional. Reverie and meditation do not belong to the ordinary man. The sadness of the world is such that the simple man will see the ladder against the white stone wall only as a tool necessary for his next task. Generations of study in economics and social philosophy teach us that it is the poet alone who disregards the purpose of the ladder. It is he who will describe the elegant geometry of the stark charcoal shapes. The gorgeous ascension of symmetrically spaced shadows is the ladder in the mind of a poet. I must show my son that the desire to see something in a certain way is as much a part of the reality of that thing as the existence or purpose of the thing itself. The thought of a thing is like the shadow of an object and this peculiar condition plague's man in his desire to know his God. I am not embarrassed by the elementary nature of this idea nor am I intimidated by the thoroughness with which it has been considered. I am a man of vision and intuition. I will show my son that it is the unexpected and inspired examination of the obvious or the familiar that ultimately leads to some undiscovered truth. As I held my wife's hand after she had given birth to our son I heard the click of the doctor's earpieces from his stethoscope. They snapped together after he removed the instrument from his neck and my wife quietly died. Two weeks later I brought my son home and I removed my wedding band to wash my hands. It hit the bureau with a single tap. It was like the quick metallic click of the ear pieces and for the first time in fourteen days my palm again felt the release of my wife's limp hand as her breathing ceased. I heard the heart monitor emit its unique flat signal; that perfunctory mechanical announcement of death. I saw the swollen circular shadow of the ring-shaped window shade handle on the opposite bed in her hospital room. The fury of the doubter's denial of the existence of the deity gains momentum at these times when our mortal frame is no more than a recording device that never tires of tormenting us by polluting the mixture of memory and perception with undeniable and seemingly unanswered sorrow. I fell to my knees and wept like a child. I cried out to my wife. I called out her name. Where did you go? I asked. Where did you go? My paroxysm of tears was so great that my hand shook. At that moment I heard the whistle of the teakettle in the next room. With an automatic gesture that I could not fathom I returned my wedding band to my finger and reached for the steam-engulfed vessel with a steady hand. As I poured the amber liquid into my cup I looked up and through the window opposite saw one large yellow leaf suddenly snap from its stem and blow with the wind to the ground. I remember that for some reason my attention was drawn to the pure coincidence of downward movement. I was most intrigued by the simultaneity of the descent of pouring tea and falling leaf. When we suffer the pain of the death of a loved one we cling to memory the way the shadows of feet remain inseparable from the one who walks. The more I remained in the presence of the memory of my wife the less inconceivable and unreal her death seemed to me.   The last embrace of the illusion manufactured by every multi-layered component of the senses where every understandable pitiful doubt and every metaphysical contradiction cry out. There is the horrible certainty of the recollection of all that we have done and said. A plaintiff but inextinguishable voice somewhere inside us whispers incessantly about those uncannily solid images that do not mix with the incorporeity of death and instead insist that we were here. It is like removing all human presence from old photographs and seeing only the objects and the space that become a peculiar host for recall and association and above all the dissonant illogic that in death everyone becomes an image. Photographs somehow exert a kind of mystical control over their subjects. There is a peculiar wisdom in the superstitions of primitive cultures in which grave objections to having one's picture taken can be found. The terror that one's soul will be "stolen" by this god of the mimetic known as a camera. It seems to me that such mortal fears of the reproductive power of the lens as exhibited by most tribal societies is instinctively if not philosophically based on this element of abstraction that I am trying to define. Animals do not experience self-recognition. A creature will not perceive its own being in the reflection of a mirror. I have heard that only the chimpanzee comes even remotely close to achieving this elementary level of existential awareness but that this is accomplished arduously after months of training. I suppose the argument put forth by anthropology is that since the chimp in most matters of cognition and behavior is our closest relation these revelations of self-perception are natural rather than coaxed. I have my doubts. Humans alone are both consciously and subconsciously fettered to the awareness of mortality. Hence our regard of a photograph in which we appear from a day ago or fifty years in the past summons in us the strangely bittersweet certitude that we have passed through space and time with little more to anchor ourselves than the elusive inner voice of consciousness. The creature does not know that it is destined to die. That is the essence of the mystery of self-recognition. The animal cannot know itself in the form of reproductive imagery (such as a mirror or a photograph) because the perceptual equipment of its senses does not include either an inherited or acquired knowledge of the inevitability of its own demise. Sometimes there is an instinctual awareness of the immanence of death. I do not know how science has categorized this phenomenon but I assume that it is prevalent among the higher animal species. A dog for example will try to remove itself from view so that it may perish away from a human audience. I remember that I sat next to our dog as it lay on its side the evening before it died. I was a young man and I stroked the animal gently while it panted with laborious effort. Yet it found the strength presumably through some primordial impulse to try and push me away with its paw. It was such a pathetic gesture and I wept for the poor creature. I did not understand or accept the necessity of its suffering and I suppose my youth caused me to question God's reasoning. For here was this poignant valiant dumb animal whose only language of compassion for its human keeper was a feeble swat from its paw. The dog wanted to die alone. Perhaps our pain in life sometimes causes us to seek God in too many places when we assume that the dying dog wishes us away for our own sake. This may simply be a reflex or some kind of imbedded behavioral code similar to the momentary digging out performed by the hind legs in the aftermath of a bowel movement. Therefore the gestural vocabulary of the dog is governed by the same forces whether it is bidding us farewell in death or evacuating its excrement. Sentiment does depend upon point of view. Yet we know there is emotive content in many areas of the dog's behavior. Who has not felt tenderness and affection and even love when a happy dog nuzzles them? The animal died in the morning and I glimpsed the dead glossy surface of the staring eyes only for a moment because I was too upset to approach it. My father covered it with a sheet until two men from the department of sanitation came to remove it. I remained in my room. I had closed the door. I cautiously rested my palm against my closed door and quietly waited for the men to leave. I wanted to believe that in its final hours the animal wished to spare me the anguish of witnessing its death. I wanted to believe that this inarticulate beast had loved me so much that it wanted to somehow soothe my desperate feeling of loss. Or was the movement of its paw simply an ancient expression of self-insulation that had generations of canine anthropology at its base? I suppose I will never know for sure. I remember the day my father brought me to the pet shop and I saw a shadow shaped something like a parenthesis appear across the face of the puppy that would soon become a part of our household. I remember the dog dashing madly across a snow-covered schoolyard as it first discovered with delightful abandon all the pleasures of dipping its snout into the cold soft overlapping white blankets. I remember that it would often nudge me when I lay stubbornly clinging to sleep. My father had laughingly bid the animal to come into my room and wake me for school. Yes. Death turns life into an image. Is it simply sentimentality and compassion that motivate me to care for the sparrows? It is not. An image has haunted me for decades. And all the living souls in this image are dead. In this image I am a small boy sneaking upon my mother and a cousin as they were about to distribute a little food for a couple of sparrows that had alighted upon a pipe just beyond the window of my grandmother's urban apartment. We were poor. These were poor people who lived in a chaotic city and there was a charm for them that sparrows should come so close to their cluttered tiny tenement home. There was a small sweet joy at the thought that they could stand so near these creatures of nature. So the impulse to show the birds kindness was laden with many things that characterized the troubles of their lives. They who rode subway trains to their jobs and climbed stone steps in their dwelling and knew surcease from the opaqueness and sterility of city life only in the form of rare and brief trips to the country or the shore. I remember that they felt a special indebtedness to these living things that had decided so unexpectedly to make their presence known. Feeding the sparrows thus became for them an act that was somehow endowed with spiritual meaning. Perhaps in the simplicity of their sincerity my family felt through this attempted act of kindness a certain affinity with God. Although still a boy my mind was keen yet it perceived none of these subtleties and concerned itself with mischief and playful disruption. I remember that my family gingerly crept about the apartment so as not to frighten the birds before they could be fed. Somehow like the lover in Baudelaire's poem who strikes his mate without hatred and compares himself to the butcher who pummels the chopping block there is the unfortunate blind maliciousness of the child who seeks out what is negative purely for its contrary pleasures. I was seized by the spiteful impulse to disrupt my family's ministrations and just before they could bring food to the birds I screamed and stomped and banged the heating pipe that was inches from the sparrows' perch outside the window. They flew away in unison and their movement was beautiful. I remember that as the birds scattered I noticed a group of stains on my grandmother's apron. There was a patchwork of brownish beige and white spots on the old material. I saw the disappointment in the release of her hand as it sank to the apron with its fistful of breadcrumbs that would now be thrown into the garbage pail. My mother bowed her head and moved away from the window in silent dejection. And my cousin who was a generation closer to my age admonished me sharply for my act of senseless cruelty. For many years I remembered her warning meant to shock the complacency of my mischievous mind that one-day I might come back as a sparrow and I would be deprived of kindness in the same way. In retrospect I can see the instructive purpose of her words for there was absolutely no virtue in my act. It contained neither justice nor courage nor temperance nor holiness nor wisdom. In fact my shameful insensitive behavior was a perfect illustration of the depths to which a misguided soul can descend by indulging in the opposite of these fine and noble qualities. My mind acting as its own camera has kept my spirit painfully aware of this display of childhood insensitivity by replaying the image of my callousness towards the sparrows. Sometimes our morality is shaped by our senses particularly in light of the sheer plasticity of an image that defines what is right and what is wrong. So I have let not one morning pass without coming to this tree in front of my house bringing food of some kind for the sparrows. It is odd that the pictorial life of my mind sustains the remorse of my past deed just as vividly as though my mother and grandmother and cousin were still alive. How many thousands of times have my grandmother's hand dropped to her apron? How many thousands of times have my mother walked away from the window in somber silence? Conscious life can be such a grim comedy of repetition and regret when it is ruled by what we remember. I must help my son understand the dangers and consequences not only of wrongful acts but also of the power they exert within the mind through the medium of imagery that is their only instrumentality. He must be shown that our connection to God can be defined only in terms that are simultaneously absolute and relative. The truth like the connection between shadow and object lies somewhere in-between. Doubles and paradox seem to characterize all religious thought. Always this notion that something internal is related in a mysteriously contradictory fashion to something external. I suppose a pragmatist would never be satisfied with such a condition. That is certainly understandable. I remember a friend of mine who often spoke of the moment of death. He worked in the emergency room of a hospital and saw many people die from accidents or heart attacks or gun shot wounds. He emphasized again and again that the moment before death and the moment after death were barely distinguishable. One moment the eyes were open and breath escaped from the mouth. The next moment the eyes were shut and the chest was still. Like sleep. Like sleep. His point was that there could be no emphatic or dramatic transition between the last moment of life and the first moment of death. I think such a puzzle is at the root of man's obsession with religion and

God. How could we be so inconsequential? How could all of those thousands of layers of content and all of the years of thought and emotion and perception and action disappear into an invisible place? There is the rumor of the so-called "last tear." My friend mentioned it but he had never witnessed it. In the moment of death supposedly a single tear is shed. This could be a physiological event that is unrelated to the soul. I wonder if it has anything to do with the controversial results of Doctor Macdougall's experiments? Those missing twenty-one grams of body weight that he claimed to have recorded after death. Evidence of the escaping soul? The last tear like a turn-key or signature of exit? A tear of sadness or joy? Answerless questions. I wondered about the sparrows for many days after they flew away. I used my imagination like a magnifying glass to create large intimate images of their presence and behavior. I imagined them sitting in their nest looking down at the scene behind the window in my grandmother's kitchen. They pecked at the twigs and nodded their heads as my family moved away from the window. I imagined their confusion and fear. I suppose their natural distrust of humans was validated by the noise and commotion I created. Yet it is certain that they associate humans with food. Many creatures do. There are times when I run a thread of mental invention through many images at once. A calming technique. Something to give me a set of associations that for one reason or another keeps my sorrow over my wife in a less accessible place. So many times the jittery twitching of the birds' heads became the tapping of my foot as I waited next to the delivery room. The shadow of the shade ring became the funereal reef on its metal stand next to my wife's coffin. The arc of the turning gulls became the blessing gestures of the priest's palm during my wife's burial mass. We must bury. I wonder if the greatest challenge to a belief in spiritual life is the ineluctable rot of mortal flesh. There is always the seemingly unsolvable mystery of the person who leaves the body behind and is (supposedly) never to be seen or heard again. *A mockery which love cannot touch.* As the poet said. Is it somehow a mockery of who and what we were that our remains decay and stink? Is the dead shell left behind an insult to the person who inhabited it? I have passed through crowded markets on unbearably hot days when the fruit and vegetable refuse lying in the streets exuded the foulest odors of death. How different is the brown mush of rotting apples and broccoli compared to their life-bearing counterparts with robust colors and enticing aromas! We take comfort from the circular reasoning of metaphor. The human husk. The animal husk. The vegetal husk. So many common characteristics and therefore we must believe that one meaning speaks through all the forms. I have tried to use this logic in my thoughts about my wife. To somehow ease the pain of loss. I do not think of her grave. Her coffin. Of the thing that remains that was her body. My thoughts have turned more and more to imaginings of the spiritual world. There are many who believe that we continue as we were in another place where body and matter are no more. I have been sorely tempted to think of my wife in this way. These beliefs however are not entirely to my liking. They dismiss the validity of religion. They posit a surprisingly simple yet overwhelmingly plausible view of existence in the after-life. One feature of this theory is that all bodily cares and needs have ended. I suppose that characteristic of spiritual being is common to many religions. Egyptology. Christianity. Islam. Judaism. Hinduism. Buddhism. Jainism. Taoism. Confucianism. Shamanism. Shinto. All of these belief systems place great faith in some form of spiritual resurrection. Another life after the body ceases to be the modality by which we experience the world. These spiritualists (if that is an accurate way of describing them) believe therefore that we are no longer burdened by hunger or thirst or fatigue. There are no financial concerns. We do not need shelter. Some of these believers supposedly possess the uncanny ability to see and speak to the dead. Of course charlatans abound who for a fee pretend to do this. It is shameful that they have persisted in duping so many. It seems to me that the mystic and the séance became a late nineteenth century phenomenon. The Dark and Middle Ages certainly held no public tolerance for those who engaged in such practices and many throughout the sixteenth and seventeenth centuries were labeled witches and put to death for attempting to commiserate with supernatural beings. Today such behavior is accepted and in certain conspiracy-oriented circles there are those who maintain that the leaders of the world's major religions know that the after-life bears no connection to the tenets of their faith but keep this secret so that their followers will continue to support them. The basis of this claim is that if the existence of God were absolutely proven to be false the world would crumble into chaos and the abandonment of human laws. I have read about those who claim to communicate with the dead and I must admit that these individuals offer a glimpse of life after death that differs greatly from the promises of most religious institutions. There is for example the notion that we are not suddenly transformed into higher beings that do not kowtow to emotion. That all of our prejudices or familiarities with people and places remain the same. A spirit who makes himself or herself known to such a gifted person will show envy or resentment or anger over situations that provoked such emotions during physical life. There is the belief that we may have more knowledge than we possessed at death but that the psychological core of our being seamlessly transits mortal life into the spiritual realm. That if a person with less than higher education spoke they would use the vocabulary and expressions (even those of a colloquial character) that they used before. Yet they could instantly know the meaning of any word in any dictionary of their native language. Therefore they may have absolute knowledge of selected subjects. A vision of souls moving through a kind of space and a kind of time. They are not bound by natural laws. They are capable according to these beliefs of using the mind in its purest form to make themselves appear in any attire or at an ideal age of their lives (twenty-seven is the prevailing theory). They can create any environment or happening that they wish. So it is tempting to assume that such spirits can conjure any scenes or aspects of nature just as they experienced and knew them during their stay on earth. They may be in front of the ocean or on a mountain or in the sky or around a glacier. To ponder the phenomenology of life after death one must combine the innocence of childhood with the longings of old age. That is to say that most of us do not want to end regardless of longevity and the rewards of life and family and prosperity. Suffering and insanity may cause a certain minority to look forward to death or in some instances to take their own lives but I think it is reasonable to say that most humans posses an indefatigable wish to continue their existence beyond the life of their bodies. Do we become the imprint of who we were once we enter this other world? I am tempted to think once again of the indexical. A footprint. An echo. A shadow. Or the notion of music as the pure expression of will. That we function and exist in the sense that music (without physical form) is the spirit and personality of the composer? Of his very being? I can understand why there are many who long to know the characteristics of this world. Why those who claim to communicate with the departed often exhibit such tranquility about earthly matters. Imagine such a level of being where thought is no longer framed or harnessed by the limitations and exigencies of mortal boundaries. I suppose that from a philosophical point of view all of this condenses into the distinction between thought and matter. The distinction between occasion and the mental being that causes occasion. Will and action. Thought and being. The physical and the metaphysical. The ages are filled with thousands of pages of meditations by all of the world's philosophers and the centerpiece of these meditations is the mysterious connection between mind and body. If we dream of walking or climbing and in our dream we slip it is common to experience the sensation in our bodies and we awaken startled as the limb performs the movement from the scene in the dream. Science and medicine have proven again and again how the mind in good ways and bad can affect our physical well-being. So it is exciting to imagine the role of thought in a world or a dimension where the physical or the organic no longer play a part. One might think of Raleigh's *The Body's Guest* to conceive of how this reverse image of our being would function. Again I ponder music in a metaphorical way. What is music? You cannot embrace music. It does not offer the corporeal experience found in the qualities of a painting or a piece of architecture or sculpture. In that sense we think of music as invisible. Yet the emotions and thoughts of the composer are conjured each time a score is performed. Therefore it may be meaningless to regard the score itself as an expressive text. The score does not have the same kind of energy as a painting or a poem or a novel. A maestro may be able to hear the notes and harmonies and structures in his mind merely by reading a musical score and thereby recreating the colors and tones and emotions of the music. That is a rare exception. The ordinary person cannot perform such incantations and for him a sheet of music might as well be a matrix of lines in a set of complex blueprints. I have often thought of the sound of my wife's voice in much the same way. Is my memory a kind of score upon which the character of her speech has been captured? I wonder if science or psychoanalytic study has determined what length of time must pass (depending upon the individual) before a deceased loved one's voice begins to fade from memory until it can no longer be summoned by the imagination. Several years after my grandmother died my mother mentioned this peculiar phenomenon to her cousin. One time when I was a boy I heard my mother speak of how she could barely remember what her mother's voice sounded like. Somehow she still knew the voice and could certainly recognize it but just as an afterimage soon melts into nothingness there no longer was any residue of her mother's voice in her memory of sounds and so the voice could not be replayed in the manner of a tape-recorder. I did not realize what this meant or what sorrow it could cause until little by little I began to forget the sound of my wife's voice. I can remember occasions or events or circumstances in particular and summon a visual memory of speaking with my wife. I can remember some of what she said. Yet the sound of the voice is gone as though she were a character speaking in a silent film. How strange it is to remember words being spoken without that always-familiar feeling of hearing the speaker's voice. We take it so much for granted how easily we identify family and friends simply by their voices. We go through the drawers and closets of the dead. We carry items of clothing away. We put treasured objects into boxes. And if the afterlife is real one wonders if those we mourn watch us. Are we pitied? Or are there a knowing smile and the kind of reassuring expression that a parent gives to a frightened child? Are the decades that may follow and the repeating moments of loss viewed light-heartedly by the ones we miss and weep for? Do so many years of sorrow lose their legitimacy like obsolete currency because incorporeal time is so immeasurable and the awaiting wealth of otherworldly compensations so vast that there is no need for pity? Our weeping and memories for thirty years are perhaps the single flap of a bird's wing in eternity and all comforts await us so therefore no torment or sorrow is permanent. A nice formula. In a way I suppose it is like the inconsolable sobbing of the cranky infant. So little usually separates the tiny body from comfort and pleasure. Any moment of frustration or minor pain is enough to cause endless cries and jerks of the body. One paroxysm of tears replaced with suckling and coziness does little to prevent the next bout of whining and stark terror that all is not well again. A never-ending cycle of feeling terrorized alternating with being enveloped by tenderness and reassurance. All the while even through the end of childhood it is the powerless adult who always knows that what seems horrific to the child will soon fade through cajolery and supervision into happiness and renewal. Powerless the way our relations and friends who are spirits may be powerless because they cannot tell or show us that the misery of our mourning and the torment it causes mean nothing in the next life and are intended only for the temporary turmoil of the body and finite time. Nevertheless I am comforted by the certainty that today was a good day. The blue of the sea was vibrant and clear. I made coffee. The aroma of the brew was strong and enveloping. It wafted through the house. Heavy scents of saline mixed into the air. Waves and sun increased in tandem until a crashing brightness became the new morning. The sparrows chirped in unison. Hovering seagulls eyed the sea. Smells of salt air coffee and my cigarette smoke filled the bright kitchen. I prepared my son for his first day of school. His special morning of tidy clothes and little book bag and hair neatly combed. As we walked down the front steps I held his hand. His footing was uncertain or at least it seemed so to me because his attention was unnaturally fixed upon the steps as though there were only predetermined spots where he could place his feet. Perhaps the dimness in the hallway contributed to this. The skylight overlooking the staircase needed cleaning because it was caked with gull droppings that had become so thick and pervasive that the sun barely shone through. There were times when the tree that bowed over the skylight was no more than a swaying dark blur. I was thinking of the best method of cleaning the skylight glass just last evening while I scrubbed the last of our supper dishes. Lately I have been trying my best to entice my son's finicky appetite by preparing a few unusual meals. Sometimes a child will eat with a little more enthusiasm if there is some element of novelty in the ingredients or presentation of a meal. I used food dye and made a pizza pie for my son that sported colors of red and green and yellow and blue! Here were this regalia of little rectangular flags sporting bright colors that I topped with rose-shaped pieces of cheese. I got the idea while I was in the supermarket. There was a little boy reaching for some kind of spinning toy and unfortunately he knocked over a large soup tureen in his attempt to grab the out of reach plaything. Luckily he was not scalded but in the cascade of spilled swirling soup and boxes of tumbled groceries I noticed several packages of food coloring and some pastry utensils that squeezed materials into flower shapes. Several feet away was a large rectangular tank filled with nine bulbous trout swimming with such animation that they gave the impression of gleeful abandon. I laughed to myself that the fish were safely tucked away within the security of their underwater abode when I noticed several plastic gull ornaments perched directly above the tank. The summer season was underway and the supermarket carried all forms and varieties of backyard decorative accessories as well as patio furniture and barbeque equipment. There was a short flight of wooden steps next to the seafood section. I found myself more than a little disgusted when I turned from the tank and its energetic fish traffic to notice several stationary ugly brown insects occupying various positions on the steps like blotches ready to advance. I was distracted by this unsightly image and momentarily lost count of the shaping utensils that I wanted. There were nine different forms including the roses and I intended to have the entire collection. As I recounted these objects and checked for duplicates I noticed some wooden patio chairs that were very smoothly sanded. I thought that a couple of these chairs would be suitable for me and my son in the weeks to come when we started spending time on the beach behind the house. Some kind of scabrous metal such as pimpled iron had been used for a large circular outdoor dining table around which these wooden lounge chairs had been incongruously clustered. As I contemplated the chairs it occurred to me that I should first consult my landlord who sometimes occupied the bottom part of the house and could often be unreasonable about such things. He was a very eccentric man who spent most of his time endlessly polishing a large set of inherited brass goblets and chalices. I remember that on one occasion I went to speak with him about some jagged bands of discarded metal that he had piled in the back of the house. My son often played there and I was concerned that he might injure himself. The man seemed completely oblivious to the existence of these objects and it required the better part of an hour for me to distract him from his obsession with polish and his coruscated antiques. Finally he acknowledged the potential danger and promised to remove the bands as he summarily ushered me out of his rooms and opened the vestibule door that led to my upper apartment. I thanked him for this gesture of mock courtesy but opened the front door instead. As I stepped outside and inhaled the early summer air I noticed a group of heavy gray clouds drifting past the afternoon sun. At that moment a long black car speeding across the road suddenly obscured the façade of a yellow house across the street. The simultaneous obscuration of sun and house gave me an impression of covering or hiding and at that moment I felt dampness on my palm. My hand was bleeding and I remembered that while speaking to the landlord I had rested my palm over some sheets of cut glass. I went back into the house to rinse out the cut and as I crossed the tiled vestibule a few droplets of blood hit the bright white tiles. I decided that there was still more than enough time for the large pieces of metal and iron to be removed from the backyard. Summer had begun but it was still early and so far the air had retained some of the chill left over from spring. There is never enough space or time in the mind to absorb and quietly contemplate all that nature allows us to experience. It seems that finally after centuries of thought all philosophical dialogue has distilled itself into one very important question. And the question seems to have divided itself between those who believe that nature confirms divinity and those who believe that nature confirms nothing. The second position asserts that nature continues to do what it does whether we experience it or not. According to this philosophy we have been imprisoned by ages of self-suggestion. We have mistakenly decided that nature exists for us because it is a living metaphor for the existence of God. A curious belief system. When confronted for example with the role of sleep in human life one philosopher I know of speaks of the difference between asking why we need to sleep and why we need to be awake. Apparently he is more interested in the latter. He is a chief proponent of the belief that nothing exists or behaves because there is some predetermined divine symbiosis between man and nature. I must confess that this point of view is not unlike my meditation regarding whether or not my dog's last living gesture was a mechanical act or an expression of love. As I dried my palm I looked through the bathroom window that faced the shore and I noticed several people preparing a large hole in the sand for barbecue cooking of lobsters and clams. When I turned the semicircular faucet on the sink to shut off the water I saw a man ignite the charcoal and the sudden emergence of the ring of bright flames startled some gulls. They flew from the shore and scanned the surface of the water. It is nature that compels man to understand himself in spiritual terms. Rightly or wrongly there has always been some contemplative and philosophical regard for the objects of nature and their relationship to human life. The scene before me was undeniably beautiful. In its sheer plasticity I found many things to attract not only the eye but the mind and spirit as well. Pale fine sand hollowed out by the campers who wore bright red and green and blue bathing suits. The swooping and swirling of the many gulls overhead and the way their gray bodies blended with the charcoal smoke. Now and then the chalky white breast of a gull shot through the gauzy brume of cooking vapors. One of the bathers stoked the fire occasionally with a long grappling hook. As he raised the pole glints of sun made the curved point glimmer and he rested it across his shoulder like a soldier holding a rifle. Part of this picnic group consisted of some teenage children who chased spider crabs along the shore and there was a confusion of splashing water covering young toes and the clutter of red spindly legs scurrying in multiple directions as the crabs jostled one another (some to the left and some to the right) as they tried to escape the children's reach. Suddenly a boy of about fourteen scooped up an unfortunate crab and ran pell-mell towards the cooking pit that had been improvised in the sand. Out of breath and beaming with wild-eyed joy at his successful hunt he flung the large crab with both hands in the manner of an amateur gymnast awkwardly releasing a medicine ball from the center of his chest. Apparently the group planned to dine on the shore. Two women were struggling with a red and white checkered tablecloth and they needed several heavy objects to keep it in place because of the strong sea breeze. The ends of the tablecloth kept lifting upwards before whipping down and swatting the legs of the wooden table whenever the strong gusts of wind caught them. The scent of cooked shellfish combined with the sea and delighted my senses. I luxuriated in the mixed powerful aroma of ocean wind and all that was fresh aquatic and saline. Juxtaposed against the horizon the drifting barbeque smoke engulfed a slowly gliding sailboat on a journey to no particular destination moving right to left in front of the slowly setting sun. How can certain philosophical minds ignore the beauty of relationships between objects in nature that seem to connect so effortlessly with the perceptions and meditations of man? That may be too simple. I have tried to reach certain irreducible truths and have embraced the many uncertainties that seem to question the existence of God. This does not challenge my faith but simply broadens its parameters. I think it is possible that every moment of sensory understanding (such as the scene I described above) creates an ineluctable destiny for the self and its morality. It is rather like saying that we are both participants in and observers of a limitless set of elements and re-combinations of elements. There is a kind of sweet pathos in the Christian credo that invisibly combines the tragedy of self with the salvation of God. How often do we feel lingering sorrow after we enjoy what our senses produce? Why? Is it because we know that the moments that connect objects and the beauty of the whole impression are so precious because so impermanent? If I live long enough to become an old man and if my memory allows it what will become of the delicate sense of dusk and shore and colors and movement that I just described? It is remarkable how many things we recall and relive when we are old. The strangeness of the sense of things and scenes and moments when nothing material remains. Memories, however separated from a world of matter, are important to any man. Memory is like a pump that continues its job even though the machine that surrounds it has long since crumbled away and vanished. Memory continues its job when even the world that surrounds the machine has gone. The philosopher who wants to challenge the ready-made assertion that we need to be awake is clever but not clever enough to realize that consciousness cannot be attenuated therefore it cannot be atomized. I suppose the core of his beliefs is that the universe is not there because it is important for man to perceive it. The world as we know it continues to be what it is and do what it does but not because we are supposed to experience it. In other words, if the universe were a play, it would have an infinite run whether it was a full or an empty house every night. A regal spider about the size of a silver dollar has reigned supreme outside the bathroom window since early spring. It is quite beautiful. I like to observe it and sometimes I lift up my son so that he too can watch the behavior of this mysterious creature. Most of the time it is motionless. There are little gray shapes similar to diamonds or pyramids on the underside of its velvety black body. Eight legs spread apart in symmetry and precision as it waits for prey to be ensnared by one of the many glossy white compartments of the web. There is an uncanny intricacy to this elaborate silken structure. One realizes how often man relies upon and copies nature when a simple thing such as a spider web is considered. Thinking about the web while looking at the ships and pleasure boats these past weeks I was often reminded of the netting of ships in past times. The rigging of the ropes in ancient ships must have been based upon the patterns and boxes of the web. At times an unfortunate fly or wasp would alight upon the deadly trap. I marveled at the magnificent ingenuity of the spider's embroidered device that was both domicile and superb hunting instrument. The instant of immobilization was a death sentence in slow motion for the fly. The spider might wait hours or even days before advancing towards its prize. Sometimes it would move in for the kill right away and devour the weaker insect alive. On particularly bright days when the spider kept vigil alongside the web I would look through the vapor-thin strands outlined against the sea and imagine myself to be a sailor checking the netting as I made my rounds. On the occasions when the spider pounced its lethal body armed for killing upon a trapped insect my reverie included an image of the heap of fishing nets cast into the waves. The nets sank so rapidly and surrounded hundreds of confused fish bolting in massive clusters against the rectangular sections of rope too small of course to permit escape. I love the sea and the beautiful energy of summer. It would be an adventure to sail especially with my son. One never tires of the mystical antiquity of sun and sea and shore. There is something about the light upon the ocean that lingers in the mind. The little curls of foam that spill up over the waves and the glistening sun that makes the curls shimmer as though they were coated with a sweet glaze. The sound. The omnipresence of the sound of the waves. The constant reminder that land has ended and the sea bangs against the shore with fists that are alternately small and large. Banging upon the shore the sea reminds you that now it wants to come through the door of land and burst into all that is secure and civilized and tame. Bursting through that door with all the energy of heat and life and an endless calling the ocean and summer unveil a prehistoric demand for release. I remember most of all the jubilation of my first trip to the beach as a boy each summer. The joy of repetition. Of renewal. The first day always seemed like a new beginning regardless of how often the rituals of beach bag packing and chair carrying and the gathering of all of my plastic digging tools had occurred. For these things became flimsy in the mind and invisible to the eye all through the long terrible deadness of winter. There seems to be no greater metaphor for the influence and presence of a divine being than the intensity and enormity of the sea. It sometimes occurs to me that humanity is drawn to the sea as if through some sense of separation anxiety. We are like mannequins or robots that have labored underground surrounded by metal and darkness and we rotate there from obligation to routine to pacification back to obligation never moving outside the circle of artificial understanding attained through artificial means. Let humans suddenly find themselves roaming carelessly across a wide expanse of beach in a tropical haze of sun and passion and we become like the salmon pushed by instinct towards a death-life union with the primordial world. One day I was particularly ambitious and had fashioned more than a dozen sand castles near the shore. I had a very large yellow pail that I packed with moist sand. Modern engineering has discovered that it is the moisture that creates a kind of webbing from sand grain to sand grain thus enabling the sound architecture that one finds in elaborate sand sculptures. My medieval structures were not that complex but I was particularly careful not to let any disturbance occur after I plopped the pail upside down upon the shore and gingerly lifted it to reveal the fat spherical tower. I surrounded my creation with large wide clamshells. My interpretation of a drawbridge. The protection that I assumed would be sufficient to prevent the waves from assaulting the castle. I remember that I wanted the top of the structure to retain its smooth level surface of tightly packed sand. I remember my chagrin when a few grains of sand loosened by the whisking shore breeze broke away from the unified drum-like top. The unsullied joy of innocence of understanding! I tried to retrieve the grains and restore them to their integral place within the mass. I remember sitting in the administrative office at the hospital on the afternoon that my wife died. I looked over at the cylindrical metal ashtray. It had a circular top filled with fine white sand. Someone had emptied it before I came into the room. There were no cigarettes there. And as I waited to sign a form that gave the hospital permission to perform an autopsy on my wife's body I stared at the sand and thought of the little clusters of wet grains that I chased long ago on the shore. The sadness of the efforts of humans to create an emotional safe house that dissolves the present. It is as if we are sets of gestures and moments of feeling coalesced into an abstraction of the gesture or the moment. That is what makes us cry out to God. That is what makes us weep for what is lost. Children playing on beaches because there is something new to do. Playing with sand and making things that the waves will eventually decompose. Making things. We move through life making things that will eventually decompose. I have strived to show my son that this exquisite sorrow of loss is itself the emblem of holy love. Think of what frightens you the most. Why do you believe that you are any different than a child who does not know the answer or the reason and is simply terrified of the unknown? Think of the joy of the little one when the light is turned on or when the strange sound is explained or when the bruise is soothed. The great fear that happiness will not last. That we cannot *become* the moment that has given us solace. Where do the moments go? This unanswerable question is chiefly responsible for the temptation to disbelieve in God. I suppose this is the origin of modern anxiety. Irrational fear devours what is rational like papers engulfed by flame. I was frightened once when I was a very small boy. Something happened around the same time as the incident with the sparrows at my grandmother's house. Opposite her apartment lived an old man who was known to my family. Apparently he had lived for many years in that building. He may have been retired. He had lost a leg but went out often enough with the aid of crutches. He had a habit of leaving his door open and I remember seeing him when I went downstairs to play. It was a peculiar image that for some reason reminds me today of a scene in a Vermeer painting. Partly because of light but primarily because of geometrical characteristics and the occlusion of space. Approximately one half of his kitchen table was visible through the doorway so the first thing I always noticed was the contrast between the vertical line of his doorway frame and the horizontal line of his shabby table. It was this contrast between the vertical and the horizontal that reminded me in particular of *Young Woman with a Water Pitcher*. From my vantage point as I exited my grandmother's apartment the surface of the table appeared about one third of the way up from the threshold. The man's doorway obscured the remainder of the table. Yet as I approached the stone stairway that began just beyond his door the change in perspective raised the level of the table to the point where it appeared to be about halfway along the doorframe. Another idiosyncrasy in the image resulted from the fact that the man's infirmity forced him to sit at the table in a very unusual fashion. Rather than having the kitchen chair positioned so that its seat faced the table the old man had turned the chair ninety degrees so that the seat was opposite the doorway. In this way he positioned himself sideways as he bended his good leg across the seat and straddled the table to read the newspaper. It was in this profile tableau repeated again and again without noticeable change that I would find him whenever I went out. But the table was positioned within the kitchen in such a way that the remainder of the man's leg could not be seen. The man's leg was obscured in the same way as the table in the painting. The man's doorway juxtaposed against his table also evoked some of the vertical and horizontal contrast in the painting such as the stained glass window that the woman appears to be opening and the table with the water pitcher as well as what appears to be a tapestry on the wall above the table. I often played with little plastic toy soldiers and on a few occasions I took one of these and tossed it into the man's apartment before hastily shutting my grandmother's door. Because I was a child this act of rudeness and disrespect seemed harmless to me. My ignorance of consequences was reinforced by the child's belief that closing a door made everything bad disappear. So I was quite unprepared for the outcome that resulted one day when I had reached the vestibule to go out and the man was coming in. He came over to me quietly. He said *Don't throw things in my house. I'll kill you.* Suddenly the comfortable familiarity of the old man with the missing leg that I had seen hundreds of times was replaced by a paralyzing fear that I could barely comprehend. I was frightened in a way that I have never experienced before or since. Terrified by this man who was so insulted that I should disrespect his home that he felt perfectly comfortable in threatening an eight year old boy with death. That was the only time I came upon the man in a mobile state and this added to the menacing quality of the situation. It was as if he came out of the frame that had been so implanted in my mind and was no longer the plastic moment of a tableau but a living creature who moved and did errands and had pride in his little apartment and who did not hesitate to use the threat of death as a means of communicating his feelings. I cannot escape the gestalt of dread that his remark caused. I have never been able to toss something without an all-consuming feeling of foreboding. The gesture itself has always produced an irrational sense of guilt and anticipation of punishment. Strange journey of this vessel of memory and body. The whole process made me realize that from this earliest time in my life I gave meaning to people and events in the same way I suppose that a photographer tries to capture a movement or an expression or some elliptical event. To preserve a visual moment that captures the ineffable or the sublime. I have always felt an unfathomable sadness. As though life was composed of only such moments. As though we are the memories of gestures and movements.

As though memory and dream are our holographs. The tap of metal upon my bureau when I dropped my wedding ring. The sound of cloth being thumped when the young doctor in humiliating frustration dropped her arms to the sides of her lab coat because I had said "I want you to save her!" when she asked me what they should do. The way the cloth made the thick enveloped sound as her arms came down on the white jacket. The way canvas bags might sound piled one upon another. They wanted to know if I would allow them to deny life support and I wanted them to save her. It was impossible to save her because she was quite brain dead by this time and would expire soon anyway. Afterwards they told me that I could go into the room and see her. After they had cleaned her up. That was how they put it. *They're cleaning her up now and you can go in to see her in a little while.* I had a great pity for the doctor. She was young and may not have experienced many deaths. I remember the pathetic look of utter impotence in her compassionate eyes. She could not save my wife and in that moment when her arms fell to her sides and I heard the soft pressure against the cloth of her jacket I felt the need to reassure her. It must be a terrible feeling to dedicate oneself to curing the sick and be unable to tell a frightened man that his wife will recover. I wanted to say something that would soothe the doctor's feeling of ineffectiveness. There was no justification for such a burden to be placed upon her. I told the doctor that there are times when someone for inexplicable reasons decides not to be saved because they need to let go. I told the doctor that I knew she had done all that could be done. I felt it incumbent upon me at this most terrible moment to release the doctor from any shame at the thought of her limitations. I think it is inexcusable that anyone should suffer because they are unfairly blamed for something hideous. I went into my wife's room. My eyes filled with tears and for some reason I became conscious of the contrast between the dripping salty drops and the immobility of my wife's body. As though my grief and the movement of the tears could somehow unite me with her lifelessness. As though the unchangeable difference between us could somehow be negotiated through my weeping. They had removed the tubes from her arms and the flesh was damaged in various places. The shade of her bruised flesh was not unlike the dark yellow plastic eyes of stuffed dogs staring trance-like in a shooting gallery. Where did you go? In retrospect I suppose it was ridiculous but after a few moments of viewing my wife's lifeless body I thought I was somehow reproaching her for not being alive. As though the terrible transition from living being to dead object was something that should not be pondered so intimately. I felt like a thief who moves through the rooms of an empty house and enjoys the illicit freedom of examining the private spaces and intimate possessions of the absent owners. I became ashamed and left the room. I remembered the death of my grandfather many years before when I was a boy. He was a funny man and often told me little stories at night. On one occasion my grandparent's apartment was being painted and there was a circular splotch of white paint on the unfinished wall next to my grandfather's bed. When I snuggled up to him inside the bed he turned the form of paint into a ghost and related it to the stories. My parents thoughtfully gave me the choice of going into the viewing parlor to see him in his casket or remaining outside and remembering him the way he was. I did not want to go inside. I did not want to experience the dreaded difference between what I knew him to be and the thing that remained still with closed eyes. So I thought of my wife in that way and hurriedly left the hospital room. On another floor of the hospital in the maternity ward was my newborn son. I was terrified of this new responsibility and naturally in a state of great shock that my wife had just died during labor. What was I to do? How could this have happened? The mature side of my being was overshadowed by my immediate fears and concerns. I felt the way I did that day at the funeral parlor when I was a little boy. I wanted to displace the present reality of my wife's death and remember her only as a living person.   I tried to immerse myself in soothing concatenated images from my childhood. Mainly images from the beach that had remained unchanged since I was a boy. Unchanged not only in the perfection of their plastic ingredients but more so in terms of their immediacy. The perfect clarity of the little dark green crabs burrowing with orange claws into the sand near my feet and the evanescent clouds of displaced grains disappearing afterwards. The dismembered orange claws strewn along the shore which later became a coat of arms upon the castles I struggled to make. Drifting pleasure boats with flags on their masts and the feeling of slow motion each time I looked to see them lazily making their horizontal passage across the sea. Giving in to the laziness of summer heat and the soft bedding of the beach blanket and smelling the salt air which did not permeate but rather jumped into one's nostrils with occasional snaps of wind. The softness of the sand suddenly replaced by the pebbly surface of the broken concrete entrance to the outdoor refreshment stand whenever I walked barefoot to get a hot dog or a soda. How the waves returned and revolved and resonated in my mind later at night under the sheets! Whenever I closed my eyes there was that transport to the joys and motions of all the waves I had jumped into or rode and again I was enveloped by their sonority and power and rhythms. And the little patches of dried sand to be found on the inside of my pail or the corner of my shovel were living reminders that the summer was infinite and that new sea-digging awaited me the following day. If we were designed by a superior being great care must have been devoted to the needs of the child. There is no time in the world of a child. Things do not "end." They overlap and intermingle like wheat or corn stalks so that one undulation interlocks with its neighbor and there cannot be any separation within the whole. So I stayed in this safe matrix of moments and images where the content remained uncorrupted by time. A matrix (true to its Latin roots) that offered pure maternal protection and solace. I did not go back to my wife's room. There were some papers to be signed. They gave me a little plastic bag. It contained her combs and wedding ring and miscellaneous personal items. Somehow it seemed to have traveled by itself because when I got home that day and saw it on the bureau I had absolutely no recollection of having brought it with me. Yet today was a good day. As always smell of the sea and flutter of the sparrows. Pencils of sunlight through the window. Miniature yellow lighthouse beams across the coffee pot. Evaporating gray branches of my cigarette smoke. A gull. Stare of the eye then sudden departure. Frightened of my hand parting the bathroom window curtains. Long white sailboats on the horizon. Large colored sails. There could have been a man on the deck in sandals enjoying his morning coffee and watching the sea. He might have been smiling as the easy waters were delicately rippled by schools of fish. It is not impossible. My son's catechism manual next to his cereal bowl. The waves seem timid as though early morning found them unawares. Yet their undulations continued. I inhaled the saline. Sipped my coffee. Took pride in my son's decision expressed to me last evening to enter the priesthood. I am happy that this coincided with his twelfth birthday. Last night I discussed the parable of The Prodigal Son with him. It was important to address my son's confusion over the text. He could not grasp the meaning of the rewards bestowed upon one who had behaved so irresponsibly. He wondered how it was possible that God favorably viewed those of us who had wandered away from goodness but found humility and asked for forgiveness. I must admit that my son asked very challenging questions. Where was the penalty to be paid for the irresponsible use of free will? Where was the acknowledgement of the devotion and obedience of the son who remained? Who toiled for and obeyed his father? Was it not pure desperation that led the Prodigal Son back to the security and reassurance of his father's world? How do we know if the son's promise to return as a lowly servant and beg his father's forgiveness was sincere? Suppose the son's resources had lasted longer and his hour of need had been postponed? What is the true meaning of the son's impetuousness and bad judgment followed by his so-called remorse and humility? How can we gauge the worthiness of his choices? What if during the Prodigal Son's absence the authority of the household had been transferred from the father to the second son? What if the second son refused to forgive his brother's reckless behavior? I marveled at the acuity of my son's mind. It was very encouraging to hear him dissect the text in this way at the outset of his decision to enter the priesthood. I tried to gently steer him by suggesting that the sanctity of the text must be respected. It was not a model for a short story that could be changed according to the ingredients of a writer's mind. There were many times when I checked my son's writing assignments and found that he was driven to write and invent. I thought this inclination to imagine beyond the literal was manifesting itself in his thoughts about the parable and I wanted to be judicious in my comments. His ruminations about the text were sincere and thoughtful and it would have been unfair to undermine his speculations. I told him that it was the Prodigal Son's belief in the power of forgiveness that had saved him. That it is easy to ignore the need for forgiveness and that causes a soul to be lost. That it requires self-recognition and a certain transparency to genuinely seek forgiveness. This is what God wants for us. My son remained quiet and reflective for some time. I hoped that my attempts to widen his perspective were successful. Suddenly he asked me something he had never asked before. And I was taken aback by the question because it contradicted the otherwise mature reflections of a boy who was often quite sophisticated for his years. He wanted to know why his mother died. Why did my mother die? he asked. I knew of course that this was not a medical inquiry. It was not the cause of death he wanted to know. That was what surprised me. Of course if that had been what he sought I could not bring myself to explain. I thought that there was still plenty of time for him to learn that there were some unpleasant things in his mother's past. A child of twelve did not need to know such things. It was a meditative or a philosophical question. And in a way I suppose that it was rhetorical. He knew that there are never any answers to such questions. Perhaps he was beginning to connect the intricacies of the case of the Prodigal Son with the unanswerable elements of life and death. I do not know. We sat silently in the bright kitchen and averted one another's eyes. There was a kind of tranquility or calmness in our silence. Somehow the absence of conversation or explanation was in itself a source of fulfillment as though my son's question and my inability to answer were symbiotically attached to one another. The mood of that moment made me think of river stones for some reason. Underneath so much flowing clear water. All that sunlight too. A smoothness that was gray and flat. The chalky quality was important. The clarity through the water because of the sun was important. As if the image were a photograph that surprised the viewer because after all these stones lay beneath water. And there was no mistaking the precision of this image. The way radar or DNA or a slide seen through a microscope was undeniably precise. Idle thoughts come from something so clear and easy and soothing. I remembered something about being calm. Sometimes a thing can make you feel calm if you care to look at it long enough. But that is not all. I wanted the river stones to become a part of my mind in a way that makes them more than river stones. The gray. Swirls of white run through them in unexpected ways and the sun amplifies this. The underwater sharpness of the stones is surprising. I wanted my son's life to absorb some of that simplicity. And in that simplicity I would like some form of peace. I expected a soothing to come from the sunlight. The clarity. The way the groupings of stones articulated the space below the water. My mind began to conjure associations that were pleasant. So there was more to the image of the river stones than the plastic characteristics of an image. But I cannot really identify what is suggested or what is suggesting it. Bizarre union between my eyes my mind and the image of river stones. The silent stones so shockingly clear in the sunlight underneath rippling water. Visions, however fleeting, are nurturing to a tired mind. Secretly I worried that the social and moral strictness of the priesthood would deprive my son of the taste and dimensions of life that were yet to be lived. Even as I gathered various pamphlets from some of the most prestigious seminaries there was a kind of regret or trepidation that I had pressed all of this upon my son. Certainly I had tried my best to be objective and liberal in my teachings and at no time did I create the impression that joining the clergy was something that he had to do. I always told my son that the decision to direct his life was his and his alone. I tried to behave in the manner of a true seed bed and offered my son the option of allowing what I taught him to take root and develop into something that grew naturally. What he did with that knowledge and growth was to be the result of his own judgment and decisions. I thought of love and the company of a soul mate and of course in my most desperate times when I mourned my wife I thought of those joys of the heart that bring both pleasure and despair and wondered if they were worth the sacrifice and if it was not better to remain unscathed by the pain of loss or disappointment or betrayal. I thought of tears and the quiet of night and the dread of knowing that the sound and the flesh of a lover no longer exist. Was my son better off in the priesthood with its sacred insulation that would surely protect him from the sorrows of unrequited love and a suicide by pistol with an unvisited grave beneath the linden tree? Was profane love merely a trap that the less spiritually advanced fall into and could my guidance help detour my son from the horrors of self-reproach that befall so many of us in the pursuit of romantic bliss? I wondered if some form of bitterness had been slowly growing within me. Was my tranquility in accepting my wife's death merely a mask? Was I in fact so infected by submerged rage that I should be robbed of my wife's love and company and the joy of raising our son together that I wanted (subconsciously) to prevent my son from knowing the comforts of romantic companionship? The thought that another self with insidious motives was secretly working against my best intentions for my son was vile and repugnant to me. There was no point in making a kind of psychic inventory of the obvious pros and cons of my life up to this point. Naturally there were endless scenarios and events that would have happened had my wife survived. Naturally there were thousands of happy moments that we could have shared. Since her death I have tried to use memory and imagery as if they were a prosthetic that at least offers an imitation of the motion (if not the reality) of the limb it replaces. Raising my son alone while constantly conjuring the presence of my wife has made me into a kind of hybrid being. I was no longer only myself and my wife was no longer my living companion. Yet somehow I had brought a vibrant sense of my wife into all of my interactions with my son. It was my hope that through my memories and recollections of my wife (which I shared more and more throughout my son's life) elements of her life and personal characteristics could somehow be inculcated into my son's world. I wanted him to know how much I had loved his mother. Therefore it seemed unlikely that my remorse over her death could transform itself into some kind of ugly subconscious scorn for romantic love especially not such a despicable desire to deliberately make my son's life as barren as possible by sabotaging what might have been a healthy and robust interest in domestic partnership. I came to the conclusion that there was no malice (subconscious or otherwise) in my exposing my son to the theological and philosophical rewards of the priesthood. As I have noted there was never one scintilla of coercion or insidiousness in my efforts. I presented these matters to my son at all times in the manner of a choice that he and he alone could make. It was never about my needs or my will. I wanted my son to be spared the pain of betrayal or (as in my case) bereavement and if this wholesome wish to protect him played any role in my suggestions about the priesthood it was probably meant to convey some of the spiritual lessons of Keats' Grecian urn. The lovely girl who can never be kissed even though the bold lover is forever nearing his goal. That she cannot fade and will always be fair yet the young man in pursuit does not have the bliss of possessing her. The perpetuity of beauty unmarred by change. The perfection of love uninfected by sorrow.

I did not want my son to have to reach into himself as I have done to find a miraculous strength to rescue him from despair. Oh Madeleine I loved you so! Memory and hope are those invisible things frozen by the suspended time on the urn. In the perfect nothingness of the eternal lies the impossibility of regret. The lover will never embrace his beloved. Yet he will never lose her. Here was the beautiful essence of Keats' vision of romantic love. It was like thirst needing to drink. It was like fatigue needing to rest. After my wife died I took refuge in the barren comfort of this hellish paradox. I took the moments that we shared and somehow turned them into a kind of alter-image. It was if they were companions to the moments that we would never share. If I needed the solace of fond remembrance in order to remind myself that I had been happy there were always the easily accessible recollections of my past with my wife. If I was tormented by her absence I used the present as if it were a screen upon which I might project images and scenes of what we would be doing at that moment had she not died. So in this way I became thirst waiting forever in the long line of those who would drink. I became fatigue forever struggling to move on without rest. I became the very air through which those two youthful creatures romped. I became the space on the urn. It was as though I could no longer live life and had to observe instead. I suppose that is why the poem appealed to me so strongly. It was the uncanny synthesis of inertia and promise. That must have been it. There was something deliciously philosophical in this rumination about love pursued and simultaneously suspended. I think what appealed to me most was the idea that desire never would be thwarted yet at the same time the goal of ultimate happiness remained in an unattainable future. I suppose there were many times after my wife's death when I imagined (much as I wish to deny it) that we were that giddy couple depicted on the urn. I wished that I had never me her in life. I wished that I had known her (as the urn so tauntingly suggests) only as a wondrous and perfect and beautiful gift awaiting the needs of the soul and the pleasures of the body. These were my thoughts as I heard the doctor's words about what time my wife's heart stopped. I had gone to the hospital so many times to visit her and as I turned away from the doctor all of the visual ingredients which formed the routine of my visits suddenly flashed through my mind. I had created and followed certain patterns of movement during these visits. There was the gift shop to the right of the hospital entrance followed by the reception desk where large plastic square passes were distributed with the word VISITOR printed on them. There was the long hallway preceded by three sets of revolving doors. There was the bank of elevators at the end of the hallway and the congested congregation of visiting family members and friends. These were the interminable ascensions and descensions of the elevator cars. There was the lounge at the end of the floor of my wife's room. All of these spaces mixed and swirled within my mind as if someone had taken the pieces and sections of an architect's model of a house and broken them apart and jumbled them together. As if the particles and sections and strips of balsa wood were dissected and spliced together so that a third of the living room became attached to a quarter of the library and half of the dining room was sutured to the entire garden. So I slowly walked away from the doctor not knowing where I was going or why I was moving and my footsteps did not seem to belong to my body. The revolving doors dissolved into the counter in the gift shop. The elevators floated into the square visitor cards. The hallway became juxtaposed against my wife's bed. I felt haunted by impressions of all that was rectangular because I associated that shape with what I expected to see. I knew that the next time I saw my wife in a supine position she would be in her coffin. And as my mind conjured images of the long narrow wooden rectangular box the similar shapes of the elevator doors and my wife's bed and the counter in the gift shop slowly dissolved one upon another like a travel-montage in a black and white film from the nineteen forties. I tried to remind myself that these associations were visceral rather than intellectual. In normal perceptual terms there was very little (if any) resemblance between a coffin and an elevator door or a sales counter or a visitor's pass or a bed. The coffin was simply a shape. Nothing more. I cannot remember the color of the dress my wife wore in the coffin. I suppose it is strange to say, "the dress my wife wore" as if it was she who put on the dress. No effort is spared in preparing the body for the viewing parlor. Anyone who has attended a wake knows this. Somehow the uncanny verisimilitude of the lifeless body gives us a sense of visiting or observing our friend or loved one as though he or she was merely enjoying a little sleep in a public place. The embalming and make-up techniques (not to mention the brand new clothing) do indeed go a long way toward evoking an impression of life and in many cases there is even a hint of younger life. The work done on my father attests to this. Dressed smartly in an impeccable charcoal gray suit with his hair and mustache tastefully dyed my father (who was only seventy-two at death) looked almost twenty years younger. Walking into the viewing parlor on the first day was extremely disturbing. That is when the so-called dream state that cradles the bereaved meets its first serious challenge. Psychiatric studies have shown that with few exceptions there is a kind of veil or coating of dreamy unreality that somehow protects loved ones from the shock of loss. We find it impossible to conceive of the permanent absence of a loved one. It is as if death was a phenomenological trick or riddle and no amount of intellection or perceptual examination can ever unwind the sleight of hand that renders it so enigmatic. The relationship (as I see it) between the movement and modalities of the consciousness and the properties of filmic spacetime is worthy of a serious critical study. I believe it is through this relationship that our inherent denial about our deceased loved ones can finally be understood. Cinema creates an uncanny synthesis of the ephemeral and the concrete. When our minds and our spirits are touched by the images and sounds of an event on film it is because the commonplace or the ordinary resonate with meaning by being raised to the level of the sublime and the metaphysical. More importantly there is in the continuousness of film projection a kind of perceptual reckoning in which the understanding of past present and future becomes synonymous with the mechanics of consciousness. Yet with or without the spiritual balm of visions there is the certainty that today was a good day. Sparrows' flutter repeated in my mind as I stirred the coffee. Sharp salty breeze through the house all of the morning. Having slept very little I was up before dawn and smoked languidly as the skinny white bunches of air slowly floated away. The pleasure of being awake. Earliness and bright sky the sound of waves. Little sails across the expanse of silky blue water. Crisp yellow that peculiar sharpness of dawn light made a caterpillar of crawling smoke inch across the floor. Nervousness perhaps thinking of my son and nearly averting an accident with the coffee pot as the top bubbled up. Jolted by sudden garbage truck noise in the front of the house. Cans rattling like someone falling down a flight of steps. Some sadness as I looked at my son's empty closet. His classes at the seminary began this week. His journey finally towards the Truth and my comfort in knowing that the priesthood will give him the answers he seeks. My wife would have been proud. I know it was so important to her that her son find the true way. Now that he has left it seems that my thoughts are more and more clustered around memories of my wife. I remember our first date. At the cafe. It was early spring and quite balmy that day. She had spoken of her love of the sea and in my naiveté about the appropriateness of a romantic gift I had collected strands of seaweed that were draped across the rocks. I let them dry and tried to fashion them into a kind of garland for her. Most of the lengths of the ocean crop were darkish green but some had turned black. Those black curls that for me had a child like beauty. Confusion and excitement raced through me like tentacles reaching into every compartment of my psyche. Was I in love? I felt such a kinship with her. I could not understand where such content had come from. The day before we met it certainly was not there. I suppose that is one of the miracles of true love. Finding a soul mate. Suddenly one's life is meaningful only if the "other" is a part of it in every conceivable way. I have to admit that just reminiscing about those lovely heady days after I met my wife has put my mind into a sort of giddy cloud. I think I heard the landlord waxing the staircase this morning. I have to pull myself together and get to the supermarket. My son sometimes stops by on the weekends and I wanted to get a case of that soft drink he likes. Memories of being in love. Such powerful combinations of magic and hypnosis. I almost feel as if I am floating. Where did I put my keys? I have to lock the front door before I go down the stairs.

The Woman: Chapter Seven

Daddy, wake up. Wake up, Daddy. Let's play.

On this screen on these pages occasionally you will see some of the moments a few of the images things the woman lying on the hospital bed did or fantasized about such as the one where she's a little girl she runs into the funeral parlor lifts up her tiny skirt pulls down her little panties suddenly she's on top of the man in the casket she rubs her hairless crotch against that man remembering her father trying to wake him she's trying to make daddy wake up now she's an adult there is a special room a large white room and she is suspended from the ceiling bound and gagged ready for punishment a special need something not to be talked about in delicate company something to be ashamed of something to be kept buried and hidden but there is a secret thrill there is this yearning that cannot be suppressed the ordinary and loving ingredients of life do not do away with these needs you know about that don't you it comes as no surprise to you because you cannot wait to see the next image how many times have you imagined it happening to you and you shudder when someone passes by as if their movement takes the shadow away from your thoughts and exposes the fantasy for all to see all to see the curtain is lifted the veil is parted the authorities have discovered the trap door someone has pushed the button that opens the secret panel there is so much to see and at night the cloak of conceit comes off at night there is too much space and it is so much easier for the dirty thoughts to move is it not just so cozy and teasing to be enveloped by these thoughts at night?

Her beloved had planned a delightful picnic in a beautiful pastoral setting. The pink blades of the grey windmill were reflected in the pond and somehow her fears were soothed by this delicate image of gentle pastel. Would he tell her that he loved her? Babbling sheep grazed nearby and she was reassured by the roses he had brought. She stared at the windmill blades and was hypnotized by the apparent aimlessness of their turning motion. She hoped that his intention was to vow himself to her. But there was uneasiness in his movements and she imagined ghosts twisting and distorting the water dripping from the oars in the little rowboat on the lake. Lacking the necessary courage he turned away when he told her; he did not love her and could not look her in the eye when he said it. In the glints of sun that sparkled upon the painted anchor on the boat she could see or at least thought she saw her expression of remorse. Her features seemed contorted like melting plastic and she could not recognize her face. All the undulations of the scene that included the rowing oars and the circling blades and winding green fields became distinct to the point of harshness and she felt startled as though waking from a bad dream. She knew he did not love her.

Lost Love & Other Short Stories.   Page 9.   Such a beautiful paragraph.   How many times did I read it? Windy night.   Lonely, cold, bad long feeling. I can't.   I can't.   Over. So little keeps us happy, so little time to do the things that could make us happy. Holding on to something in the silent room, like part of the boat, so cold and windy at sea. Try to hold. To be loved. Long unbroken dream. Fiction dream, fiction time, but utterance is not a guide. Inside the dream of words, who can say what is real and what makes it so? Outside the illusion of words, what is the purpose and the direction of our heroes? Who is he? Where is he? Slipped away at the last moment. Away in a dream. All of the sea. Quiet comfort, sea and darkness. Why so much guilt for Woman? Sorrow fable. Endless fable guilt. Take me away. Ancient idea that we are guilty. As Eve was guilty, I suppose that is where it comes from mostly.   I think that thoughts are private but who can tell. Consciousness of guilt. Before life, before time. Invent the natural law of death. Inevitable banishment.   Some say it depends on how you look at it. Not this tree. Where does the knowledge of good and evil lead us? Holy seal is broken then there must be Time and

Death. Novel idea. Divine energy creates supernatural being; supernatural being defies divine energy by acquiring forbidden knowledge, then suddenly and eternally perception becomes banishment in human form. Very finely conceived idea of retribution, wouldn't you say? It seems that punishment comes for allowing the image to live a life of its own. All the centuries filled with so many unhappy souls passing through time like pictures in an endless series of projections. Deranged Magic Lantern box gone insane with misty notions of what to do when you are corporeal. Punish woman. Purity. Lost divinity in the soiled movements of limbs needing things on earth. What is woman? Why is she guilty? My beloved. It cannot be. All that day, I remember that day; I knew there would be nothing for me. You left. Scattered throughout, beautiful blanket, the picnic things, but you left and I saw the windmill all the way across in the fields. You wanted no more of my pain. Dread of woman, terrible dream, we are all searching but nothing happens. Quiet. Sleep. All cold in the sea. Plaything for the darkness. For thoughts, for guilt, so much guilty sea. I loved you so. Temptation for man. So much to search for when the day turns into night. Reach for life. Take the fruit. Know how much there is to know. If your senses give you the light, then it must be more light, more life, anything is there if you perceive it. Shame, finally; indecent independence of perception and thought. That is where it starts. I suppose that is the best explanation they can give us. Loveliness of the pastel. Sweet fruit, all colors, so reserved and gentle, such dreamy colors for woman. Woman and color. Monochromatic patriarchal law, so afraid of woman and her colors. Stay inside this place where decisions are made. Wretched box of inflexible doctrine. Take away the colors. All sea is quiet now. My beloved lost to me forever. I am punished, so seek pain; savor the endless toil of the body used for lasciviousness. I will go there now and remain. The endless rebuke for the offer of sexual love. That's why we are so ostracized; we tempted man with the fruit of knowledge, didn't we? If it's total depravity that they're after then they shall have it, unencumbered by any form of earthly reason. Unfettered, I would rather have Pelagius as my spokesman, but they cast him down, there is no neutrality, it was sin all right and the fruit is logic. The awareness is damnation. All of it passes age to age with woman as the emblem of spiritual decay. No! We are sirens of hope, not destruction. So much of a woman's heart remains unknown because of the energy of man's ego. An often-misdirected energy. We are torn away from what we know to be true because our lives are cornered and driven by forces outside our love. Let woman give what she has. There is goodness there. Comfort and rest. Comfort and rest.

"It was the most repulsive thing I've ever witnessed," said the mortician as the young girl's hysterical mother was led out of the viewing room. No one who had come to pay last respects to the dead man, friend or relative, would ever think of him in the same way again. Such an explicit, horrific display of misguided trust and desire could only cast deeper and stronger suspicions. "Oh yes, we've thought something was wrong with that child for a long time," a cousin eagerly volunteered to the investigative reporter.

There was always something wrong with the way she responded to her father. Now the world at large would know a thing or two about it. There would be images on the television screen. There would be photographs in the newspaper. There would be interviews and commentary and discussion. At home, supported by shocked family members, the young girl's mother reaches for a bottle of sedatives with shaky hands at the same instant that a newspaper reporter, sitting at his computer in an office far away, strikes the keyboard to finish a sentence in his feature story about the funeral parlor incident. The reporter has covered domestic violence and abuse stories for decades and an excess of cynicism causes him to smirk as he works on the piece. He is thinking of the utter obscenity of the event and does not care that it amuses him. How ridiculous, he thinks to himself, that at the man's wake, where his dapper corpse is surrounded by mourners and flowers and colorful religious cards inscribed with Pauline messages, there should be not only this graphic disclosure of a forbidden sexual exchange between child and father, but that the girl's cotton panties, once they had dropped past her ankles, had been forgotten and were therefore sent into eternity inside the coffin with the man who had so often removed them when he was alive. This was a part of the story that, much to the reporter's chagrin could not be published.

Like so many people in the newspaper business, he had contacts and informants who, for a price, frequently provided information that was not officially available. His man at the funeral parlor for example, who often supplied him with private details when organized crime figures were waked and media access to the viewing parlors was of course denied as a matter of Christian decency, told him that immediately after the young girl's half-nude form was unceremoniously yanked from the body, the casket was hastily closed and sealed. Always spying for the reporter, the assistant at the funeral parlor took special note of the fact that the panties now rested upon the deceased's foot. The reporter would have liked to include something in his story about how the dead man might stumble during his first steps toward Paradise. Something along the lines of "If Thine eye offends thee, pluck it out!" would be equally suitable, only in this case, following Christ's advice for passage into eternity might necessitate the use of crutches. The journalist chuckled when he considered that an entirely different, though no less active, area of the man's anatomy would surely fall under the heading of offensive liability, so to speak, and while said bodily part would have been most sorely missed by the dead man in his mortal life, entering Heaven without it, with his daughter's panties wrapped around his foot, seemed to be a more spiritually reassuring equation than hobbling around consecrated ground minus a foot but with the corpus spongiosum at the ready.

The child's mother has spilled water on her sweater-blouse. Her hand trembled so much as she tried to swallow the pills that half the glass poured away from her mouth and drenched her bosom. It will require the calmative effects of the drug to produce enough composure for her to question her daughter. For now that delicate task and the diplomatic sensitivity that it requires are beyond her fragile state of composure. Her sister and some female cousins have taken the girl into her room and are cheerily speaking with her surrounded by the Mobiles that hang from the ceiling like foliage in an Amazon rain forest. The little figures of decorative cardboard evoke a jungle theme: elephants and giraffes, alternating in size, height, and angle according to the architecture of the Mobile. Somehow an elephant form is suggested by the shape of the water stain on the mother's dark grey top. At least that is the impression of the woman's cousin who stares at the sweater as she leans over her supine relation. The cousin sits next to the woman's bed, holding her hand and applying a damp towel to her forehead, trying to give her some reassurance that the little girl does not seem overly disturbed by the atrocious event. The behavior that caused it, the indoctrination of sexual intimacy between father and daughter, is not discussed.

The reporter, having finished his story, leans back in his chair, smoking a cigar that produces gelatinous circles of velvety smoke that slowly twist around the display cases filled with numerous journalism awards that have graced his career through the years. A frustrated novelist who was never able to interest any publisher in his fiction, the reporter nurses a long-standing bitterness that is only superficially relieved by his success in a field of writing that never particularly appealed to him. Unfortunately there is little in the man's philosophical point of view that gravitates towards anything more sophisticated or sensitive than repellant subjects of abduction, sexual torture, and the typical literary conventions associated with pulp detective and murder mystery fiction. His bookcases at home are filled not with volumes of classic world literature but detective novels from the 1940s; hundreds of such books with melodramatic titles and lurid color illustrations of men in trench coats hiding blackjacks or syringes in the shadow of alleyways, silky buxom women smoking cigarettes with holders, covered in jewelry and fur. He is an innately voyeuristic person who thrives on any image or understanding of an event that comes to the observer through questionable or immoral means. He is not above spying on his neighbors. He spends his evenings looking through binoculars or a telescope at the apartments across from his living room. It had to be murder or depraved sex or suicide or any other deformed and wretched behavior that obsessively occupied his mind. Why would a man who had experienced no great personal misfortune or tragedy, who had received the benefit of higher education and was comfortably entrenched in a long career as a noted journalist, leave his apartment three times every evening to try to convince his neighbors that he was not home, only to sneak back into his apartment where, in total darkness, he would set up his equipment and watch the surrounding apartments until every light in them had been extinguished? For some reason the arrangement of persons and objects, within the artificial confines of the circular frame, imposed upon the reporter's neighbors through his telescope, gave him a peculiar thrill. It was as though the comings and goings of these people, and all of their ordinary behavior, such as making a pot of coffee or sitting in front of their television sets, acquired another dimension when viewed in this way. In a sense, the reporter hoped for the macabre, the dangerous, the unusual. He wanted to see something vulgar or violent. As images, even banal domestic activities provided the reporter with endless interest, especially, of course, when some of the female neighbors disrobed. Unfortunately the reporter fell into that category of persons identified by modern psychiatry as being addicted to sex. Like an alcoholic, they suffer from a craving that knows no limits. Never married and for the most part a solitary creature, the reporter lived in a world of sexual imagery, real and imagined; he was, of course, no stranger to prostitutes and pornography. In many ways, his spying on the female residents of the opposite building supplemented his obsession with pornographic imagery. There was a great, unfathomable loneliness in the man that was somehow converted into a kind of intellectualized cynicism, a psychological defense mechanism that probably prevented him from committing suicide.

The journalist kept a large collection of pornographic videos alongside his array of vintage detective novels. He had a predilection for the bizarre and the unusual; his tastes in erotic imagery led him towards bondage and sadism. Filling the topmost shelf of his bookcase was a series of S & M movies that, like the western and science fiction serials of years ago, such as *The Perils of Pauline* and the *Flash Gordon* serials, featured the same principal character cast into an ever-changing stream of predicaments. These films starred a female heroine who always seemed to be a victim of kidnapping, bondage, prolonged sexual torture, and rape, unlike Pauline whose misadventures usually involved rescue from the deep sea, hot-air balloons, horse and motorcar races, and so forth. This character, known as *Virginal Val*, was left at the conclusion of each film in some dire situation from which escape or rescue seemed highly unlikely; yet, at the beginning of each new entry in the series, *Virginal Val* was free once again, engaged in another adventure based on a completely different occupation and situation. In one installment, she was a forest ranger inspecting a camp site for fire hazards when she was abducted by escaped convicts, taken to an abandoned cabin, and brutally raped for days; in another episode, she was a gym instructor who disciplined three of her female High School students by keeping them after school; they retaliated by locking her in the shower room, taking turns sodomizing her with batons.

In the most recent film, she played a research scientist. Working late in the lab one night, she was attacked by the courier who delivered the weekly biological samples. He had been eyeing her for a long time and was enraged that she turned down his incessant requests for a date. The relentless harassment made her so uncomfortable, she had complained to the owner of the messenger service that employed him. As a result, he was suspended for a week without pay. The messenger company hired many unsavory characters and never checked the background of its employees. This man had been committed for several years to a mental institution. He strangled his puppy when he was ten years old. Violence and deranged sexual behavior (he had masturbated into his younger sister's cereal) had characterized his actions for many years. After delivering the samples, he snapped. Using chloroform to render *Val* unconscious, he dragged her to the basement of the facility.

He was a very large man. Standing five foot eleven inches, he was about one hundred and seventy-five pounds and very muscular. He liked to work out with nautilus equipment and spent most of his free time using all kinds of weights. His brutality towards women, beginning with his mother and sister, was life-long and vicious. Left in his care when their parents went out, his sister was often subjected to long hours of painful bondage. He would threaten her with beatings, even death, to keep her silent. Now forty-two, he had become an expert in bondage and could use rope in intricate ways to secure a woman in an extremely painful, lewd, sexually vulnerable position.

While she was being stripped, gagged, and tied, *Virginal Val* began to regain consciousness. In her semi-anesthetized state, she confused the metallic sounds of the man's footsteps with ship chains flowing onto a dock. The man wore thick, heavy work shoes equipped with specially designed steel tips and metal taps on the soles. There were many pipes lining the basement ceiling and these gave the man several options for selecting a spot to tie *Val's* hands above her head and hoist her upwards.

The dangerously disturbed messenger remembered his sister as he pulled the rope, standing face to face with *Val*, raising her so that her voluptuous, delicate toes were about an inch above the ground. He was deeply excited by the perverse, sexualized infantilism of a woman's dangling feet; that image reminded him of the way a toddler might swing her legs while sitting in a high chair. *Val* fully regained consciousness just as the messenger reached into his large, black knapsack and pulled out a thick paddle. She began to moan and sob desperately, but the gag suppressed the wet sounds, allowing only the garbled murmur of her anxious, stifled breaths.

Val had good reason to be not only shocked by the bizarre situation that she was awaking to, but to be afraid for her life, that is, her physical survival from the ordeal that the messenger was about to subject her to. For as her tormentor came closer, holding the paddle at arm's length, she saw glints of metal on its surface and realized that, like the bed of nails used by Fakirs in India during meditation, the tips of numerous nails had been affixed to the wooden, oblong shape. The rule of physics whereby an equal distribution of many closely grouped nails prevents the skin from being broken, when one lies upon the studded bed, did not apply to the messenger's paddle. It had more widely spaced, longer nails which, assuming enough hitting force was applied, could easily penetrate flesh, especially Val's tender, naked, quivering buttocks. The messenger approached Val slowly, the clang of his heavy footfalls echoing in the cavernous basement, his hulking form a matrix of intersecting pipe shadows cast by the glaring bulbs, like the crisscross patterns of plaid material or the large, wide netting in the cargo bay of a commercial ship.

In spite of his abnormal psychological tendencies, or perhaps because of them, the messenger was an amateur writer. He spent much of his time sitting on the waiting bench at the messenger service, during the lulls between delivery calls, scribbling in a small, narrow, ringed notebook, much like the kind used by reporters hurriedly capturing the details of an event or quotes from an interview. *Val* saw the notebook, jutting out of the back pocket of his filthy dungarees, when he set the paddle down on the concrete floor, nails facing upward.

The unfinished piece that the messenger had been working on began with a man having a nightmare in which the amplified buzzing of thousands of bees seemed to be coming from inside the man's head.

The messenger's dreaming protagonist was in fact insane. It was difficult, given the messenger's twisted perspective on life, to determine whether or not this was an intentional ingredient of the narrative. He had described the room in which the man slept as having what appeared to be rubber walls, creating the impression of an institutional padded cell. Also, the man in the story wore a straitjacket and his ankles were secured to the foot of the bed by restraint cuffs. Gripped in the vortex of his nightmare, the man screamed loudly in his feverish sleep.

He saw a man and a woman in a car driving along the sinewy paths of a mountain road. It was late at night; sheets of heavy rain were battering the vehicle like a car wash and the man, who was driving, was having great difficulty seeing. Perhaps because of the anxiousness produced by such hazardous driving conditions, and the gloomy surroundings of woods, rain, and night, the man suddenly remembered a recurrent nightmare that plagued him when he was a boy. Each time he awoke, he was inexplicably overwhelmed by the sharp smell of pepper, despite the fact that nothing in the nightmare had anything to do with the spice. He wondered if there was some kind of mathematical necessity within his subconscious, a kind of mental formula or schematic that repeated the narrative of the nightmare so minutely. He was always terribly frightened, running away from someone or something. It was a feeling of utter dread; a kind of primal fear, an unnamable fear. The setting, of course, was always the same: he was in the woods, there was a furious rainstorm, it was night. The illogic of dream-space and dream- time made it possible for him to run at full gallop, without even the spotty, occasional illumination of moonlight, and still find his way through the blackness of the forest. Somehow he always managed to move forward without tripping or running into a tree.

The little girl sleeps, covered by her blanket that is decorated with seagulls. The elephants bobble slightly, slowly circling above the child's bed. Caught in flight by the embroidery on the blanket, the gulls seem frozen in space. The child enjoys arts and crafts at school; she is clever with paper and there are several dolls made in the Origami style sitting in various positions on the windowsill.   One of the paper dolls seems to be reaching for a rubber ball lying next to it. That appears to be the mother's impression as she looks from the windowsill back to her sleeping daughter and reaches, perhaps in imitation of the doll's gesture, for the girl's head to stroke her hair. Grateful that the girl has fallen asleep, the woman anticipates with absolute dread the conversation that she will ultimately have with the child.

The girl dreams of the shore, where the seagulls are released from cages of ice, melted by the sun; they fly to the rocks after stabbing their beaks into the ocean, trying to catch fish. She is probably still thinking of her summer vacation, filled with numerous trips to the beach with her father, interrupted just recently by his sudden death. It was very disturbing to the family, particularly because the man was so fit and suffered a broken neck from a fall down the stairs. As the girl skips in her dream along the water's edge, she sees something that she would use when school resumed. One of the assignments was to paint pictures showing what the children had done over the summer. The child saw a man, sitting in a beach chair, who had snuffed out his cigarettes in the sand. These white cylinders reminded the girl of towers and conjured for her the proverbial image of castles in the sand. That became the subject of one of her paintings. Her teacher would regard the visual metaphor as a very sophisticated idea for someone so young. She would immediately recognize that the child's interpretation of the cigarette shapes as towers demonstrated a hunger for associative thinking that should be nurtured. The instructor would certainly see the early signs of genius in a budding artist or philosopher. There was a special auditorium, named Ruggieri Hall after the benefactor who donated funds to the school, where prized projects, such as artwork or science experiments, were displayed. Here the little girl's "tower" portrait of the man on the beach would be hung between a scientific report on how the human body breaks down during starvation and a sculpture depicting a large spider devouring its young.

On that day of summer fun, recreated and transformed in the young girl's dream, was another child of approximately the same age who played with a large rubber ball. The children quickly became playmates.

There is something about the season of summer that compels childhood camaraderie, imbuing it with a kind of Dionysian abandon. The beach especially, on a particularly hot and sunny day, with all the raw nature that sea and sand and salt air bring to even a youthful consciousness, creates an uninhibited emotional atmosphere for children who start conversations with one another and jointly engage in castle building or ball playing or wave riding or shell collecting as though they had been friends since birth. The playground and the schoolyard do not engender this instantaneous social harmony, this western Mecca where, each summer, hundreds of little devotees gather to carry pails of seawater or to create sluices in the wet sand or to crown the towers of elaborate castles with captured crabs. The girl played with her new friend and they shared the ball in the water. The little artist who would make the painting that would so impress her teacher, looked over at the man in the beach chair and noticed that up along the shore, so far undisturbed by the widening reach of the tide, the ends of the cigarettes he smoked still protruded from the sand, randomly positioned like pegs in a board.

lying on the hospital bed she's a victim she's in a coma all of the equipment the entanglement of life-support apparatus is connected to her body but she will not wake up she cannot wake up there is the snap of the ear pieces the doctor's stethoscope as he removes the instrument from his neck sometimes on these pages there will also be a record of things that occur outside the world of the mind of the woman not necessarily a real world but that is up to you to decide after all there is truly no absolute way of knowing what does and does not register itself in her consciousness after all it has been observed that someone in a coma while uncommunicative nevertheless hears all that occurs around them so it is as if the woman were a filter through which other realities can be known always through a framing device if you will or let's say a medium of some kind and we know that adds to your pleasures the funhouse could not entice its audience were it not for the manipulation of the normal that is the bait that is the trick we want what is normal to be disarranged and distorted that is why you paid the price of the ticket isn't it?

"Wasn't that what you said?"

"When?"

"You know, about that guy, the new intern, you said he was cute and you liked him."

"Oh, yeah, he's dreamy, ain't he? I think he's a little stuck up, though, don't you think? He's too serious all the time. Never says anything nice to me, anyway."

"Hey girl, you can't expect miracles! Give him a little encouragement, y'know?"

"I did, I did, I mean, y'know, I flirted with him a little bit but, like, I'm not gonna make no fool out of myself trying to get his attention and all that, y'know? Seems to me that if he's interested he woulda got the message by now and said *somethin'* to me."

It was quite unlikely that the handsome intern would say anything romantic or flirtatious to the nurse. He took what he was doing very seriously. There was no time in his life for dating or any other kind of recreation. He knew what his parents had sacrificed to save the money to send him to medical school and he felt an all-consuming dedication to them. "Maybe he don't pay you no mind 'cause he one of them pretty gay boys!" giggled the other nurse as she replaced a chart in the metal container behind the nurse's station. The chart, recently returned by the doctor who did rounds on this floor of the hospital, the intensive care unit, contained what little new information could be gathered about a brain-dead young woman who had been admitted several months ago. There was gossip amongst the nurses about this woman, partly out of sympathy and partly out of sexual curiosity. "Wasn't she some kind of S & M prisoner or something like that? Some guy kept her tied up and did wild things to her?" asked the nurse whose attempts to interest the dutiful intern had so far proven unsuccessful. The doctor was approaching the station to ask for another chart; the nurses immediately and transparently changed the subject. The intern, however, who had just joined the doctor during the examination of the woman in question, had overheard the nurse's comments. He stared at her with disapproval that the smitten nurse mistakenly took for evidence of sexual interest. She tossed her hair back and smiled at him as she straightened herself from the hunched position in which she and the other nurse had huddled for their private discussion about the unfortunate patient, thrusting her chest forward to showcase her breasts for the indifferent intern's benefit.

"You've hardly touched your dinner. What's wrong?" asked the intern's mother as she removed his plate from the table. The curtain by the kitchen window suddenly blew about when she returned the dish to the stove. It had gotten much colder by the time the intern returned from his shift. Walking from the train station, he had doubled his scarf and hunched his shoulders to make the fit of his coat snugger. A gust of wind had burst through the open window and the blue and yellow triangular tassels of the curtain fitfully twitched in the frosty night air. The woman still thought of her only son as a child and attended to his needs from that perspective, just as she had done when he was asleep in his crib and she wiped the saliva that had dried on his face. Smiling at the roses that he had brought for her, she was reminded of the red and pink pinwheel toy that, at night, remained motionless in a corner of his room. During her pleasant reverie, the steam rising from one of the dinner pots momentarily engulfed the woman's face. It was very late. The intern rarely returned before two a.m. Below in the streets were the closed stores. Decorative flags strewn between them appeared colorless in the dark. "Today was a little rough for me, mom" answered the intern. "There's this young woman who's in a coma, she was in labor and her entire system shut down. The baby's all right. In fact the father just picked him up today. I couldn't help feeling so sorry for the woman. And there were these really vulgar nurses talking about her. There's all this gossip in the hospital, because this woman, supposedly she was into something weird. I really don't want to say."

The intern's mother was aware that her son would sometimes experience painful things and she knew when not to question him further. As she busied herself at the stove, he stared at the bowl of soup. It was very hot and waves of steam rose up from the bowl in moist swirls. He was exhausted and still thinking of the woman who succumbed during labor. There was a kind of dreaminess or unreality in his mind and the pattern of roses that decorated the soup bowl began to change. An illusion of swirling and mixing occurred and the roses, some red, some pink, some yellow, began to melt and blend into one another, as though the heat from the steam had released them. He thought of the equipment in the woman's room, the respirator pump, the I. V. drip, the heart monitor, the e. k. g., everything that was mechanical and automated, as though they were metal and plastic extensions of the woman's vital organs, living another life outside her body.

The more the intern stared at the bowl of steaming soup, the more its hypnotic power affected his thoughts. He remembered an incident that occurred many years ago, when he was a small boy on a trip with his parents. They were in their car and the intern, fascinated by the disappearing road and the many lanes of traffic, was transfixed in the back of the vehicle, looking out of the rear window. He played a visual game inside his head. Every time his father turned a corner on the freeway, he closed his eyes and wished away all of the following vehicles. Having imagined that every car behind them had been magically removed from the road, the boy suddenly opened his eyes and gave himself little shocks of perception. In his mind, the lanes and the cars were gone. Seeing everything reappear, realizing that the highway and the vehicles (seen through the rear window of the car) were still there, was very strange to the boy. The image of emptiness that he created in his mind became more jolting after being suddenly replaced with reality when he opened his eyes.

He played this little game, amusing himself for many minutes until, with his eyes closed, he heard a terrible, pained yelping sound immediately after a screech of brakes and a loud impact. Apparently, at that moment, they were passing an area of the freeway that stood about a hundred feet from a park. A young boy, probably around the same age as the intern, had been playing with his dog, throwing a ball far away, making the animal charge after it and return. Somehow, this time, the ball found its way out of the park and onto the freeway, with the racing dog, seemingly impervious to the highway noise, madly dashing after it. There was something sickening about the successive sounds of the thud, the brakes, and the yelp. It was like a kite being yanked away by the wind, thought the frightened boy as he opened his eyes just in time to see the poor animal whisked to the right of the automobile, landing against some bushes near the freeway rails. For many years, in fact until this moment as a mature man, the intern wondered about the fate of the helpless dog. He wondered if the animal survived the accident, although he realized, even when he was a child, that such an injury would have been fatal. He wondered what became of the dog's body, and if the family that owned it was at least able to retrieve the remains. At that moment the intern's mother, who had been rubbing the calluses on her palm, flung away some particles of dead skin. This gesture made her charm bracelet jingle slightly. The image of the car passing the dog's carcass, an image that the intern stubbornly held in his mind, flashed through his thoughts during the gentle tinkling of the bracelet. Since the vehicle was moving so rapidly, the intern could not be sure if the animal's body was still moving. He picked up his spoon and began to eat the soup. As he broke the surface of the hot broth, the filmy, overlapping images of the dog's accident loosened and evaporated from his mind. The intern shook his head as he contemplated his fixation all through the years on the outcome of the incident. Surely, he thought, someone must have found a way to retrieve the animal's body. There was something obscene about the idea that the desiccated corpse would have been left to rot alongside the highway, flattened more and more by the endless traffic. Perhaps it was the fact that suffering and death confronted the intern on a daily basis, and so his thoughts carried him toward images of a more positive nature. He liked to imagine the dog as a puppy. It may have been that his mind, recently trained to think in visual terms, as a result of his long, highly detailed studies of anatomy and internal medicine, had generated thousands of pictures of organs and blood vessels and other, intricate, otherwise invisible mechanics of the body, so it was a natural impulse for him to vary and elaborate upon images from his past, as if he were imagining the cardio-vascular system or the synapses of the brain. So as a calmative and distraction from the disturbing idea that the dog's body was left behind, he thought of it as a puppy. He saw the shreds of wet newspaper covering the bottom of the cage; a porcelain, white water bowl in the corner; a soft squeaky toy in the puppy's mouth; bits of food and excrement stuck to its fur and smeared along the newspaper. He saw an odd-looking man leave the pet shop after chatting briefly with the manager. He somehow had the impression that this man brought bundled newspapers to the shop and left after exchanging some small talk with the manager. As the conjured images of the imaginary past of the dog unfolded within the intern's mind, it seemed to him that the manager, for some inexplicable reason, was annoyed with the man who left the newspapers. In fact, the manager, while appearing to be pleasant and treating the man politely, had an acute distaste for this character that was acquitted of sexual crimes against a young woman who had died after lingering in a deep coma for several years. The store manager recalled reading about the trial; it was a well known case and almost daily coverage appeared in all of the newspapers. An ironic component in this peculiar connection between the unsavory man and the manager was that many of the newspapers brought by the man were multiple copies of the very newspapers which reported the salacious details of his trial and which the manager, without realizing how much his own sexually repressed (floridly perverted) imagination was titillated by such details, had been greedily consuming each day of the trial.

The manager was the type of person who maintained a facade of decency: he was kind to children and compassionate towards the animals in his pet shop; he would immediately return money whenever a clerk or cashier had erroneously given him too much change; he supported several local charities with generous, annual donations; he fed pigeons in the park across from his store, when he took his little, neatly squared, home-made sandwiches there and ate lunch; he disliked violence and moral turpitude. Yet, in private, at night in his home where he lived alone, his double-edged pathology illuminated a reverse image of sorts. It was as if one were looking at the same scene and the same objects, and finding new and different content in them, just as in the optical illusion built into the Surrealist painting of what seems, with one view, to be the profiles of two human faces, and with another view, a chalice. Similarly, the manager somehow released himself from his public persona, and indulged in thoughts and acts which would be repulsive to his conscious being. For example, he was degenerate in the degree to which he felt entitled to engage in prolonged voyeuristic behavior; usually he would spy on his female neighbors while in the nude; he was also capable of stalking a woman who had rejected him. Yet, in a social setting, he would be the first to criticize such behavior because of its emotional immaturity and psychological defects. It might not be going too far to say that the transition from the man's social behavior to his private actions constituted a kind of hypnotic state in which what mattered most to him from an ethical and moral point of view was involuntarily discarded.

He would disrobe immediately upon entering his apartment. All of the windows had been covered with dirty, old sheets, conveying a sense of desolation to anyone who, from the opposite building, happened to look across at the manager's apartment. It was as though an infirmed bitter old man lived there, or a murder had been committed, or the space had been condemned due to some horrific violation of public health codes. The man was not content with the privacy afforded by most window treatments; in fact, in one of the rooms he kept for storage were the split and ripped remains of wooden blinds and canvass shades that, in a fit of screaming rage, he had destroyed one night, feeling violated because he had convinced himself that he was the recipient of unwanted attention from his neighbor's prying eyes. Only thick, dark sheets would suffice; he had nailed them along the sides, top and bottom of each window.

All of the domestic and decorative ingredients which enliven a home had been systematically stripped away. There was a terrible, lingering sadness in the place; one had the feeling that the house had become a kind of emotional mausoleum for the man, so palpable was the sense of loss, regret, and unrecoverable love. A child had been raised there, but the walls and tables and shelves did not contain celebratory mementos, objects or photographs, of a beloved child's life. In the midst of all of the heaps of things gradually shifted from one room to another, producing the disarray one finds in houses where someone has died and everything of importance has been wrenched from its place and thrown into a jumble where it does not belong, was a solitary photograph of the man standing in the street with his daughter. It had been taken many years ago; unaccompanied by any other totemic object or harmony-inducing ingredient of the child's existence, its presence seemed artificial, like a bowl of plastic flowers or cheap lawn ornaments. Thus it remained as an oddity or incongruity; as a reminder of something that no longer existed.

He was divorced and equally estranged from his wife and adult daughter; he had lost the love of his child, and her permission to see his grandchild. He attributed this to a lack of sensitivity on the part of his daughter; hadn't she summarily discarded her intended just before the wedding, with an utter lack of humanity towards the poor fellow? There was no end to the self-serving formulas and rationalizations he used to escape any honest appraisal of his own behavior, to lay blame and find fault with what he believed (in his delusion) were psychological and emotional foibles in the other person. Therefore, as far as he was concerned, in his perception of matters and his judgment about them, he could never be wrong. Like a vulture circling a massacre in search of carrion, he went about the social business of dealing with people with one motive only. Given his innately misanthropic nature, which he went to great lengths to disguise, what he wanted most from any form of social interaction was to find what he believed were flaws in the personality or actions of others which he could then categorize and critique. Nothing in his soul, which, deep down, contorted with self-reproach and self-hatred, would allow any bubbling of thoughts towards the surface of consciousness where there could be the slightest cognizance of personal responsibility for the resentful, often hateful reactions of those individuals (family or friends) who were close to him. If one listened to the man complain of his daughter's decision to disallow contact between himself and his grandson, given the surface ingredients of the situation, as the man chose to explain them, one could not help but feel pity for him. In reality, this was a form of thanatosis; he was very much like an insect or animal that played dead so that nothing harmful would come its way. For the man, that meant avoiding the revelations of someone else's penetrating attention, someone who might realize that, with words and deeds, he had destroyed his daughter's affection for him; that he and he alone had caused the severance of all contact between himself and his family.

There is a term in forensic psychiatry, the mask of sanity, which is often applied in the analysis of the behavior and personality of many serial killers. When one of these killers is apprehended, and the horrific details of their murders are made known to the public, the most common reaction of those people who knew the murderer, whether they are family, friends, or coworkers, is frequently shock and disbelief. It is through this mask or veneer of sanity, of normalcy, that the individual manages to deceive everyone who has known him, especially during the period when the murders took place. We often hear of how kind and generous, how beneficent and personable, how trustworthy and helpful these killers are. In reality, these people have no conscience; they have no remorse; they think of their victims as objects or toys. They do not possess the most fundamental layers of humanity, which, in even the most casual circumstances, give individuals some sense of spiritual communion with another human being. This reflex, this humanitarian instinct, has not been activated in their psyche. It is as if something fundamental has been left out at birth, as if a car were assembled without a chassis, as if a house were built without insulation running through its walls. In much the same way, the manager suffered from moral and ethical vacuity. His was a mask of civility, a superficial social disguise which allowed him to project the appearance of a caring, gentle, introspective man, whereas, in the emptiness of his soul, nothing could be farther from the truth. He was mean-spirited, cruel, resentful and envious of others, and incapable of selfless, caring love towards anyone or anything.

He was a retired teacher. For many years, he had yearned with great frustration and despair to be a writer. He wrote works but did not believe in them; he did not believe in himself; rarely would anything he had written leave the dusty darkness of his desk drawers, to be read in the light of day by another soul. Perhaps this was *The First Cause*, the core of the bitterness that pervaded his life; a bitterness that gradually turned into resentment and hate regarding all aspects and dimensions of his life, but which compounded itself all the more intensely whenever he was forced to recognize that he was paralyzed by fear of criticism, fear of success, fear of exposure. So all of this baleful envy of those who created but were not shackled by his fears, all of this bottomless self-hatred, which projected outward, became cleverly disguised as critical acumen and educated taste. So he used his academic knowledge of language and textbook skills of correction as a way of finding flaws in the work of others, whether that meant his students or even some of those who were published writers and had reputations of critical importance. But there was no intellectual camaraderie in this; there was no attempt to kindle talent, when he saw it, to guide a budding young writer closer to a path of self-discovery and originality. Had he been true to his profession, had he approached the youthful talent he encountered without guile and jealousy, there would have been a kind of living *bildungsroman*; there would have been a glorious coming of age, a genuine nurturing of someone who had a natural talent for producing literary imaginings, for finding new ways of understanding and describing experience. His envy, almost like a dangerous potion, did away with his nobler aspirations, replacing them with destructive hateful sabotage. Therefore, sadly, without ever realizing it, he did not correct a text for the purpose of helping its writer to capitalize on what was already a plenitude of instinctual facility with language; rather, he refused, with pathological insistence, to address any item of imagination, style, concept, or ideas in the work. Moreover, he used the need for mechanical correction in matters of language usage as a way of belittling the author, as a way of bullying him down to a place where he, the manager, could feel safe and superior to any evidence of the imagination that the writer exhibited which, of course, the manager so fiercely resented and coveted. It was like someone who brings first aid to a fallen skier, and then directs him to a bridge that is about to collapse. He would often be heard, claiming with a twinge of victory, as if he had defeated an adversary, *I've read everybody*. He found a twisted satisfaction in believing that there was always something, some blind spot of execution or conception or style, whatever it may be, that only he in his perfect understanding of what literature should be, could observe and understand and articulate. He could not see that this was really the ugliness of jealousy; it was the kind of infected energy that is produced by self-contempt, when one insists on something being so, only because the undisguised truth of one's own fears and limitations and lack of imagination is simply too terrible to behold. He was like a weed that masqueraded as a bright, innocent flower. He sulkily watched his neighbors, using his temporary, counterfeit colors to deceive, to create a compassionate surface, to encourage the trust of those things that, robust with real, natural beauty, escaped the suffocative grasp of his destructive tentacles and united themselves so purely and effortlessly with the prodigious rays of the sun. He was like the inglorious miserly offerings of the selfish Cain; his soul was hollow, like the smoke from those offerings; acrid, sterile smoke. Like Cain he held back what he felt was rightfully his; yet he still expected the rich embrace of God's love. It was poison, not sincerity, that he brought to everything he touched; just like the weed at night, trying to contaminate the soil; trying to strangle the roots, but all in vain.

The manager was not a writer. He could not create a piece of original writing if his life depended on it. He could assimilate; he could reflect; he could absorb. There was a categorical exhaustiveness in his talent for stock piling the ideas of others and trying to cobble them into a work of his own. But there was no creative spirit; there was no inspiration; there were no eccentric or unique strokes, which revealed a style that was his alone. He was like the auto mechanic who can take apart a highly sophisticated sports car, and put it back together, wearing a blindfold, but who could not successfully drive the vehicle in a race; he would have no understanding of the beauty of the machine being made to perform, to make sharp turns, to reach high levels of speed; in other words, there would be no symbiosis between the poetry of the machine and the man at the wheel. Therefore the manager, with his superior attitude towards language and literature, which served as a shield against his deep, self-loathing over having no imagination as a writer and being pathetically insecure about his work, perfectly embodied the notion that knowing everything there is to know about how language works has absolutely nothing to do with knowing how to write creatively. By the same token, knowing how to write creatively does not necessarily include an absolute understanding of how language works. The car mechanic knows the sports car more intimately than the driver could ever expect to know it, in a hundred lifetimes. Yet, the mechanic lacks the driver's intuitive talents for making the car do extraordinary things.

This was a man devoid of compassion; emotionally remote parents had stunted his empathic impulses. They were long deceased. The manager always spoke of them as if he was reading sacred words from a holy text, but there was never any real detail in his remembrances;

there were no spontaneously conjured, happy anecdotes or vibrant memories of the things they may have done together. When he spoke of his parents, it was as if the manager was mechanically repeating the broad outlines of some ancient myth. There was no core of verifiable reality; only the idea, the pretense of some great thing. The adult, worshipful of his parents, belied the pathetic heroism of the rejected child who pretended that his parents' psychological abuse did not exist. Thus the manager revered his past as a set of idealized images; he turned it into legend and left the heartbreaking reality of his parents' insults and insensitivity, the tragedy of his fragile, belittled ego somewhere else, someplace far away in his mind. And in what is commonly referred to in such cases as an unbroken chain of rejection and abuse, the manager, as the first victim of his parents' inability to foster emotional intimacy, acted out the demeaning behavior of both mother and father. Powerless as victim, he would become victimizer, and the new targets of this serial subjugation became his wife, his daughter, and a teenage boy who was one of the manager's students. The great sadness of it was that the manager believed in his innocence; he felt wronged by his wife and daughter; it was they who had misperceived and misjudged him. That was not true. Over the years, with unrelenting, unendurable anal-retentive nitpicking, it was the manager who, in ways small and large, constantly made his wife and daughter feel that they were inadequate or unreasonable or irrational. Nothing in their nature or their behavior or their decision-making was worthy of the manager's approval. Everything they did, thought, or said was, according to the manager, riddled with some form of emotional immaturity, intellectual shortsightedness, and psychological abnormality.

Finally, after so many years of ridicule and belittlement, the manager's wife and daughter found peace in the renewal of their lives, based largely upon their permanent separation from him. They found, at the end, that they could easily live without the corrosive effects of the manager's private nihilism; they realized, as if having gone through a kind of trial of self-discovery, that the manager was a bitter, self-serving creature who needed to deflate the aspirations of others in order to feel less inferior and less impotent. The same abusive scenario had played itself out in the manager's relationship with the young woman, the one he had stalked. She, too, could no longer bear his insufferable, claustrophobic treatment; she wanted release; she wanted to be free. And the manager, feeling some kind of possessive entitlement, as if it was his right to know where she was, and have access to her, drove her nearly to madness in his repeated attempts to contact and locate her, until this relationship, too, ended in acrimonious rejection of the manager.

Now in his early fifties, the teenage writer who had met the manager long ago, as a student in one of his classes, had sadly reached the same conclusion. Through the years, how often had the student, maturing more and more as a writer, and finding new and different forms of expression in his works, hung his head in dejection, because, as usual, the best of his efforts was merely fodder for the manager's shameless negativity; the more the manager was impressed by what the young man wrote, the more deeply he would try to question, to cancel out, the underpinnings of the work. This realization, coming so late to the writer-former student, was very disturbing; perhaps the man, having placed his faith in the manager at such an early age, and having maintained that faith for so long, could not accept or was not willing to believe that the manager, whom he had loved, could ever think of him, or especially his works, in anything but sincere and supportive terms; the writer could not fathom that the manager was not what he appeared to be; he had trusted him so completely for so long. And the suspension of that trust, the disappearance of that faith, coming to the writer so unexpectedly, and in one wave of hardcore, never-before-experienced revelations about the manager, was not just the destruction of a cherished innocence; it destroyed an intellectual bond that the writer, for the first time, saw in its undisguised form. From the beginning, when he shared his work with the manager at the age of fifteen, until just recently, as a middle-aged man, the writer had worshipped the manager's input; he had placed him upon a pedestal of exegetical authority; he needed drops of approval from the manager, to support his delicate ego.   But this was not, and had never been, a bond of mutual respect; it had never been a question of reciprocal admiration. The more the manager respected and admired the writer's work, the more he despised himself, for his lack of imagination, his lack of courage. He resented the writer with an even greater ferocity and, concealing his real opinion of the work, he focused all of his energy and attention on finding flaws and faults, to discourage, to distort, and otherwise try to cripple the writer's spirit. What a truly tragic and wasteful end, thought the writer, to a friendship that originally gave so much joy. Once the facade disappeared, all of the hypocrisy and hollowness from years of the manager's comments came rushing into the writer's mind, finally revealing the manager's true nature; his real character. It was like a voice-over in a film, and the audience is listening to a criminal during a police interrogation. The man is giving his version of events, describing the scene where he came upon a body, stating that he had nothing to do with the murder. The scene is shot with a moving camera, and as it weaves in and out of the spaces described by the murderer, the audience sees what he has really done, realizes he did commit the crime, and so the camera makes a mockery of all his false words. That was the writer's last feeling; that of having been grandly duped; of having been monumentally deceived. Torn between pity for the abject machinations of the despicable manager, and contempt for his inability to be transparent and give honest praise and encouragement where such things were deserved, the writer felt, ultimately, a great sense of relief. He had outlived the self-doubt and, in the aftermath of these events, had earned a healthy, perfectly balanced sense of self, which meant his sense of himself as a creative artist, a writer, since that was the essence of his being, his reason for living. And the importance of the manager's opinions of the writer's work faded, just as the writer's images of the manager faded, until he became a hooded shape, like one of the figures of the hypocrites in Dante's eighth circle of Hell, a silent, wandering thing.

When the writer closed his eyes, he saw the manager in this way, and he thought of the reason for the hypocrites' punishment, and the golden shine of their beautiful flowing robes, the radiance magnified the way the hypocrites' outward attitude shined with encouragement, and the heaviness of their tread, as they walked like living corpses, the insides of their robes lined with lead, all the dead, life-stealing heaviness of their deceit.

life-support equipment because of the attack all the violence things that were done to her that are too horrible to repeat but somehow there is the suspicion that these things will come out you are hypocritical you will be disgusted yet privately thrilled somewhere along the line you will want to know and the main thing is that her mind is like a screen a moving thought a set of images one by one they can be plucked out and brought into harmony with something like a panoramic view like Nietzsche's ideal spectator an omniscience of some kind will govern the selection and arrangement of this scandalous material her mind is like a screen there is perhaps the metaphorical image of a fly's eye or the installation piece of a video artist let's say a hundred screens grouped together in a gigantic square pattern of ten rows of ten monitors a symptom of viewing in the modern age let's say it is a trick of simultaneity that satisfies a desire to multiply the point of view until nothing is left out we wouldn't want you to be disappointed after all it is essential that nothing be left out isn't it?

I don't know where it comes from. I don't know. I get excited by it, that's all I know. I've always been excited by different kinds of sexual violence. Since I was little. I liked being spanked. Daddy was the one who spanked me. I think he liked it, too. It made me tingle down there, you know. After a hard spanking, I mean, that night when I was put to bed, I always played with myself, always. I think there were times when I must have kept it up half the night, sometimes until the alarm clock went off in my parents room and I knew it was time to get up for school. I was almost unable to stand up. My legs were so tired, twisting and flexing all night, from all the orgasms I remember giving myself. Everything was sticky: my fingers, the sheets, the covers, my panties which were usually stuffed somewhere all the way down the bed. Sometimes daddy helped me find my panties in the morning. He'd whisper in my ear about what a good girl I was, that I got spanked because he loved me, and that he'd make sure to rub my bottom that night, with the lotion, because the next day, after a long hard spanking, it was always so red and sore. I trembled when he said that. The lotion was slippery and cool and I liked to be rubbed with it. The remainder of the day would be a slow dreamy thing that seemed to take forever to end. I wanted it to be night again. I wanted to—-

The little flap of tape spun around on the take-up reel, hitting the play-head of the machine and producing a "plap plap plap plap" sound that was substituted for the woman's voice. Cut off in mid-sentence by the end of the reel, her monologue during one of the visits with the psychiatrist left some members of the jury uneasy. It had taken several months of arbitration, but the lawyer defending the man accused of raping and torturing the woman, who had just succumbed to a coma and was therefore unable to testify, had been granted permission from the court to play these tape-recorded psychotherapy sessions. The defense argued that the victim had been a sexual masochist all of her life and, most importantly, that she had entered into a mutually consenting relationship with the accused. The burden for the prosecution, apparently, was to prove that the carnal brutality that had resulted in the woman's present condition was something that she had not desired or requested. As a new reel of tape was threaded onto the machine, the jurors looked at a set of photographs in which the victim was naked, hog-tied, and bleeding across her lower back, buttocks, and upper thighs.

One of the jurors was a professional photographer and his interest in the exhibits was keen. Like many people who learn the technical side of something that provides entertainment for the layman, he was less interested in the subject matter, that is, he brought no moral or ethical context into the experience of the pictures. It did not concern him at all that these were brutal images of a woman who, supposedly, craved sadistic treatment to such a degree that she wanted her body hurt and abused in an extreme manner. He was like a record producer who no longer hears style or content in music but is drawn to the nuances and shadings of recording and tracking; or an architect who does not care about the functionality of a structure, only the symmetry and eccentricity of design.

In one of the photographs, the man noticed that the woman's body, occupying the far left of the frame, was not at all the center of attention. Over to the right, in the far-ground, was a large window that gave access to a multi-lane highway. It occurred to the juror that the photographer, who was probably the woman's tormentor, was either a very poor judge of how to use the frame to anchor the importance of a subject, or he had deliberately used the woman's swinging body as a visual aside or diversion, intended to make the window more interesting and important to the viewer. There was a complicated matrix of lanes beneath an overpass with traffic coming in the opposite direction.

A young married couple was having an argument in one of the passenger cars. The man was nervous and chain-smoked as he changed the radio stations by repeatedly hitting the little rectangular buttons. Apparently, they had been out (twilight was approaching) and the woman was concerned that their new baby was all right. There was no answer at their home and the babysitter should obviously be there.

The teenaged girl hired to look after the couple's child had been murdered. Two men, wearing white gloves and carrying burglar's tools, had broken into the house while the girl was watching television. She was fond of documentaries and had been enjoying a program on carnivals and amusement parks. There was a long sequence on the history of the Ferris wheel. Apparently, the filmmakers wanted to create a sense of flowing motion in their depiction of the different sizes and locations of the large, colorful, circular rides. They had used many crane-shots, where the camera was mounted onto a mobile, extremely flexible apparatus that could sweep through space, creating long, moving shots of the cars in the rides, the design of the structures, the swarms of people waiting in line and seeking out other pleasures and attractions. The camera gave panoramic views of the swinging cars; it swayed and panned from left to right as the cars slid back and forth. There was one very pronounced angle where the crane allowed the camera to view all of the people on the ground. It made the babysitter slightly dizzy because of the vertiginous view. There were all of the amusement park goers, moving along at a slow pace, eyeing the attractions. Suddenly a father came rushing over to a young girl, presumably his daughter, lapping at her ice cream cone. He looked around, over her head, and seemed somewhat alarmed, as though she had been in some kind of danger, or was being watched. Taking his daughter by the hand, the man searched the immediate area for a police officer or a security guard. He kept looking over his shoulder, as though he was trying to keep someone or something within his field of vision and did not want to lose his concentration, so he would be able to point out whatever it was to someone of authority.

After a short while, he located a park security guard who alarmed him with the information that the entire area was saturated with plain clothes detectives because there was surveillance of a suspected child killer who might be in the park. The man, quite shaken, explained that he had just seen a very unsavory individual, a man in his late thirties, appearing quite disheveled and acting strangely, who was looking at his little girl in a most disturbing manner. Unfortunately, at this point, when the man tried to find the threatening figure, he was no longer there. The park guard led the man over to a trailer that was normally inhabited by grounds personnel but had been temporarily set up as a communications center for the police. One of the amusement park managers, a man who supervised some of the more esoteric attractions where a performer swallows swords or eats fire, passed these three in a state of agitation. He was angrily mumbling something and rubbing his hand, as though he had just injured himself. The man with his daughter heard him saying something like "Damn bitch!" and there appeared to be some wet sticky substance on the man's shirt and another stain on his trousers that looked like fresh blood.

Inside the house the robbers discuss what to do. They did not intend to commit murder and are very disturbed by what has transpired. They had been watching this house for some time and thought that the routine of the couple that lived there had revealed itself to them. In other words, it never occurred to the thieves that the couple had an infant; that they would go out and have to provide a babysitter for their child. They wondered how such circumstances could have escaped their attention. The blow against the girl's head was meant only to render her unconscious. They are very agitated; have almost forgotten their intended robbery, and are concerned only with the disposal of the girl's body. It would be far too risky to take the corpse with them and find some way of getting rid of it elsewhere. On the other hand, this solution appealed to them more than leaving her in the house. If they took her body she would remain missing, and no definite conclusion could be drawn about her whereabouts. The thieves go through her pocketbook and remove any items of identification, such as the girl's driver's license. They drag her body, an uncooperative lifeless mass, down the long flight of stairs that leads to the basement. They remove her clothing and burn it in the furnace. It occurs to them that if they took the body with them, and drove very far away, they could dump the nude form somewhere in the woods, or on the shore, and it might take days, even weeks, for the body to be found. The corrosive effects of the sea or the carnivorous habits of small animals and insects would go a long way toward disfiguring the face of the girl, probably making positive identification very difficult if not impossible. One of the robbers, the one who is apparently in charge of plans and procedures, ponders this possibility while they both rest on some old rocking chairs near the furnace, the nude body sprawled between them on the cement floor.

The decision-making robber smokes a cigar as he thinks, and gelatinous waves of creamy smoke waft through the room, sometimes appearing as a gauzy curtain in the reflection of the glasses of the other thief, as if the girl's death and her body were a play, and the first act had concluded, with the curtain gliding across the stage.

Once inside the makeshift command center, the man told his daughter to go sit with her ice-cream cone and wait for him to speak to the detective. The man saw a very distraught woman sitting in a corner with another man, apparently her husband, while a different plainclothes detective spoke to them. A cup of coffee had been placed in front of the woman but she did not appear to have touched it. The other detective explained to the man that the couple had been at the carnival with their young daughter, a girl of about seventeen.

The pair of murderers decides that immolation is the answer. After all, as the one with the cigar suddenly points out, there is the blazing furnace, right in front of the body, ready to be used for the purpose of disposal. There remains the odious task of how to insert the corpse. The docile partner believes that since the girl is rather petite, it should be easy, if they hold the body from end to end like a large fireplace log, to stuff her through the furnace aperture. They agree that this is the safest and most expedient way of disposing of the girl's body. The dominant robber shifts gears, increasing the speed of the car as he drives himself and his partner down the moonlit country road. There is dried blood on the vomity handkerchief that the driver's accomplice continually applies to his mouth. The pair had remained in the basement until the girl's body charred to the point of brittle blackness. It was the driving man, the older, more experienced and callous thief, who had opened the furnace door several times and with a fireplace poker checked the stages of incineration. He was not satisfied until the flames had rendered the girl's body unrecognizable. There is a fresh bruise just under the left eye of the younger criminal. The contusion, caused by a blackjack, had begun to swell and the purplish-yellow tissue resembled some of the violets just beyond the road. The driver speeds along; he fails to notice the flowers, therefore he does not think of the ironic relationship, the off-beat connection between brutal violence and the beauty of nature suggested by the similar colors of bruise and flowers. *Goddamn asshole! You were supposed to make sure no one would be there!* The younger man, still nursing his wound, hears the other man's angry words in his mind. He winces, as if replaying the rebuke from his mentor somehow re-inflicts the pain of the black jack. "Guess you never went to a lot of barbeques, huh?! Ain't smelled too much cooked flesh, huh?!" The thief in the passenger seat submissively shakes his head, looking down at the handkerchief soaked with the evidence of his inability to cope with the stench of the girl's burning flesh, then staring out of his opened window, watching the side of the road which is illuminated in rushing spots by the van's headlights and little rods of moonlight which occasionally penetrate the thick foliage of the high trees.

They have to restrain the screaming mother. No one noticed that she stepped out of the trailer to get some fresh air. Unfortunately at that moment, a group of detectives and police had just returned. The woman's husband, sobbing uncontrollably, tries to keep his wife's hands away from the top of the zipped black body bag as a state trooper grabs her by the waist. His flashlight falls off his belt during the struggle. During the final search of the police teams, it had rained over the perimeter of the carnival. The flash light rolls off of the slick rubber surface of the bag at the same instant that one of the woman's shoes loosens and, falling from her foot, becomes half-imbedded in the sloppy folds of mud that have collected just beyond the trailer. The trooper is equipped with communications gear and his live walkie-talkie microphone transmits the woman's pitiful, elongated cry of *Nooo!* into the trailer. Filled with static and accompanied by heavy footfalls of work boots as other personnel rush down the metal trailer stairs, her cry is reproduced by the tiny speaker on the table, next to the woman's cup of untouched coffee.

The driving man has pulled over to the side of the road. He is tired.
He wants to rest for a moment and have a smoke. On the seat between
the older man and his timid, penitent passenger lies an open pouch of
hand rolling tobacco. Inserting the freshly rolled cigarette into a long,
tortoise shell holder, he lights it with a thick kitchen match, igniting the
sulfurous red tip with a flick of his stained, overgrown thumbnail. The
younger thief's malignant fear, nervous mind, and frenzied imagination
produce some kind of unnatural connection between aleatory elements:
somehow the droning, echoing, one word note of despair uttered by the
mother transforms into the *Hooot* of an unseen owl, concealed by the
crisscrossing patch work of leaves and branches. It makes the younger
man shudder as the older man looks upon him with derision and contempt,
blowing trunks of cigarette smoke upon the stinking handkerchief still
held in the other man's shaking hands.

The state trooper retrieves his flashlight from the thick mud,
crouching as he wipes it. He watches the woman, her arms and legs
akimbo, being led back into the trailer. Her husband has become so
overcome by grief that he has lost all awareness of his surroundings.
With an expressionless stare, he walks in a small circle, occasionally
stomping his feet in the slick mud and splashing his trousers with it.
The trooper stands and regards the poor man with great compassion;
he is too ashamed to go to him and try to provide some comfort. He
had desperately hoped that tonight's stakeout of the carnival would
capture the killer and prevent another victim from being killed.

The driving man puts his snub nose "bulldog" revolver back into the
glove compartment. There are a few tufts of his rolling tobacco on the
vacant passenger seat. These strands of dark tobacco resemble the
protruding clusters of nose hairs belonging to the timid partner who is
slumped against a tree trunk about twenty yards from the van where,
with the motor running, the older thief is spraying the blood stained
windshield with Clorox. A single bullet hole, approximately the size of a
dime, is in the center of the accomplice's forehead. Two separate

streams of thick blood, issuing from the man's nostrils, have begun to dry. The blood closest to the nostril openings is still moist. It reflects thin strands of moonlight across the dead man's face, giving the bullet hole, if the corpse were viewed from a few feet away, the appearance of a tiny insect trapped in an iridescent spider web. *Fucking asshole! Think I'm gonna get the chair 'cause you fucked up?!* In the final seconds of consciousness, before his brain completely stopped processing, the angry words of the disgusted partner may have repeated in the mind of the dying younger man. Some research has demonstrated that, even in the event of extreme brain trauma, such as a bullet wound to the head, the brain continues to live, if only for a few seconds, with commands and other information still being transmitted to the body. It is also believed, as in the case of beheading, that the victim will hear and perhaps even see for about thirty seconds. So it is possible that as the older man dragged his partner from the vehicle, these last words of contempt, uttered just before the driving man pulled the trigger, replayed in the other man's fading consciousness, like the after image of a drifting sailboat, or a dog leaping to catch a ball.

The red gleam of a traffic light burns like an ember in the deep furrow of the state trooper's hat. He is on his way to the morgue; in fact, he is about two blocks away and his hat rests on the passenger seat, fading into shadow as if covered with a blanket when the light changes to green and the state trooper drives on. Like the expressionistically delineated figures on a Kabuki stage, the singular, disturbing, and plastically concise images of the murdered girl's father mindlessly walking in circles, and the mother being slowly led towards the trailer like a broken kite carried away, her arms and legs at angles contrary to voluntary motion, sting and repeat inside the trooper's mind. He feels a personal responsibility for the tragedy of this night; he cannot rid himself of a deepening sense of guilt over the murder of the girl; he cannot reconcile himself to the grief of the parents. His mind is filled with visual and aural figures of anxiety and repetition, over which he seems to have no control: accordions stretching out in an agonized, screeching discord; blenders overflowing with a menacing buzz; fans spinning out of control, releasing their blades into the air; stalled motors shifting gears, reaching a sirens' chorus crescendo of frustration and noise. He is determined to gather as much post-mortem evidence as possible; he hopes that his presence at the morgue, as the autopsy on the girl is performed, will make any new clues immediately available for the officers still examining the area where the girl's body was found.

The older thief, overcome by fatigue, arrives at the little cabin where, for many weeks, he had planned this robbery with his ill-chosen accomplice. Just before he exited the main highway, he had passed a film production studio where several editors were having an all-night session injecting new material into a documentary they had recently broadcast on a public television station. Due to its enormous popularity, they were revising and refreshing it so that it could be re-aired next month. It was a visual essay on the history of amusement parks; many viewers had reacted quite positively to its original broadcast, and the editors, locked into a tight deadline, were working feverishly to enliven it with as much new footage (plus voice-over narration) as they could find. Meanwhile, extinguishing yet another cigarette in an ashtray next to his favorite drink of raw egg yokes, the older thief, still fuming over the waste of the evening, and full of self-reproach over having recruited such an incompetent side-kick, flings his boots against the cabin wall, causing a large bird, nestled in a tree just beyond the cabin, to jump from its branch and fly to another tree. Sitting in his armchair, exhausted not by the two murders he committed this evening, but by the long drive, the older thief spits a clump of tobacco-stained phlegm into his barrel glass of yoke slime, places the glass by his foot, leans back and immediately falls asleep. His subconscious quickly casts him about in nightmare, as if his tranquil mental state was a poorly manned sailboat that suddenly finds itself buffeted by the winds and waves of an unexpected, deadly storm. Perhaps that is too great a liberty of narrative. The older thief was a man with absolutely no sense of right and wrong. He killed his pregnant wife because he did not want children, murdering her by applying a blow torch to her vagina in the back room of a Mexican whorehouse, while a backer for one of his robberies stood at the bar wearing a derby, smoking little twisted, perfumed cigars. He did not have a sand grain of remorse over the killing of the babysitter or his young partner. His bad dreams must have been caused by something unrelated to the day's events. The knots of ugly phlegm nestled against a ball of egg yolk at the bottom of the glass.

she will not wake up her parents just left they were in tears once again they cannot agree should we sign the papers let her die no she's my baby there is only the clarity of the next image such as the one where the woman is naked and tied by the arms she enjoys pain and submission and shudders from the thrill of expectation as a large hateful muscular man moves towards her with a nail-studded paddle her heartbroken parents have not the slightest idea give her soul rest let her die in peace says her father he cannot bear to see her this way all the equipment that is necessary to sustain physical life the respirator pump the I. V. drip the heart monitor the E.K.G. everything that is mechanical and automated as though they are metal and plastic extensions of the woman's vital organs but she will not wake up inside her mind living a life of imagery are all of her sessions of bondage and pain she swings to and fro covered in blood from all the whipping and paddling her mind drifts away to the traffic sounds beyond the window and her mother sits by the bed hoping for a miracle holding a photo of her daughter in the playground on the slide when she was ten smiling at her mother in the background was a man talking to another girl he told her that she had such a pretty ball

"You've wanted this for a long time, haven't you?"

"Yes."

"You must say, 'Yes, Master.'"

"Yes, Master."

"You must realize now that you are worthless, don't you?"

"Yes, Master."

"You do not deserve the pain I am about to give you."

"Yes, Master. My pain is your gift. I am worthless. I do not deserve this gift. You are generous to give it to me."

He used this room for her punishment. She loved the circus and the carnival. Her tormentor had taken photographs of circus scenes and enlarged them to poster sizes. The images were laminated upon the floor, walls, and ceiling, sealed with sheets of clear plastic. The man grinned at his handiwork, admiring the bizarre mosaic he created. This space, a simple, ordinary room, had been transformed into self-enclosed portals that gave access to a world of enchantment and innocent fun. Gazing around, he saw the baroque animation of carnival colors and objects; the elephants, the ringmaster, the clowns, the jugglers, the tents, the midgets, and all the rest of this arrested world of a young girl's joy brought to bear against the woman's desire for humiliation and pain. It was a morbid juxtaposition, thought the man as he put on his leather mask, moving very slowly and deliberately. Her arms had already been tied behind her back and her body hoisted up by the pulley. He reached for the paddle and pressed the button on the tape recorder. Her plaintiff, naked form swayed helplessly as the recording of loud bees filled the room. Her torturer imagined that he was floating, gripped by a kind of beatific frenzy, his eyes rolled back, transported by visions of insects devouring a dog's corpse, of infants being executed with swords of divine justice. It was time for her punishment. An image of the rivulets of blood that he knew would fall across her lower back and buttocks had already formed in his mind. In this image, he was carrying her limp body in the rain; droplets of blood became beads of rain and he knew there was justice in the punishment. He saw the dog suddenly resurrected and there was a blinding light that filled the room. The animal's jaws snapped open as it drew back its jowls in vicious anger and the glaringly bright teeth projected fierce light across the room. Infants came into endless sacrificial chambers, transported by leather conveyor belts; the infinitely perfect harmony of the machinery of death. Every infant occupied a position on the conveyor belt that was perfectly matched by a suspended machete that snapped down with fascinating precision. The arrangement of one machete for one infant gave the man exquisite satisfaction, that the blade descended just as the body passed. This occurred so precisely that each beheading, and each lifting of the blade to its original position, happened within seconds of the next head moving into position for the next decapitation by the next machete. Distracted by his visions, the man thought he heard the woman begging for her punishment, but for some reason the volume of the bee noise seemed to be escalating beyond the plausible range of amplification of the tape recorder's speaker. He remembered films he had seen of the ancient Greek amphitheatres and coliseums and the expanse of the buzzing seemed to have that kind of spatial dimension. When he was a child, he would sometimes weep for no apparent reason and it seemed at the time that there was some kind of unfathomable pity or empathy that filled his young soul with sorrow. On one such occasion, when he was about twelve years old, there was a family holiday gathering. Mysteriously and suddenly overwhelmed by melancholy, he went into a room by himself. The inevitability of the death of every loved one in the room had overwhelmed him; he could not connect his remorse to anything more specific than that. The room was his young cousin's bedroom and the walls were decorated with pictures of the circus. In fact, he had joined his cousin in a visit to the circus that was supervised by the mothers of both families. They saw many things that day, including a cavalcade of clowns that emerged from an automobile as if there was no logical end to their number. The man wondered about the private lives of the clowns, picturing one of them sitting alone at a make-up table. He imagined that the man who became the circus clown was a little boy running through the woods. There were many clouds overlooking the trees and the air was chilled and bitter. Consumed by this thought, the woman's tormentor saw a peculiar relationship between the wet grasses that enveloped the boy's naked feet and the dry straw that littered the floor in this room he had designed for the woman's punishment. There were owls perched on all the branches and they watched the boy with ominous attention, as though the scene were some frightening passage in a children's fairy-tale. For some reason, the man wanted the little one to escape. It was not possible to see who was pursuing him, but somehow the man knew that the child was terribly frightened; he was certainly running away from someone or something. There was a cabin in the area; pairs of eyes glowed in the moonlight that shone on the cabin windows. The boy was being watched. The slowly swaying woman suspended by thickly knotted rope appeared to the man as a pendulum swinging in an old grandfather clock, standing in a dusty corner of the cabin. Mice scurried around the clock, making tiny scratches with their feet. The man wanted to help the boy and regretted that he could not determine who or what was pursuing him. He wished that he could see into the woods, and thereby make some determination as to what kind of threatening force was making its presence known and frightening the child. Finally, he decided that the best way to help the boy would be to investigate whether or not the cabin was a trap of some kind or an unexpected safe haven.

Of course, judging only by outward appearance, the cabin seemed rather foreboding. There were ugly, black trees with spindly, gnarled branches that reached across the roof from all sides. Moonlight made the windows glow and, at least from the perspective of the fleeing boy, gave the impression of human eyes staring from inside. These could merely be several reflections of owl eyes since the branches here, and throughout the woods, were filled with the vase-shaped, yellowish-brown birds.

The terrified child saw a very tall oak tree with an extremely wide trunk. He needed to rest for a moment, at least to catch his breath, so he dashed over to the mammoth tree and crouched behind it, trembling.

His attention was drawn to the texture of the tree bark, and he noticed the intricate pattern of furrows in the thick skin. This reminded him of his visit to his grandfather's house. The old man spent much of his time in South America and was always deeply tanned. The boy remembered running up to his seated grandfather and jumping on his lap. As they embraced, the boy kissed the old man and saw how deeply wrinkled his dark forehead had become.

The man had just returned from a trip and fondly recalled how he had been greeted when he arrived in the small town. His host, who immediately led him to a café, had respectfully carried his suitcase. Inside, sitting on a stool, was a large jovial man in a cream-colored shirt. In the breast pocket of the old man's shirt was the package of cigarettes, with a peculiar decorative pattern of black diamonds and squares that the corpulent gentleman, an acquaintance of many years, had given him before he left. The little boy smelled the peppery tobacco as he hugged his grandfather and wondered about the little package with the odd geometric shapes.

More business than pleasure, this trip was a kind of unofficial investigation of sorts. The boy's grandfather, who was a retired private investigator, agreed to look into a disturbing case, as a favor to one of his other friends. Apparently, his friend's granddaughter, who was only nineteen, was leading a double-life. She was murdered and there were many unpleasant sexual overtones in the killing. Her nude body, covered with welts from some kind of whipping implement, was found in the local area, a coastal fishing village. The only clue, a book of color photographs of women in bondage, was found next to the girl's body. When her corpse was discovered by a small group of fishermen returning to the shore with their catch, a jolt of wind violently ripped open the book, flipping back its pages in rapid succession. In the volley of skipping pages little snatches of images could be seen. One of the fishermen picked up the book and leafed through it slowly until his companions chided him for disturbing evidence. He placed the volume back on the wet sand next to the girl's blanched form. The young man was in his late teens and had never seen a woman in the nude. Even though her corpse was bloated from exposure to the sea, he was excited by the sight of her body. The teenager wished that he had made this discovery by himself; then he would have been free to touch the body wherever he desired; he would have taken the soiled book of pornographic images home, so that he could view it in privacy in his room after his parents went to sleep. He was obsessed with sexual thoughts. Each night, before he masturbated, he made an entry in the secret journal he kept:

Sunday, December 24th

Awful today. Rain and mist mostly through morning. Went to the tackle shop for supplies. Saw the owner's daughter playing behind the counter. So lovely. So tiny. Thought of how I would spank her. Maybe across my lap but then when she struggled it would hurt all the sores on my kneecaps. Could tie her to Mama's four-post bed. I'd like it better that way. Saw that last week in a magazine. Or maybe just tie her arms so I could see her legs kick up and down. Better. Crippled old bastard on the boat today wouldn't give me a moment of peace. *Throw the nets! Hurry up! Where's the fillet knife?! C'mon let's go!* I'd like to kill that old bastard. Not much of a catch today anyway. We thought we'd have a good haul in time for all the Christmas Eve markets but it wasn't enough. So many thoughts at night lately. Naked angels floating above my bed spreading their white legs to showcase their behinds. An unnatural whiteness, like the face of Queen Victoria or a Kabuki actor. A dream last night where I lived in a gigantic stone house on the shore. It was limestone. So light and airy. The house on an embankment overlooking the sea. A circular pool surrounded the house. No doors or glass in the windows. A carousel-like structure which created pathways and apertures throughout and each one gave access to the pool. The house was orange. It was limestone colored orange. It had a peculiar combination of building materials and architectural design. For the materials were indigenous to Mexico; the gravel, the stone, the fusing together of part to part, all of this evoked native Mexican building. Yet the design, the endless passageways and alcoves and marvelously intimate cul-de-sacs, were of distinctly European origin. In my dream I wandered throughout the house; I felt the peace that comes from living by the sea; I luxuriated in the delight of pastels and sun and the endless hum of churning waves. The fruit colors of a summer world, the orange of the house, the blue and white of the wooden deck chairs along the pool, the green and pink furniture, the echo of my voice that blended with the warm salty wind. I recognized the woman on the beach. I said nothing. If I'm careful, all will be well. I should have weighted the body. Too late. I'm always thinking of remedies long after the damage is done. If I had killed her in the carousel house, everything would have gone smoothly. I'll know better next time. We saw some sharks that day and I was confident that they would stay in the same area. I suppose I have much to learn about the sea. Thinking I had thrown the corpse over the boat while in the same general area as the sharks, it is entirely possible that I was in fact miles away. I'm not a very good navigator. It doesn't matter. No one saw me. It's that old man I have to watch. The visitor. They said he knows things because he was a great detective. But she was naked. I even burned the belt I used on her. It was very dark that night and mama was snoring away when I left the house. I even burned the clothes I was wearing that night. I put the ashes of the belt and my clothes together and ate them. The buckle I threw into the sea. I buried my stool from the following two days. The first day would have been sufficient but, as I said, I wanted to be careful. That night. What was it that made me determined to kill her *that* night? I remember she was very pretty. She spoke to me at the bar and was flirtatious, too. I guess she liked me.

The boy's grandfather was a veteran of police work. He had spent his thirty year career in homicide and after his retirement maintained a private detective practice specializing in missing persons. He was reluctant to speak to his friend just yet; the shock of the murder was enough of a mental strain for the poor man. The ex-detective knew, for example, immediately upon examining the girl's body that many of her bruises were too old to have been caused during her murder. In other words, this girl had been engaging in all sorts of sado-masochistic sex long before she was killed; the ex-detective had examined hundreds of bodies, and he knew right away that many of these wounds, scars, and marks were much more than twenty-four hours old.

The girl was covered with many small tattoos. Apparently, she was fond of insect imagery. She seemed to favor deadly insects. Her lower back displayed a Preying Mantis; on her left calf was a Black Widow spider; a Tarantula, with hairy legs splayed, formed a disturbing still life across her stomach. Perhaps, thought the boy's grandfather, her submissive sexual tendencies made her identify with these creatures. Maybe her desire to be physically abused had created a need to surrender her body to images of physical threat, as if she were a sacrificial victim being prepared for some prolonged, sinister ritual of pain and death. The ex-detective pondered this interpretation as he viewed the largest tattoo. It was like an enlarged panel from a comic strip and extended between the girl's shoulder blades, terminating just above the Mantis. The old man, trying already to fashion a preliminary profile of the girl's private life, wondered what kind of thematic connection could be drawn between the images of these things which stung and killed, and this picture of the inside of a confessional booth. The old man was immediately struck by the peculiar omission of a supplicant. There was the priest, sitting on the left, with hands serenely folded in front of his stomach, eyes cast downward, as if attentively listening to his parishioner's confession. Yet the other side of the confessional booth was empty; there was only the faintest spot of light illuminating the vacant seat. Was this girl particularly religious, thought the old man? Or was the incongruity of the image of a priest in an empty confessional booth meant as an ironic comment on the girl's self-image, that, perhaps, she felt condemned to a lifetime of domination, a lifetime that could never be redeemed or vivified by salvation?

The priest was despondent. He sat alone inside the dim, empty booth because he had been thinking about his father's death. Depressed as he was by these thoughts, he was most deeply disturbed because his religious career was chosen as a remedy for unrequited love and not (as his father had hoped) because he was influenced by his father's nurturing, gentle, religious and philosophical teachings. The priest was tormented by the wish to leave the priesthood. Even long ago, before his father's accident (the unfortunate man had fallen down a flight of stairs and broken his neck), the priest had been struggling with conflicted feelings about his purpose, his usefulness, about the very foundation of his faith. His father had been so proud of him; he was overjoyed at his decision to go to the seminary; to enter the priesthood. But over the years, ugly urges and desires had filled the priest's mind; there was an unrelenting bitterness in him. He found that he could no longer suppress memories and feelings about his one true love, the girl who had rejected him when he was a young man.

In recent months, dressed in civilian clothing to avoid unwanted attention, the priest had been visiting video arcades where pornographic movies were shown. His original joy at having found the woman who, he thought, was his soul mate, had degenerated into rabid feelings of hostility, expressed more and more by his predilection for films that depicted sexual sadism. He returned again and again to the same viewing booth, to watch the same S & M video in which a woman, tied and suspended in a hog-tied position, was brutally paddled and whipped.

He may have been suffering from some kind of nervous malady or mental breakdown, especially since his father's passing. Although there was no logical or rational basis for his thinking, he blamed himself for his father's death. Having digested the images of his favorite film so thoroughly, he would return to his room in the rectory, lie on his bed in total darkness and, with eyes closed, reconstruct and endlessly replay the erotic images. But he would invent new imagery during these perverse reveries; he would use the framing effect of the video monitor as if it were an ever-changing painter's canvas, focusing on something, or creating an imaginary detail, then using a kind of mental zoom lens to enlarge that detail until a new scene emerged within another frame, with its own logic and ontological rules.

There was a long staircase in the house where the priest grew up. He had lived there, with his father, until he entered the seminary at the age of twenty-two. His formal religious training was in full bloom, and soon he would become ordained. But, unbeknownst to his father, for the previous year he had been leading a kind of double life. While browsing through some large, coffee table size photography books in his favorite bookshop, which had a lower level devoted to photography and cinema, he had met a woman who utterly fascinated him. He kept her existence from his father, just as he kept his beloved completely unaware of his preparation for the priesthood. Consumed by guilt on two emotional fronts, that he was deceiving both his father and the woman, the young man became more and more detached from reality, and less and less certain of which path to take.

With an odious combination of tragic sadness and venomous contempt, he remembered the last time he saw his beloved. He remembered how he had planned to declare his love, to propose and leave the seminary. But she could not love him, and he sat alone on the picnic blanket as he watched her walk away. How quickly the beauty of the pastoral setting, with its quaint windmill and soothing brook, faded from his mind already seething with the painful loneliness of rejection! *Please don't leave me... Please come back...* He silently mouthed the words, like a mute zombie staring meaninglessly into space. He continued watching her as she walked across the field, occasionally side-stepping other lovers spread upon their blankets, lying arm in arm under the reassuring, warm summer sun. When she reached the vanishing point, where the picnic area ended, near the parking lot, and she was no longer visible, he closed his eyes and tilted his head back, letting his face absorb the glaring rays of the sun.

The heat instantly warmed his face while the sharp light, somewhat diffused by his closed eyelids, created images in his mind of tall streetlights. He saw an endless series of the lampposts, like the infinite echoes of facing mirrors. And as she turned away from the picnic site and got into her car, all of the large fluorescent bulbs in the lampposts turned on, each one casting a wide, circular pool of light on the ground. It was as though an ironic voice within his consciousness felt compelled to amplify his despair and humiliation by inventing these innumerable urban streetlights, incongruously mixed into the country scene. It was the finality of his loss, and the darkness of that finality, which the multiplied public lights so cruelly mocked.

let her die no that will not do there would not be any more fun we have too much to do here you and I there is so much more to tell and show for example on the screen there is an image right now of what she wanted to do that day when she was only ten and she saw the construction worker it was a hot day it was the end of summer but still very hot all the sweat and his muscles it was so exciting and forbidden she hurt herself that night in the shower she probed herself very deeply the attraction of the forbidden will never fade she will always be a conjuror of the most taboo erotica and in her mind there is no limit to the sexual pain she can enjoy she is more than one person her fantasies give her the option of living in a coma after birth so that the images can continue then in another version she died during child birth and her spirit hovers over her heartbroken husband she watches him pour his tea the breeze from the sway of her spirit hand causes a leaf to fall from a tree there is no reason the image has moved beyond that and it enjoys absolute freedom

Dear Diary:

Tomorrow my husband will take me to the hospital because our baby is due this week and I must be admitted. We moved just recently to this wonderful house by the beach and to bring our child home with the ocean in our backyard will be so enchanting and joyous. I have had more dizzy spells and I don't want to worry him about it because he frets over everything so easily but the doctor said we'd need to do another cat scan. I'm not going to say anything and I'm hoping it's nothing so the best thing is to just get it over with and have the baby and come home. Sometimes I think I married a saint he's such a religious man and he wants to give our child as much wisdom and guidance as he can. But I know he won't force him to accept things because he's not strict like that. He'd rather be a gentle teacher and I'm sure he'll be very loving. I hope the dizziness isn't serious enough to interfere with the birth in any way. Oh God! That would be terrible! My shame over what I have done in the past and maybe that's why I might be sick now? Please God don't let it be that. Anything but that. Maybe all those terrible things I couldn't refrain from doing with men and all the physical things that were done to my body before I was married will come back now to make me pay a terrible price! If I must die please God take me but let my baby live. Should anything happen to me I know my husband will love our child with a mother's love and it will be that same eternal, desperate clinging to that which is your self.

"What do you remember most about that day?"

"I'm not sure. It's so painful to remember."

"Well, let's try to break it into little parts, all right?"

"Yeah. OK."

"He called you that morning, when, when he suggested the picnic, or was that before?"

"I think it was that very morning. It was a good day. We were hungry. The previous night's storm was violent but that morning it was hot and there was lots of sunshine so he thought we should have a picnic and talk. I was greatly disturbed by his behavior the night before. Of course, I became obsessive and reconstructed it, I mean, our conversation, the whole conversation, in my mind. But that day there was much sunshine. It was beautiful. I could smell the salt air. The rhythm of the waves was like a confirmation of good things, it made me feel confident."

"Were you happy about that?"

"Yes, yes, I, well I thought this was going to be the big day, y'know? Like he was going to propose to me or at least say that he wanted us to stay together and try to work things out. He had told me recently that he was trying to avoid pornography, that he realized that he had become sort of addicted to it, kind of like what you had said when we had that session together, last month?"

"Yes, when he came with you that time? What do you think he came away with, after that session? Did he go into any detail with you?"

"Yes, very much. We talked about it that night. He said he realized that many couples get into a sexual hang-up if they watch too much pornography, like the example you gave of the couple you treat that started losing their sex drive because they watched too much pornography before they had sex and then they thought they would achieve what you said, what did you call it?"

"Instant ecstasy..."

"Yeah, right. They expected that instant ecstasy to happen and like they wanted to make each other come in a few seconds and couldn't see that those orgasms are faked and the porno actors are not really coming and all that phony stuff like the looping you said they do."

"The way they take two or three segments of action and repeat them at various places, so the whole production takes less time, and they re-use the same footage."

"Yeah...that it's all an illusion, even that the images which you think are happening for the first time, they're, they're all really identical, the same parts again and again, but put in at later times, and if you don't look very closely, you think it's continuing with something new that they're doing to each other. You made me laugh with one thing you said about it..."

"Oh, you mean the 'endless blow-job'?"

"Yeah, that's it! The woman who never comes up for air and keeps blowing the guy from the same angle, and she doesn't get tired!"

"Yes, that's the magic of editing!"

"Yeah!"

"Then what happened?"

"He came by in his car to pick me up, about an hour or so after he called. I got ready. I wanted to be so beautiful for him, to please him, y'know? I wore a fashionable silk dress and several pieces of bright jewelry. I knew that would be obviously overdressed for a picnic, but I wanted to look special that day. The air had grown chilly by the time we left but I chose not to wear a hat because I felt it would spoil my appearance. I dressed methodically, consulting with great satisfaction a large mirror hung behind my door. Its dull metal frame was cracked and dented. Isn't that weird? I remember such little things, like the marks on the mirror frame. Why is that? Why do people hold on to such tiny things?"

"It's all part of the mosaic. Everything connects to everything else, whether we realize it or not. So, when you got to the picnic area, were you, were you nervous, anticipatory?"

"Oh yes, very much, very much, I could tell there was, I don't know, at first I thought I was just suggesting it to myself, but I could tell he wasn't at ease, he didn't seem relaxed. When he spread out the blanket and took all the things out of the basket, he didn't even look at me. He hadn't looked me in the eye at all, from when he picked me up, all the way there."

"So you sensed that something was wrong? It wasn't self-suggestion...you were using your instincts and you realized that he wasn't being emotionally honest with you. You can give credit to yourself for having that awareness, for seeing what was there."

"I know...I know...but it was so scary, I loved him so very much. I didn't want it to be like that. This was his "Good-bye" ceremony. That's why he wanted to take me there. I kept thinking, I guess I was doing the projection thing, that you said I do so much, I kept finding things in the scene, physical things, y'know, like they were symbols or manifestations of good outcome or like they were the physical expression of what I was thinking, the way I wanted things to be, like the sheep and the roses, I told you about that, and there were, I guess there were some clouds for a bit, and there were shadows that crisscrossed upon our blanket, so I thought this meant our journey towards one another would be difficult, like it was a sign of hope, that we would struggle to find our love, but there was nothing to hope for, there was no love to find, the jumble of shadows was the inevitable result of sunlight shining through the tree and its leaves, our blanket lay in its path, and he, after he told me he didn't love me, he left me sitting alone, he wanted no more of my pain, it, it was the last time I saw him..."

"That was very callous of him. He didn't even bring you home, then? He left you there?"

"He was ashamed, I suppose. He didn't want to face me anymore. He left me money for a taxi and said never mind about the picnic things. He just wanted to leave."

"Do you think he was entitled to treat you that way?"

"I know what you're thinking! No, I'm, I'm not being self-demeaning now, I didn't feel happy about what he did, the way he did it, or excuse him for it, no, I'm, I guess I'm just trying to explain what he must have felt, and that's why he did what he did."

"As long as you appreciate that you didn't deserve to be treated so superficially..."

"I realize that. I really do."

"I noticed while you've been explaining all this...I wondered if you are conscious of it. Your speech is a little peculiar...you switch from a more formal language and tone to a somewhat more casual and conversational language. Are you aware of that? Is it from your diary? Is the pseudo-literary aspect coming from that?"

"You pick up on everything, don't you?"

"That's what I'm here for."

"I keep the diary, yes, I mean, I'm still writing in it. You mean that when I talk about that day, there's something, something..."

"Something contrived about it, yes. As if you were repeating lines you had written."

"Yes, yes, yes! Oh God, you see that, don't you?"

"Well I'm the one who is listening…it's not that difficult to notice. Do you see this as more obsessive behavior? Why do you think you chose to quote something you've written about that day in order to talk about it? I mean, as opposed to just letting thoughts and emotions and any details just come out as you remember them, in ordinary conversation?"

"Do you mean that I'm censoring or filtering my feelings?"

"Is that what you think you're doing?"

"I wanted to be as accurate and as clear as possible. So, I mean, I had already written some of those things in the diary, when they happened, and of course I OCD'd on it, and read it and reread it dozens of times!"

"Do you think that taking these lines, using them as a sort of substitute for spontaneous conversation…does this bring you closer to or farther from what you really feel?"

"I'm not sure I know what you mean…"

"I mean do you—"

"I told you how I felt, what, what else can I say about it?"

"Do you see the use of the prewritten, controlled diary language as a way of avoiding honest confrontation with the pain of being rejected?"

"You mean that I'm trying to anaesthetize my pain with visions?"

"Exactly."

"I never thought of it that way before. That's interesting."

"Now we have something that we can compare to your feelings about your father, for example. Do you see yourself doing the same thing there?"

"That's still so hard to figure out. There's so much negative and positive stuff wrapped together in it...I..."

"I know, I know...there are some terribly sensitive feelings to sort through. That would be the case for anyone who experienced what you did. But if you are still conflicted about your reactions to the sexual abuse that your father subjected you to, we have to start to figure out why you have such an attraction to being a sexual masochist. Is there a particular spanking scenario or fantasy that is extremely stimulating or exciting for you?"

"Yeah. Kinda. There's one that I think about a lot. I mean, I masturbate to it pretty much. But I haven't tried it with anybody yet."

"Would you like to talk about it?"

"Do we have to?"

"No, not if you're uncomfortable."

"Well...Maybe it would be good to tell you. I've never told anyone. You're my doctor, right?"

"Right. Sometimes just vocalizing something helps to bring about a healthier or a clearer perspective. And I wanted you to know that many people get turned on by a safe, consensual expression of sexual violence. That's fine. But you are unhappy with your own sexual wishes. Where do you think the conflict comes from?"

"I don't know where it comes from. I don't know. I get excited by it, that's all I know."

No! For woman there is nothing. To hold her heart man turns away from everything she needs. Did they not use the Pear of Anguish for the innocents who conducted miscarriages? Are all of the screams of the tormented women collected in some vessel buried deep in the black conscience of man? In the Father there is remorse; in the end there is nothing. I want the sea. Completely I

*am in the sea. Who was the first man? Did he come from the sea?
My beloved. He is told by God that if he eats of the tree of knowledge
of good and evil, he will die. The terrible doorway! Such mystery
for us in halls and rooms! Rooms within rooms the chilling nature
of it. Yes because they said that death entered the world through
the sin of Adam. Adam is that door. And the fruit of knowledge.
Eve's sexual love. Finely wrought dilemma such a battle between
consciousness and life. Why didn't you just kill us in the first place?
All the sorrow of knowing in advance that we are finished before
we start. The animals don't know. How happy they must be! Mute
and remote. Mute and remote. Slowly all float down gentle dream
into the sea. The gurgling, the gurgling, the little dead room at the
bottom of the sea, sealed metal walls, silence without breath, silence
without breath. Quiet endless hope from the ignorance of mortality.
Not for us. And woman so alone in her spirit that intuits what is
needed for happiness. Struggle to prove that she knows. Dragged
to the pillars age after age all types of stone for these pillars where
she is shackled and punished for offering her love. The heat and
the hatred in the energy that stalks woman. Branded and pilloried
for all ages and kept in disgrace for her wanton temptations. So
much to give. Discarded. My beloved unknown to me forever, in
brutal loneliness he discarded life's feast, relishing debris instead.
Why? Why so much confusion and waste? The creak of wood
against the floorboards. The old man rocks himself by a window.
The light. Bright sunlight. Days that have vanished. There is a
grassy field beyond his window. He sees children play there. Their
voices are sweet and filled with wonder. He loved once. He is old.
There are so many things that remain unsatisfied by devotion to
what is logical. You who ask reason and logic to speak, what
answers come to comfort you? What music do you hear in the
dark when everything you tried has failed? Are you afraid to
remember your mother's embrace? Do you smell her perfume and
hear her voice? What regrets do you keep hidden under layers of*

propriety and self-deception? Your lost love will not return. You mourned for her. You wept for her. What did you accomplish? If happiness were a condition of true comfort, why do so many seek it without result?   My beloved. And for woman there is nothing but doubt and error and condemnation in the desert. Lifeless patches of dry desolation. Where is the salvation of dear Beatrice? Dante's conviction has evaporated; he has lost his way. Yet even now sweet Beatrice shows him divine compassion. There is hope in the beautiful night sky; and Love moves the sun and the stars.

Eve Returns To The Sea: Epilogue

so there you have it *That's All Folks* that was what you wanted wasn't it to make the fact that this guy was a priest can work for us or against us given the recent climate concerning the Catholic Church but I think we can find some interesting angles to play it from nevertheless we have many ways of viewing our material don't we or maybe this one's gonna be like the corsets with The Uptown Stuffer but I wouldn't count on it because nobody came for a week and it was the middle of the summer I bet you loved it when you found out it was that crazy Chinaman with the wolf-man mask he made out of incontinence bags yes I remember Mike Jauntley came in when the forensic boys lifted the body off the pipe yes I remember the cool darkness of the enormous theatres filled with circuitous passageways and shadowy alcoves and he said that the deception of the frame edges was like the imposture of the senses like the corruption of pure mind when it succumbs to what is apparently real but inherently false it does not surprise me that the authorities could not understand you were such an enthusiastic audience most of the time you had that abstract gaze on your face like the guy in the fish market when he looks at the new catch twistin' on the cuttin' table yes we have thoroughly examined the mystery of the outline and I fully understand how the radiant delicacy of traps and compartments fascinated you maybe you would have liked the Trireme ships the nomadic search of the ancient travelers unaware of the distant lands but wait a minute your Honor may we approach the bench for a side bar you see what we have here is a failure to acknowledge that the viewer will also see the long attachment coming down from the fluorescent lights to which a microphone is connected so that everything the coroner says is recorded in real time as he conducts the autopsy so were you surprised by the fact that the freshly removed vulva fitted well into the tissue defect of the body so since we're talking about images and illusions let's not forget that the camera is placed directly under the coroner's face so that only his lips appear in an extreme close-up and that most of this mutilation was inflicted upon surface regions instantly visible to the naked eye that's a good one isn't it the naked eye as if there could ever be such a thing as pure vision there is an aural bridge that links them so of course he was obsessed with this revelation of a kind of hidden time you know that deliriously modern notion that matter behaves on several planes at once we have witnessed this haven't we our victim and our son and our father and our screen writer have served as the background of the scene containing the detectives and the flame-strewn fountain was a huge billboard depicting a man coming into a new town and being greeted was it him was it the right son you know he's been charged and he's about to stand trial for at least nine serial slayings did you figure out that the obsession with the sparrows is an even more extreme example but have you been an honest observer I think I heard you say that these things never cease to disgust me is that because my father's blood crept through there it moved across the geometric tiles shining with the same sunlight as the mailbox did you wonder how many wept because of lost love knowing that the sweetness of her gestures is irrevocably gone and his figidity impatience overcame him once again and he immediately shifted the buttons in a manic survey of every possible selection and of course we know that has been the key the multiplication of the ways of seeing for example he saw rows of pentagons a geometric plane of porcelain tiles rigidly outlined by thin black lines even though the sparrows had not yet perched on the branch in spite of the fact that her eyes were not her eyes and my hands were not my hands yes isn't it charming the surprising domesticity of the animal kingdom the natural interdependence of the male and the female you are a good observer and if we push this button we also see the DJ inside the booth mouthing words that cannot be heard but isn't the investigation also focusing on another man in the East I saw that same man under the boardwalk and without really knowing why the importance of a thing always depended on its visual content for example behind him the cloudy mixture of distant but familiar carnival sounds and the child scurries back to his annoyed parent as the murderer suddenly opens his eyes and the shadow takes her by the hand and leads her away and as another used to say only at twilight and acting as a one-man Greek chorus submitted for your approval is the Final White draft of Commentary from Victims' Families that occurs outside the prison shortly before the execution and of course there are times when I believe that popular culture is a mirror for the collective subconscious so which conclusion did you draw attentive reader did you end up saying I hope he's tortured until the end of time and then have it start all over again while the clang of the spinning wheels becomes metallic laughter echoing from clown mouth to clown mouth perhaps you asked yourself did I kill life with my bitterness or did you long for innocence the way the child takes his father by the hand looks up at him with an adult's understanding no do not despair just press the button again change the selection another scene within the scene always be wary of those who claim that it is important to note the simple presence of God within the moments of one's everyday life you see sometimes there is no warning or logic and sometimes there is an instinctual awareness of the immanence of death I remember a friend of mine who often spoke of the moment of death do we become the imprint of who we were once we enter this world we might go another way take a different path there was a short flight of wooden steps next to the seafood section there was a barker claiming that memory continues its job when even the world that surrounds the machine has gone yet you must be cautious when you look because the man's leg was obscured in the same way as the table in the painting such a pity all of the stifled longings and fears we cannot go back to the place where there is no time in the world of a child that is why I always told my son that the decision to direct his life was his and his alone fiction dream fiction time but utterance is not a guide do you see how this begins do you understand the process of transformation now see somehow an elephant form is suggested by the shape of the water stain on the mother's dark grey top she can't wake up and it was quite unlikely that the handsome intern would say anything romantic or flirtatious to the nurse instead he liked to imagine the dog as a puppy and she was fond of documentaries and had been enjoying a program on carnivals and amusement parks oh how she loved the circus and the carnival but the man had just returned from a trip and fondly recalled how he had been greeted when he arrived in the small town a feeling of waves repeating returning unfurling in the moonlight should anything happen to me I know my husband will love our child with a mother's love and it will be that same eternal desperate clinging to that which is your self like waves unfurling is the pseudo-literary aspect coming from that do you feel protected by that surface you who ask reason and logic to speak what answers come to comfort you that was very callous of him to give the son so many levels of omniscience especially since we moved just recently to this wonderful house by the beach and to bring our child home with the ocean in our backyard will be so enchanting and joyous for the little boy smelled the peppery tobacco as he hugged his grandfather and wondered about the little package with the odd geometric shapes you must realize now that you are worthless don't you just like her husband has become so overcome by grief that he has lost all awareness of his surroundings it made the babysitter slightly dizzy because of the vertiginous view he saw an odd-looking man leave the pet shop after chatting briefly with the manager he stared at her with disapproval that the smitten nurse mistakenly took for evidence of sexual interest we are building a nice little pocket of seamlessness here that is a bonus for you a little something extra thrown in at the end he wanted to see something vulgar or violent if it's total depravity that they're after then they shall have it unencumbered by any form of earthly reason so that most of the lengths of the ocean crop were darkish green but some had turned black it makes one wonder what if the second son refused to forgive his brother's reckless behavior they wanted to know if I would allow them to deny life support and I wanted them to save her there seems to be no greater metaphor for the influence and presence of a divine being than the intensity and enormity of the sea waves repeating waves pushing forward he is a chief proponent of the belief that nothing exists or behaves because there is some predetermined divine symbiosis between man and nature waves returning backward are the decades that may follow and the repeating moments of loss viewed light-heartedly by the ones we miss and weep for they know how we take comfort from the circular reasoning of metaphor yes we have learned through these pages how death turns life into an image haven't we have you ever felt yourself gently compelled into mystification when you consider the duality of shadows and things yes I can almost touch it now the jumble of shadows was the inevitable result of moonlight shining against the wrought iron gate a coffin is simply a shape a kiss is just a kiss the priest clasped and unclasped his hands many times while he spoke maybe he didn't do anything seems unlikely they should do it the way they used to in ancient times they should cut off his arms and legs and scatter them to the four corners of the earth and then leave his head on a post for the birds to pick I think justice is being served but I get disgusted by the way the media turns these things into a circus I mean who cares about the discoloration of the coroner's nicotine stained fingertips similar to the paint stripped floor buttons of the vibrating lift do we have to be told that the echo of metal rings eerily within the long hall of slabs also metal also cold while a cluster of slugs nestles within the protein rich bed of semen and blood on the underside of the cotton panties or like this killer I know the way the philosopher knew his candle in dream in memory in perception the reality may be translated but it remains irreducible why yes that seems to have been our theme all along the kind of thing that might appear in some controversial film about damnation or the dissolution of religious belief but look press the selection button a man is watching an afternoon movie in another city in the same state and now Mrs. Vargas begins changing the channels but discovers that other stations are presenting the same material she does not know that there is a very large coffee mug in front of the disc jockey but of course our hero knew better just listen to his thoughts that day so I rushed away from my father to see my beloved to declare my love to pronounce my devotion to her and her alone it is not impossible that the gulls became frustrated by a fierce wind sweeping the shore we have longed to play with what is possible and what is impossible haven't we to luxuriate in the fleeting superimposition of this thin band of radiance for a moment made the brown splotchy step appear less ugly and here is one of our concoctions some of the raw ingredients turned into our metaphysical soup when he swam he moved continuously without resting and because of this perpetual motion the blood could not conceal every splotch on every step I held my father's hand one day when we stopped to look at the dressed lamb its face smeared with saliva there is a section on death row reserved for extremely violent prisoners who have been restricted to special confinement for varying periods of time the bloodstains were removed from the tiled vestibule floor it was simply a matter of procedure in the determination of the validity of an insanity defense certainly there are schizophrenic tendencies here but I haven't spent enough time with him to be sure yeah that's easy for you to say who really knows what shadows lurk in the hearts of men five doctors sit at a circular table each with their own set of files and notes her strained faculties had regrouped ready to continue their search for enjoyment the waves the repeating forwards then backwards the eternity of the waves on several occasions they had both stopped at the water-fountain at the same time but never spoke as the man reached over to open the cage he shifted his weight and his pocket change gently collided with his keys return to same extreme close-up of coroner's lips he is illuminated because only the glaring fluorescent lights above the table where he works are on so there is a good deal of shadow in this shot at that moment the frail old man was pushing his little hot dog stand away from the house from time to time he rolled his tongue around his mouth and the reflective planes of the fat lozenges captured fragmented slivers of the scene the illogical landscape of the imaginary a devotion to the spell of falseness sometimes the labyrinth is heaven not hell as long as there was something to see outside of myself I could bypass the arid vacuity of my life when I was finished I looked up I will include what I choose the edges of the frame were the key like the movement of the waves myths are the most potent source of terror and this was all done with a pocketknife you never know about these nuts tell him to puncture his ass with the receiver for ten minutes he must be sleeping only a few hours a week there is however some cut-away material as you'll notice yes long slow tracking shots of the ocean beautiful slow rhythms of the waves the repeating waves moving outside time moving forever the back and forth flow of the eternally moving waves